CiTY·SMaRT™

Portland

Third Edition

Robin Klein and Paul Koberstein

Lighthouse
- Heceta Head Lighthouse
(Highway 101 north of Florence, Oregon)

CANNON beach → North of Portland
South of Astoria
Eugene

**AVALON
TRAVEL**
publishing

Acknowledgments
Thanks to the many Portlanders who contributed to this book in one way or another: Nicole Vanoni, Keith Goodman, Charlie Hales, Keith Kullberg, Albert Reda, Greg deBruler, Julia Puzikova, Lenna, Jake, Rick, Sabrina. Special thanks to Marc Zolton for his help as well as his writing.

Dedication
To Ernie, who thought Portland's a cool city.

CiTY·SMaRT: Portland
3rd edition
Paul Koberstein and Robin Klein

Please send all comments, corrections, additions, amendments, and critiques to:

CiTY·SMaRT™
AVALON TRAVEL PUBLISHING
5855 BEAUDRY ST.
EMERYVILLE, CA 94608, USA
e-mail: info@travelmatters.com
www.travelmatters.com

Published by
Avalon Travel Publishing
5855 Beaudry St.
Emeryville, CA 94608, USA

Printing History
3rd edition— September 2000
5 4 3 2 1

ISBN: 1-56261-530-0
ISSN: 1530-8378

Editors: Ellen Cavalli, Leslie Miller
Copyeditor: Deana Corbitt Shields
Graphics: Erika Howsare
Production: PerfecType, Nashville, TN
Maps: Mike Ferguson, Mike Morgenfeld

Front cover photo: © John Elk III—skyline
Back cover photo: © John Elk III—*Portlandia*

Distributed in the United States and Canada by Publishers Group West
Printed in the United States by Publishers Press

CONTENTS

MAP CONTENTS

Restaurants, hotels, museums, and other facilities marked by the
& symbol are wheelchair accessible.

See Portland the CiTY·SMART™ Way

The Guide for Portland Natives, New Residents, and Visitors

In *City•Smart: Portland,* local authors Robin Klein and Paul Koberstein tell it like it is. Residents will learn things they never knew about their city, new residents will get an insider's view of their new hometown, and visitors will be guided to the very best Portland has to offer—whether they're on a weekend getaway or staying a week or more.

Opinionated Recommendations Save You Time and Money

From shopping to nightlife to museums, the authors are opinionated about what they like and dislike. You'll learn the great and the not-so-great things about Portland's sights, restaurants, and accommodations. So you can decide what's worth your time and what's not; which hotel is worth the splurge and which is the best choice for budget travelers.

Easy-to-Use Format Makes Planning Your Trip a Cinch

City•Smart: Portland is user-friendly—you'll quickly find exactly what you're looking for. Chapters are organized by travelers' interests and needs, from Where to Stay and Where to Eat, to Sights and Attractions, Kids' Stuff, Sports and Recreation, and even Day Trips from Portland.

Includes Maps and Quick Location-Finding Features

Every listing in this book is accompanied by a geographic zone designation (see the following pages for zone details) that helps you immediately find each location. Staying near Pioneer Square and wondering about nearby sights and restaurants? Look for the Downtown label in the listings and you'll know that statue or café is not far away. Or maybe you're looking for the well-known Catholic sanctuary, the Grotto. Along with its address, you'll see an Eastside label, so you'll know just where to find it.

All That and Fun to Read, Too!

Every City•Smart chapter includes fun-to-read (and fun-to-use) tips to help you get more out of Portland, city trivia (did you know Portland's MAX transportation system has the deepest light-rail tunnel in North America?), and illuminating sidebars (for a tour of Portland's microbrew styles, for example, see page 98). And well-known local residents provide their personal "Top Ten" lists, guiding readers to the city's best sights, places for kids, and more.

PORTLAND ZONES

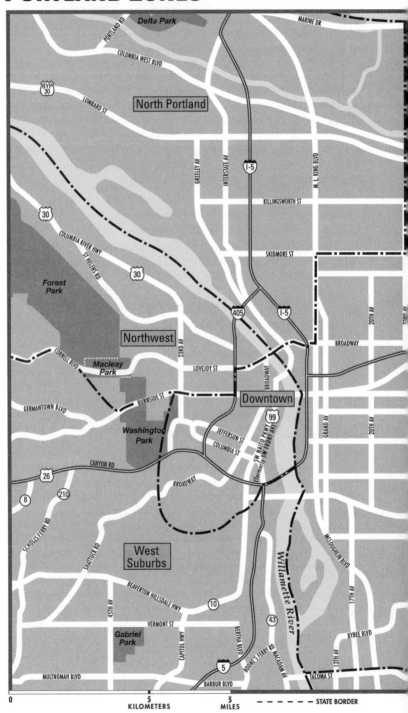

Delta Park

COLUMBIA WEST BLVD

MARINE DR

PORTLAND RD

BYP 30

LOMBARD ST

North Portland

GREELEY AV

INTERSTATE AV

I-5

M. L. KING BLVD

KILLINGSWORTH ST

30

COLUMBIA RIVER HWY

ST HELENS RD

30

SKIDMORE ST

Forest Park

405

I-5

20TH AV

23RD AV

Northwest

BROADWAY

CORNELL BLVD

LOVEJOY ST

Macleay Park

BROADWAY

GERMANTOWN BLVD

BURNSIDE ST

Downtown

99

GRAND AV

20TH AV

Washington Park

JEFFERSON ST

COLUMBIA ST

SW MACA PKWY (formerly SW FRONT AV)

CANYON RD

26

BROADWAY

8

210

West Suburbs

MCLOUGHLIN BLVD

SCHOLLS FERRY RD

SHATTUCK RD

Willamette River

17TH AV

BEAVERTON HILLSDALE HWY

10

43

BYBEE BLVD

45TH AV

VERMONT ST

CAPITOL HWY

BERTHA BLVD

13TH AV

Gabriel Park

5

BOONE'S FERRY RD

MACADAM AV

TACOMA ST

MULTNOMAH BLVD

BARBUR BLVD

0   5
KILOMETERS   5
MILES   – – – – – STATE BORDER

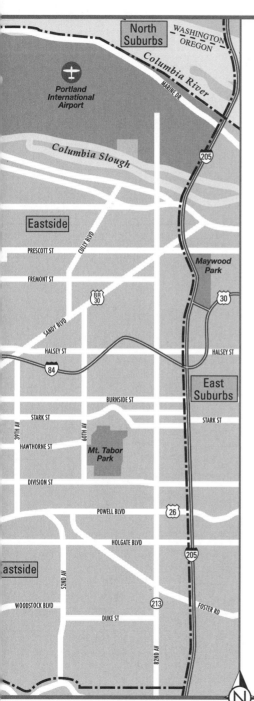

PORTLAND ZONES

Downtown (DT)
The area south of Burnside and west of the Willamette River. It includes some of Old Town. The southwestern border loosely follows Portland's West Hills.

Northwest (NW)
Bounded on the south by Burnside, on the east and north by the Willamette River, and on the west by the West Hills and Forest Park. It includes the Pearl District.

Eastside (E)
Bounded on the east by I-205, on the south by Tacoma Street, on the north by Skidmore and the Columbia River, and on the west by the Willamette River. It includes the Lloyd District, Hawthorne, and Sellwood neighborhoods, and the airport.

North Portland (NP)
Bounded on the south and west by the Willamette River, the north by the Columbia River, and the east by Martin Luther King Jr. and 33rd Avenue.

West Suburbs (WS)
The area south of the Downtown and Northwest zones and east of the Willamette River. It includes Lake Oswego and Beaverton.

East Suburbs (ES)
The area east of I-205 and south of Tacoma Street and the Columbia River. It includes Clackamas, Gresham, and Oregon City.

North Suburbs (NS)
Includes cities north of the Columbia River, including Vancouver, Washington.

Portland Oregon Visitors Association

1

WELCOME TO PORTLAND

First-time visitors to Portland often anticipate a dreary, rainy, provincial, quiet city. And without fail, they discover just the opposite. Portland has a progressive beat, rich in life, culture, and politics. And, while overcast throughout the winter and spring, the city has exceptionally gorgeous summers with reliably clear skies straight through to October. Portlanders know how to exploit those fair-weather months with countless European-style outdoor cafés, beer festivals, waterfront activities, open-air musical performances, a Saturday market, and hikes in the city's old-growth forests and in the spectacular surrounding mountains. And they love their gardens. In fact, for many in this city, gardening is an obsession. Whether strolling the ever-blooming Rose Gardens or the serene Rhododendron or Japanese Gardens, or simply admiring neighborhood vegetable patches, when the weather gets warm, Portlanders find those green sprouts and new blossoms irresistible.

While Portlanders indeed celebrate fine weather, they are highly adept at keeping busy when the rain does come. Buzzing coffee bistros abound. Bookstores and libraries are everywhere. The largest, Powell's Bookstore in downtown Portland, occupies an entire city block and spills onto adjacent ones. A staggering number of microbreweries makes Portland the nation's brewpub capital, and the city is credited with leading the microbrewery revolution in America.

Home to Nike and Adidas USA, and one hour from year-round skiing and snowboarding on Mount Hood, championship windsurfing in Hood River, and the breathtaking Oregon coast, Portland is an adventure-sports town. But it's also a booming major-league city with its NBA Trail Blazers. Kid-friendly and clean, Portland boasts great schools, no sales tax, old-fashioned gas stations, the only volcano within city limits in the continental United States, and both the largest and smallest city parks in

There are few quicker ways to stand out as a foreigner than to mispronounce "Oregon" or "Willamette." To trick the locals, be sure to place the emphasis on the right syllable. Say "OR-uh-gun," *not* "or-uh-GONE," and "wih-LAM-it," *not* "wil-uh-MET" or "WIL-uh-met."

America. It also has a thriving art scene with first-rate exhibits, music, and dance.

With expanding bus, light-rail, trolley, and streetcar lines, getting around is easy in Portland's many urban neighborhoods, each of which has character and charm all its own. The city has also produced one of the most successful downtown renewals anywhere: Portland's Old Town has truly become the city's hub, full of vitality and excitement. Come explore this city soon, for the secret about the sunshine has gotten out.

Getting to Know Portland

Situated in the Willamette Valley between two great Northwest mountain ranges (the Coast Range and the Cascades), Portland, in Multnomah County, is divided geographically into quadrants. The Willamette River runs south to north through the city separating the east side from the west, and Burnside Avenue splits the north and the south. Addresses are easy since they include a SE, SW, NE, NW, or N designation that readily identifies the city quadrant.

Bordering the city to the north is the mighty Columbia River and, on its opposite shore, Washington State. The "West Hills" of Portland loosely define the city's western border, with Washington County and the city of Beaverton beyond them. Interstate 205 and 82nd Avenue mark the city's eastern boundary, although technically the "city" stretches east to 242nd Avenue or so due to annexation.

Portland History

Portland sits on land that was originally the home of Chinook Indians. Various Native American dialects were spoken there: Multnomah, Clowella, Clackamas, and Tualatin. The Multnomahs lived along the Columbia River while the others resided in the Willamette Falls area (now Oregon City). Interestingly, the word "Boston" came to mean English or American in the language of the Chinook during the fur trade with American and British Canadians, probably due to early visitors from the New England city. Sea otters were sought by the fur traders but soon were found to be scarce in the Northwest, leaving beaver fur to become the region's choice commodity during the first half of the nineteenth century.

Early in the nineteenth century, the Columbia River captured the explorer's imagination of one Thomas Jefferson. During an expedition (1803–1806) set forth by President Jefferson, the famous explorers Lewis and Clark came across the site that became Portland. It was little more than a clearing in a forest on the Willamette River, halfway between Fort Vancouver and Willamette Falls, and it was a rest stop for fur traders and Indians en route between those two places.

Ocean commerce up the Columbia and Willamette Rivers brought settlers to Portland in the 1840s. Oceangoing ships favored the deep inland port, which today is the largest inland port in America, 100 miles upriver from the mouth of the Columbia. The city's earliest plot plans in 1845 called for small city blocks—each 200 feet square—so that more corner lots could be sold. The corner lots were more desirable and could command a higher price. The result of the reduced block size, still noticeable today, was a feeling of small-city ease and livability.

Portland grew rapidly—so much so, in fact, that in 1847 there appeared to be more stumps (from the clearing of trees to make streets) than residents, and hence the city acquired the nickname Stumptown. Pioneers arriving in the state via the Oregon Trail met a fork in the path where one road went south to California and the other headed for the Willamette Valley and Portland. Those searching for gold and adventure, typically those from the Midwest and the southern United States, went south, while those looking to settle, typically people from New England and New York, continued on to the new city.

To encourage growth in the new frontier, Congress passed an act in 1850 that gave 320 acres of land to every adult white male settler residing in Oregon. The act was in direct conflict with a 1787 law that promised not to take Native American lands without prior consent, and it set off a series of devastating wars. By 1851 half the Willamette Valley and all of the lower Columbia was surrendered to the United States through a series of 13 treaties that guaranteed Native Americans the remainder of the land. By 1855, however, the Indians of western Oregon had all been relocated to reservations east of the Cascade Mountains.

In a shameful 1844 statement typifying attitudes not unique to Portland or Oregon, the commissioners of Oregon's provisional government explained the decimation of the Portland–Oregon City Indian population as a divine act. "This country has been populated by powerful tribes," the statement went. "But it has pleased the great dispenser of human events to

1993 Oregon Trail celebration

Oregon Tourism Commission

reduce them to a mere shadow of their former greatness." By the 1870s the natives of the Willamette Valley had been virtually wiped out.

Over the next 50 years, Oregon struggled with rampant racism. In 1843, with the creation of Oregon Country, slavery was outlawed. Unfortunately, however, so were blacks. The first exclusion law in Oregon, passed in 1844, required all blacks to leave the territory within three years.

In 1857, after three failed attempts, Oregon voters chose to make their territory a state. In that same election, in a seeming paradox, voters overwhelmingly opposed slavery but reaffirmed the exclusion clause that prohibited blacks from residing in the state. Despite the fact that the law was never enforced, it remained a part of Oregon's constitution until 1926.

Sometimes called the New England of the Pacific Coast, Portland was a haven for white Protestants fleeing ethnic and racial encirclement. Still, according to Gordon Demarco in *A Short History of Portland* (Lexikos, 1990), "That was only one side of Portland. The other side was of a crowded melting pot. In 1890, 37.5 percent of residents were foreign-born, many not speaking English. Portland's ethnicity at that time ranked second only to San Francisco."

The Twentieth Century Dawns

Portland grew rapidly at the end of the nineteenth century, fueled in no small way by the completion of the transcontinental railroad in 1883. Inextricably linked to the railroads were the timber barons, who essentially controlled them. At the turn of the twentieth century, bogus land sales entangled the timber giants, city officials, and businessmen in scandal. "We are . . . witness to a spectacle of public and privateness that is almost without precedent in the annals of the country," wrote William Wheelwright, president of the Portland Chamber of Commerce at the time and president of Pacific Export Lumber. Portland's infamous Timber Fraud Trials of 1904 brought 33 convictions.

Still, not all of the lumber barons were entirely wrongheaded. Simon Benson, for instance, was also a philanthropist. In 1912 he commissioned for the city 20 elegant freshwater drinking fountains, now known as the Benson Bubblers, because he was concerned that his thirsty mill workers were drinking too much beer for lack of available fresh water. Beer consumption in the city reportedly decreased 25 percent after the fountains were installed. Visitors can still use the original bronze bubblers as well as the many others that have been added in the years since.

The greatest Oregon fair, the Lewis and Clark Centennial Exposition, was held in 1905 and brought people and attention to Portland from afar. The Olmsted brothers of New York, who designed that city's Central Park, were hired to design the Centennial Exposition, but they wound up designing a comprehensive park system for the City of Portland with playgrounds and waterfront parks.

After the fair, the city underwent another spurt of tremendous growth. The Broadway Bridge opened in 1912 to link prestigious northeast neighborhoods to the downtown and riverfront. Portland's great neighborhoods were also connected by streetcar lines, which once stretched for more

Salmon Homecoming

The Pacific Northwest is where the salmon live. It is home to the chinook, coho, sockeye, pink, chum, and steelhead. These majestic species are born in high mountain streams, spend two or three years at sea, and then mysteriously find their way back home to spawn. But everywhere, the wild salmon are in danger, and their possible extinction has triggered a rescue effort unlike any the world has seen. The cost is approaching $1 billion a year.

Before Oregon became a U.S. territory, more than 10 million salmon returned to the Columbia River each year, swimming up from Astoria, past Portland, to spawning grounds as far away as Montana and Idaho. Today dams block passage to all of Montana and parts of Idaho, Washington, and Oregon.

The Portland-based Bonneville Power Administration (BPA) started developing power from the Columbia River's dams during the Depression. Years later it learned that those dams were causing mass salmon declines. Nevertheless, at the BPA's visitors center at Bonneville Dam, you will see Woody Guthrie's words to "Roll On Co-lumbia, Roll On," his tribute to the social and economic benefits provided by the dams. You will also hear serious discussion of taking some of the dams down in a last-ditch effort to save the fish.

It's a tradition every spring for hundreds of boats to take to the Willamette River, from downtown Portland to Oregon City, for a chance to catch a 30-pound chinook. Increasingly, however, Port-landers are less interested in hooking the big one than in giving it a fighting chance to make it back.

than 200 miles throughout the city. The Columbia River Basin in general came into its own with the completion of the major rail lines: Union Pacific, North Pacific, and Great Northern. The years between 1905 and 1913 saw Portland's population double to 276,000.

As part of that era, Portland's trendy magnetic appeal drew a little-known motion picture industry three years even before Hollywood was

A Toss of a Coin and Portland Is Born

Despite Portland's history as a great American port city, the city's naming had nothing to do with its role as a port. Rather, the story goes, Portland's first settlers, Francis Pettygrove and Asa Lovejoy, each wanted to name the new settlement after his own home city back east. Lovejoy wanted to call it Boston, after his hometown of Boston, Massachusetts, and Pettygrove wanted to name it Portland, after Portland, Maine. They couldn't come to an agreement, so they tossed a coin. Pettygrove, obviously, emerged the winner.

invented. From 1916 to 1925, with three local movie studios and Hollywood producers looking for locations, Portland enjoyed a rich filmmaking boom. Today Portland continues to be a choice location for shooting movies. Among the better known from more recent years are *Drugstore Cowboy, Breaking In, Mr. Holland's Opus,* and the Willem Dafoe–Madonna flick *Body of Evidence.*

Oregon's racist history haunted it well into the early 1900s. In 1920 the state's legislature passed a resolution urging the U.S. Congress to prohibit "Orientals" from gaining citizenship—a none-too-subtle attempt at preventing Japanese from acquiring too much land. The KKK came to Portland in 1921, with Roman Catholicism and the parochial school system as its primary targets.

But Portland also had its progressives, who, in the early 1900s, profoundly shaped thinking in the region and beyond. Reed College was a cornerstone to that advancement. Established in 1911 by Unitarian minister Thomas Lamb Eliot with the support of his wealthy parishioners Amanda and Simeon Reed, Reed College has become one of the nation's preeminent institutions of the liberal arts and sciences.

The Growth Continues

Terry Schrunk was elected mayor in 1957 and represented a Portland "conservatocracy" typical of the city's early years. However, he stood out from his predecessors in his quest for urban renewal and forward-looking city planning. In 1958 the Portland Development Commission was established. The commission bulldozed 84 acres of old dilapidated buildings in the south part of downtown, uprooting the largely Italian and Jewish ethnic communities there. At the same time, it launched the construction of parks, gardens, fountains, the Civic Auditorium, and high-rise apartment buildings.

The Willamette Riverfront was rediscovered after 1965—chiefly through the vision of Oregon's maverick governor Tom McCall, who took office in 1966 and held it until 1974. Governor McCall's famous catchphrase, "Come and visit us again and again, but for heaven's sake, don't come here to live," remained Oregon's sentiment, fueling an undeserved "inhospitable" image that persists today.

In 1973 McCall pushed through state legislation that created the nation's strongest land-use laws. Urban growth boundaries were established for all Oregon cities, large and small, making it okay to build up but not out. In Portland, growth is confined within a designated 362-square-mile area. The idea is to protect Oregon's precious farm- and forestland from the ravages of sprawling, low-density development. But clashes between environmentalists and developers have compromised some of the protections.

Oregon's Environmental Movement

Protecting the environment has been important to Oregonians since the start of the last century, when a citizens' vote made sure that all the state's ocean beaches would be kept public forever. Today Oregon's beach law means that private condos, surfside motels, and developers cannot block access to beaches in front of their property.

In the 1930s Oregonians began to realize that the Willamette River, which flows through the western part of the state and bisects Portland, had been used as a toilet by industry and communities. Though *National Geographic* heralded the cleanup as a rousing success in the 1970s, the job remains unfinished. The U.S. Environmental Protection Agency has said a segment of the Willamette through the heart of Portland is still so contaminated it belongs on the Superfund list among the nation's most

---

The Vanport Flood

Portland has always been vulnerable to flooding. Every few years, the combined punch of heavy snowfall in the mountains and quick spring warming periods causes severe damage. One such instance actually wiped out a whole community, the neighboring town of Vanport. In 1948 the Columbia River and its tributaries rose drastically, flooding Union Station (in Old Town along the waterfront) and Vanport City, a town of 17,500 built to house wartime workers, 25 percent of whom were African American. The decision to locate Vanport on the Columbia floodplain had been questionable, and the subsequent poor treatment of the flood victims has been considered a public scandal.

PORTLAND TIMELINE

1792	Robert Gray "discovers" the Columbia River.
1807	Beaver trade begins in the Pacific Northwest.
1830s	Protestant missionaries begin to arrive.
1843	The first land claims are filed by Asa Lovejoy and William Overton.
1844	Portland is named after Overton sells his share of the land to Francis Pettygrove.
1845	Portland is officially founded.
1846	Fort Vancouver is considered to be on American soil due to new border definitions.
1848	The Oregon Act is passed to create the Oregon Territory. The act reaffirms a 1787 law promising not to take Indian lands without prior consent.
1850	The Oregon Donation Land Act is passed, granting 320 free acres of land to every settler arriving before 1852.
1852	South Park Blocks are set aside as a haven from urban stress.
1858	Congregation Beth Israel is founded.
1859	Oregon becomes a state.
1860	A daily stagecoach service is started between Portland and Sacramento.
1861–63	Oregon's "Gold Rush"
1863	Portland's first brewery is built.
1879	African Americans organize the Portland Colored Immigration Society to increase black settlement in Oregon.
1887	Morrison Bridge, the first bridge across the Willamette, opens.
1891	The Port of Portland is established.
1892	The Portland Art Association is founded.
1904	Portland appoints its first African American police officer.
1905	The Lewis and Clark Centennial Exposition is held.
1908	The first female police officer in the United States, Lola Baldwin, is appointed in Portland.
1912	Women's suffrage is adopted in Oregon.
1912	Philanthropist and lumber baron Simon Benson donates drinking fountains to the city. The fountains become known as the Benson Bubblers.
1916–25	The "Golden Age" of the Portland motion picture industry

George L. Baker, a theatrical producer known for his bigotry and inciting Red scare, is elected mayor.	1917
The KKK is organized in Portland.	1921
Beatrice Cannady becomes the first African American woman to be admitted to the Oregon bar.	1922
The Japanese-American Citizen's League is established.	1922
The Bonneville Dam is completed.	1937
The shipbuilding boom begins.	1941
A Memorial Day flood destroys Vanport City.	1948
Dorothy McCullough Lee becomes Portland's first woman mayor.	1949
Maurine Neuberger becomes the first woman senator from Oregon.	1960
A freeway between Salem and Portland is finished.	1961
The John Day Dam is dedicated.	1968
Portland's Transit Mall opens.	1977
Mount Saint Helens erupts, leaving Portland in ashes and darkness.	1980
Bridgeport Brewery, the city's first microbrewery, opens.	1984
Columbia River National Scenic Area is established.	1986
MAX, Portland's light-rail system, opens.	1986
Oregon Vietnam Veterans Living Memorial is dedicated.	1987
The northern spotted owl is listed as a threatened species, heating up the war over Oregon's old-growth forests.	1990
Barbara Roberts becomes the first woman governor of Oregon.	1991
Oregon holds the first statewide vote-by-mail election in the United States.	1993
Metro Council approves the Stream and Floodplain Protection Plan.	1998
Westside MAX light-rail line opens.	1998
Metro Washington Park Zoo is renamed the Oregon Zoo.	1998
Metro Council makes first major changes to the urban growth boundary.	1998
Fortune magazine names Portland among the nation's top 10 boomtowns.	1998
The lavish new Classical Chinese Garden opens, sparking hopes of a Chinatown revival.	2000

polluted places. Studies have found that the deformed fish in the river may have developed as a result of pesticide use on upstream farms. The river is considered safe for swimming in most places, but no one would recommend drinking from it.

The beginning of the modern environmental movement arrived here in 1966, when Oregonians elected Tom McCall as their governor. Over the next eight years, McCall passed new laws requiring the recycling of beer and soda bottles (the "Bottle Bill") and statewide land-use planning. The Bottle Bill credits Oregonians with a nickel for every empty they return to the store. In this state, "Keep Oregon Green" is more than just a slogan.

In the 1980s, however, as many of the last remaining ancient forests in the state were targeted for clear-cutting, a new wave of environmentalism captured the public's attention. Lawsuits filed by the Oregon Natural Resources Council, the Portland Audubon Society, and others halted virtually all logging in old-growth forests. Groups like Portland-based Ecotrust emerged, advocating a new economy more consistent with conservation and sustainability.

Meanwhile, it has become apparent that years of abuse of the land have decimated the salmon. In 1999 the federal government placed salmon and steelhead that swim up the Willamette through Portland on the endangered species list. That decision kicked off a campaign in Portland to make sure that people, developers, government, and industry become "salmon-friendly" as they go about their lives and business.

Today, many people in Portland are joining local groups working to protect and restore their city's famous livability (1,000 Friends of Oregon, Alternatives to Growth in Oregon), its air quality (Northwest Portland District Association, Environmental Justice Action Group, Oregon

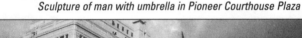

Sculpture of man with umbrella in Pioneer Courthouse Plaza

1999 Chuck Pefley

Portland's Ethnic Composition

According to the 1990 U.S. Census, Multnomah County's population of 615,000 breaks down as follows:

> White: 535,951
> Black: 37,774
> Asian: 33,925
> Hispanic: 23,425
> Native American: 7,350

Environmental Council), and the river (Willamette Riverkeepers). As other cities choke under unbridled growth, people here debate whether they want any more growth at all.

The People of Portland

Portland, if nothing else, is loaded with quirky character and a strong sense of community. But it is no "small-town USA." Portlanders on the whole are among the most highly educated in the nation. Maybe that's because the schools are among the best, or because the rainy weather and abundance of bookstores entice Portlanders to consume more books per capita than citizens of any other U.S. city. Portlanders also appreciate fine food and like to go out. Portland has among the highest number of restaurants per capita in the nation. The competition keeps restaurant quality high.

Portland is surprisingly developed and diverse in the arts for a city of its size. And, while still largely a white Protestant city, Portland's rich strands of culture seem disproportionate to its relatively small minority populations. Portland residents today promote diversity and support their ethnic communities.

Portlanders are also very political and often strangely polarized. Animal-rights activists live next door to hunters, atheists next to religious fanatics. But somehow, for the most part, they get along. It is hard not to feel a sense of community in Portland, a place where neighbors know each other and get involved. Citizen activism is nearly a way of life in Portland, where people still feel they can make a difference. And they do. At election time, political lawn signs can be seen everywhere. Politically, Portland is often seen as a bastion for liberal progressives and tolerance amidst an Oregon that, for the most part, is very conservative, homogeneous, and often intolerant.

Famous Portlanders

Jean Auel—author
Louise Bryant—socialist, artist, and activist
John Callahan—cartoonist
Matt Groening—cartoonist and Simpsons *creator*
Hazel Hall—poet
Phil Knight—founder of Nike, Inc.
Ursula K. LeGuin—author
Linus Pauling—Nobel Prize–winning scientist and vitamin C
       advocate
John Reed—socialist and activist
Gus van Sant—filmmaker

Religious devotion runs deep throughout Oregon, including much of Portland. This most likely stems from its early Christian missionary roots. Today, however, the city has a growing, active Jewish community. Another example of the city's diverse nature is the prominent gay and lesbian communities that have flourished within its bounds. Portland's lesbian community is commonly considered the largest in the United States.

Portland's ethnic diversity has been steadily increasing. Italian culture and products are definitely in vogue. African Americans comprise only about 6 percent of Multnomah County's population—up from 1 percent in 1960 and up from .02 percent in 1900—but maintain increasingly significant political and cultural influence on the city. Japanese residents, too, have come a long way from being banned as landowners. The progression can be seen, for example, in the legacy left throughout the city by Japanese developer and philanthropist Bill Naito. The city's Chinese population, once Portland's largest ethnic minority, has watched their Chinatown shrink from the bustling laundries, bazaars, exotic shops, and opium dens that were once centered at downtown's Second and Alder in the late 1800s to a few blocks of Chinese restaurants in Old Town. Many hope that the September 2000 opening of the lavish Classical Chinese Garden will revive Chinatown.

Weather

Yes, it rains a lot in Portland—three-quarters of the year anyway. But that can be better appreciated if you consider that Portland is in the heart of a temperate rainforest. The climate is lush and green and misty, and thus rainy. If it weren't for the rain, Portland would likely be a desert (like eastern Oregon, for instance, on the other side of the Cascade Mountains).

But, in Portland it hardly ever rains from mid-July to September, and it's not uncommon for summer weather to continue through much of October. Winters can vary widely in severity. Some years are quite mild with mostly rain and little else. Other years can bring terrible ice storms, bitter cold, and freezing rain. While snow is plentiful at higher elevations, Portland usually has only a few days of snowfall each year.

When to Visit

If you enjoy the outdoors, the best time to visit Portland is in August or September. Still, that's not the only time. Go to the coast in early October and you'll find sunshine but few people. Or go in February to watch whales or fierce ocean storms. In spring you'll find beauty in a train ride through the apple orchards of Hood River Valley. And if you travel to Portland in the darkest of winter, you can gleefully ski or snowboard all day long at one of three nearby resorts.

Dressing in Portland

Portlanders, above all, dress casually. That's not to say that Portland does not have a sophisticated side or is not stylish, because it is. It's just that self-expression overwhelms the conformist "uniform," whether it be a dressy business suit or the simple T-shirt, jeans, and sneakers. Portland has character. And Portlanders dress with attitude.

The city has a distinctly bohemian feel to it. Nose rings and tattoos are everywhere. Spiked hair and the Goth look are common. Snowboard and skateboard garb with the super-baggy pants are standard street clothes for young people throughout the city. And hippie clothing is pedestrian in the Hawthorne district. Because of the small size and diverse nature of the city, highly fashionable artists and business types can be seen downtown wearing sleek cosmopolitan clothing, while in locales just minutes away frumpy is the prevailing look. Name-brand sportswear is also everywhere. Really, in Portland, anything goes.

Portland sign at the Broadway Building

C. Bruce Forster

Portland Weather

	Avg. High Temps (°F)	Avg. Low Temps (°F)	Avg. Inches Rain
January	46	34	5.35
February	51	36	3.68
March	56	39	3.54
April	61	42	2.39
May	67	47	2.06
June	74	53	1.48
July	80	57	0.63
August	80	57	1.09
September	75	52	1.75
October	64	45	2.66
November	53	40	5.34
December	46	35	6.13

Calendar of Events

FEBRUARY
Heritage Concert, Northwest Afrikan American Ballet: This once-a-year concert is not to be missed—dynamic dance and drumming that's irresistible. Arlene Schnitzer Concert Hall, 503/287-8852.
Portland International Film Festival: Oregon's major film event showcases 100 films from more than 30 different countries. Various downtown theaters, 503/221-1156.

APRIL
International Women's Day: This one-day event draws more than 3,000 people for live entertainment, retail vendors, international cuisine, a free health room, and a family resource center. Portland Conference Center, 503/972-0630.
International Vancouver Discovery Walk Festival: Three days of non-competitive walking events. Vancouver, Washington, 360/892-6758.
Earth Day: Celebrate the diversity of the planet and learn how to protect a fragile global environment. Pioneer Courthouse Square, 503/223-1613.

MAY
Jefferson Dancers: Annual showcase of talented young dancers from the acclaimed Jefferson dance program of the Portland Public Schools. Newmark Theatre, Portland Center for the Performing Arts, 503/248-4335.

Cinco de Mayo Celebration: Celebrate the culture of Mexico with Hispanic entertainment, music, and food. Tom McCall Waterfront Park, 503/222-9807.

Portland Youth Philharmonic Spring Concert: Conservatory Orchestra and String Ensemble perform a variety of classic works. Civic Auditorium, 503/223-5939.

Asian Heritage Month Celebration: Many Asian community organizations take part in this event at Pioneer Courthouse Square, with cultural displays, food, and performances. Contact the Commission on Asian Affairs at 503/227-7514 or e-mail asian.affairs@state.or.us for additional information.

JUNE

Portland Rose Festival: This monthlong festival is a family favorite. Highlighted events include parades, an air show, car races, dragon boat races, an arts festival, and a waterfront carnival. Tom McCall Waterfront Park, 503/227-2681.

American Choreographer's Showcase Oregon Ballet Theatre: Oregon's premier ballet company performs creative pieces in this showcase at the end of its local season. Oregon Ballet Theatre, 503/222-5538.

Portland Rose Festival Grand Floral Parade: Tickets for the Grand Floral Parade go on sale six months before the event. Reserved seats are available inside and outside the Memorial Coliseum. 503/227-2681.

Portland Arts Festival: This festival features 120 regional and national artists, music, theater, and hands-on art for kids. South Park Blocks, 503/227-2681.

Strawberry Festival: German-style dinner, music, and lots of shortcake. Frog Pond Church, Wilsonville, 503/682-0339.

JULY

Waterfront Blues Festival: Celebrate the Fourth of July weekend on the green alongside the river. Eighty blues acts perform nonstop on three stages over five days, with loads of vendors and foods. Tom McCall Waterfront Park, 503/973-FEST.

Fort Vancouver Fourth of July Show: The largest fireworks display west of the Mississippi caps this daylong celebration. Fort Vancouver, Washington, 360/693-5481.

State Games of Oregon: Oregon's statewide Olympic-style, multisport event is open to athletes of all ages and abilities. Each sporting event takes place at a different location throughout the state, mostly in the greater Portland area. 503/520-1319.

The Gorge Games: A weeklong sporting extravaganza and music festival. Top athletes compete in sporting events, including kayaking and paragliding. Spectators are also invited to participate. Hood River Expo Center, 541/386-7774.

Summit to Surf: This challenging cycling event features a 56-mile ride (with optional 12-mile climb) that begins in Welches and follows Highway 26 to Highway 35 to Hood River. Starting point is Welches Grade School, 503/736-2770.

Division-Clinton Street Fair: Annual fair including a children's parade, vendors, sidewalk sales, and other special events. Division and Clinton Streets in the southeast, 503/774-2832.

Oregon Brewers Festival: North America's largest gathering of brewers. Music, entertainment, and 90 different brews. Tom McCall Waterfront Park, 503/778-5917.

AUGUST

Washington County Fair and Rodeo: More than a rodeo, this event also includes nightly music performances by national headliners, a showcase of horses, a circus, and more activities. Washington County Fairgrounds, 503/648-1416.

Mount Hood Jazz Festival: Oregon's largest jazz festival features world-renowned artists. Mount Hood Community College, 503/231-0161.

The Bite—A Taste of Portland: Listen to Northwest bands and sample offerings from Portland restaurants. Tom McCall Waterfront Park, 503/248-0600.

Homowo Festival of African Arts: Music, dancing, crafts, and foods from several African nations highlight this festival. South Park Blocks, Portland State University, 503/288-3025.

Oregon State Fair and Expo: This event offers exhibits, entertainment, horse shows, a carnival, and fun for the whole family. Oregon State Fairgrounds, Salem, 503/378-3247.

Festa Italiana: Italian food, wine garden, and entertainment. Pioneer Courthouse Square, 503/771-0310.

Hood to Coast Relay: This 195-mile relay race starts at Mount Hood and ends up at the beach. Timberline Lodge, 503/292-4626.

SEPTEMBER

Art in the Pearl: A Labor Day arts festival for the whole family, with entertainment, food, and fun. Portland's Pearl district, 503/722-9017.

Belmont Street Fair: Live music, games, puppet shows, sidewalk sales, and more. Southeast Belmont Street, 503/788-4992.

Annual Portland Creative Conference: This gathering of writers, directors, and luminaries focuses the spotlight on the human creative process and its award-winning results. Past presenters have included Spike Lee, Matt Groening, and Gus van Sant. Portland Center for the Performing Arts, 503/234-1641.

PICA's Annual Dada Ball: An elegant evening of mayhem and merriment to benefit the Portland Institute for Contemporary Art. PICA, 503/242-1419.

North by Northwest (NXNW): The three-night NXNW music festival allows you to discover the best new bands and solo acts from the Pacific Northwest, across the United States, and around the world. Schedules and locations vary, with most concerts taking place in downtown Portland. 512/467-7979.

OCTOBER

Portland Marathon: This family-oriented event features a 26.2-mile run or

High Technology in the Silicon Forest
by Keith Kullberg, president of STEP Technology, a Web and software development firm

The Portland/Beaverton metropolitan area, dubbed the Silicon Forest, is the third-largest high-technology center on the West Coast, just behind Silicon Valley and Seattle. More than 40,000 people are employed in high technology, making it the largest sector of the Oregon economy.

The largest of Portland's high-tech companies is Intel, where many of the leading computer microprocessors, such as the Pentium, are designed. Other significant local high-tech firms include Mentor Graphics and Orcad (electronic design-automation software), Sequent (high-performance multiprocessor computers), Electro Scientific Industries (wafer etching systems), InFocus (the leader in computer projection systems), Lattice Semiconductor (the leader in programmable array logic), Concentrix (electronic banking software), and numerous others.

Portland has a number of Internet companies and startups, although it has yet to produce a home run like Amazon.com, from Seattle to the north. Some of the more significant companies on the Internet scene include: 800.com (the consumer electronics zone), cameraworld.com, creativepro.com (vortal for creative professionals), Webtrends (Web site metrics and management software), Webridge (e-business solution frameworks), Sapient (now a division of webmd.com), Sight and Sound (electronic airline reservation systems), EasyStreet (Web hosting), Rulespace (Web content filtering), and STEP Technology (a leading Northwest Web development firm). With all of this activity, the demand for Internet and software engineers is at an all-time high—hiring them is difficult.

If you'd like to meet some of the city's Internet professionals, attend the Portland Pint (www.pint.org), an industry cocktail party held downtown every fourth Thursday evening. Also consider attending the Portland Creative Conference (www.createcon8.org), a national conference of film, video, advertising, creative, and Internet professionals held every September.

walk, a 5-mile run, a 10K Mayor's Walk, a wheelchair race, a noncompetitive 2-mile kids' run, and a 2-mile Special Olympics run. Downtown Portland, 503/226-1111.

Annual Greek Festival: Imported gifts, food booths, a tavern, live entertainment, Greek folk dancing, a gourmet bake shop, cooking demonstrations, and church tours. Holy Trinity Greek Orthodox Church, 503/234-0468.

Salmon Festival: This annual festival for all ages features guided salmon-viewing walks, environmental exhibits, children's crafts and activities, wagon rides, music, food, and more. Oxbow Regional Park, eight miles east of Gresham on the Sandy River, 503/797-1850.

Dragon boats,
Portland Rose Festival

NOVEMBER

Christmas at Pittock Mansion: This three-story elegant Portland landmark is extravagantly decorated with a different theme each year. Pittock Mansion, 503/823-3623.

DECEMBER

The Grotto's Festival of Lights: A light show, living history, and other holiday activities highlight this event. The Grotto, 503/254-7371.

Zoolights Festival: The zoo celebrates the holiday season with thousands of lights, a decorated zoo train, animated animal silhouettes, costumed characters, and music. Oregon Zoo, 503/226-1561.

Business and Economy

Several industries dominate the Portland area. Besides the sports-clothing giants Nike and Adidas/Salomon, there's a sports-garment district in the close-in Eastside. Suburban Beaverton, home to "Silicon Forest," supports a booming high-tech industry. Software companies spring up like weeds in Oregon. And of course Portland has become the country's microbrewery capital and beer hub in the last decade, with more small breweries than any other city in the world. The Port of Portland is also a busy gateway.

Cost of Living

The cost of living in Portland has increased with the city's recent growth, but it's in no way off the charts. On the ACCRA cost of lliving comparison, Portland scores 112.5, a bit above the national average of 100 but far below New York's rating of 231.8 and the Bay Area's 156.6. Note that the state of Oregon does not assess a retail sales tax. Here's what you'll pay for some typical goods and services in Portland:

Five-mile taxi ride:	$10
Hotel double room:	$120
Dinner for two:	$55
Movie admission:	$7.50
Daily newspaper:	$.35

Housing

Housing prices are average, with a two-bedroom home selling for around $128,500, a three-bedroom for $173,300, and a four-bedroom for $259,400. Old Portland Craftsman-style homes have become popular, and many have been restored. Older homes range from small bungalows to grand view homes such as those found in Portland's West Hills or the Alameda or Mount Tabor neighborhoods. Newer homes can be found in the suburbs, and swank brand-new condos have sprouted in the northwest's Pearl district. Apartments tend to cluster near the pedestrian-friendly shopping districts, such as the Hawthorne/Belmont area and Northwest 21st/23rd.

Schools

Portland boasts an educated population: 79 percent graduated from high school with 42 percent of those attending college. In 1993 Oregon high school students in general ranked highest in the nation on Scholastic Aptitude Tests, and Portland Public School students today score above the national average (520 verbal compared with 505 national, and 525 math compared with 511 national). Some programs have suffered in recent years from budget cuts, especially in the arts. However, efforts are underway to try to revive some of these programs. One goal of the school district is to have all students begin learning a second language in the first grade starting in 2000–2001.

Tri-Met

2

GETTING AROUND PORTLAND

Portland is, in almost every way, pedestrian-friendly. Most streets are laid out in a logical rectangular grid pattern with ascending numbers. Others line up in alphabetical order. City blocks are small, and the public transportation network is impressive. Consider leaving your car behind and using MAX (Portland's light-rail), Tri-Met public buses, or the city's new streetcar. Better yet, walk. Once you're in the city, nothing is far away.

City Layout

When trying to find an address, it's best to think of Portland in terms of quadrants: southeast, northeast/north, southwest, and northwest. Numbered avenues are parallel and run north-south, with street addresses starting from the Willamette River (which divides east and west) at zero. Named streets are also parallel and run east-west, with Burnside dividing north and south. Addresses on these streets can be readily found by the number. For example, 2450 Southeast Ash Street would be in the southeast quadrant between Southeast 24th and 25th Avenues. But, while the coordinates and rectangular grid layout make for ease in locating addresses, people who really know the city refer to its districts, or neighborhoods, which vividly bring to mind so much more.

Each of Portland's neighborhoods has its own feel, its own flavor, its own character. Get oriented in Portland by becoming acquainted with its neighborhoods.

Downtown Neighborhoods
Old Town is home to excellent secondhand clothing shops, a huge

crafts bazaar known as Saturday Market, a bustling nightclub scene, and Chinatown.

The Pearl, Portland's gallery/loft district, has undergone the most dramatic renovation of any part of the city in recent years. Dives and drug dealers have given way to pricey lofts, art galleries, and coffeehouses. Real estate has skyrocketed as the district continues to attract trend-setting magnets like advertising giant Weiden and Kennedy.

The Portland **Riverfront** neighborhood, with its unobstructed view of the Willamette River, is not just a treat—it's a must, especially for warm-weather travelers. Visit it for a stroll, to dine, or to sip refreshments in one of its many outdoor cafés or restaurants.

The neighborhood around the **PSU/Performing Arts Center** is Portland's established art and music hub, its cultural center. Lining the graceful South Park Blocks are the Portland Art Museum, a ballet school, and elegant concert and symphony halls and theaters, as well as Portland State University and its library. The city's beautifully renovated Central Library is just blocks away.

Eastside Neighborhoods

Hawthorne Boulevard, in the **Hawthorne/Belmont Dairy** neighborhood, has long been considered Portland's hippie street. But it is really much more than that. A busy street with a laid-back feel and good breakfast joints, unique shops, and alehouses, Hawthorne draws people from all over the city. Nearby Belmont is Hawthorne's up-and-coming sister street. Centered around the Belmont Dairy, a renovated brick building on a block that houses restaurants, bars, an upscale grocery store, and affordable lofts that cater to a young Gen-X or Gen-Y set, the neighborhood has sprouted. Teahouses and funky secondhand stores round out the area.

Ladd's Addition is a quiet neighborhood of old Portland residences. Beautiful old homes are laid out in a maze of curly streets and flowers.

The residential neighborhoods of **Laurelhurst** and **Mount Tabor** are each centered around gorgeous inner-city parks, Laurelhurst Park and Mount Tabor Park. One has a beautiful and graceful lake at its core; the other is perched on a volcano and includes spectacular views of the city.

Alameda and **Irvington** are two other old Eastside residential neighborhoods. Top public schools and beautiful old homes on streets lined with huge trees have brought many families to these adjacent communities.

Next to a golf course, prestigious Reed College, and the beautiful

When approaching Portland from the south, do *not* take the exit marked I-84E/I-205. This will route you completely around the city, and you will miss the portion of Interstate 84 that goes through east Portland. Rather, take the second exit, marked I-84.

Crystal Springs Rhododendron Gardens, quiet **Eastmoreland** is an established neighborhood with large homes.

The old southeast neighborhood of **Sellwood,** while not as close to the city core as the other communities, has become a destination for antique lovers and gourmets. The business district teems with antique shops, restaurants, and quaint cafés. Nearby, you'll find the city's only amusement park, Oaks Park.

Northwest Neighborhoods
Bustling **Northwest 23rd Avenue** is a popular destination for Portlanders as well as visitors. The street has a distinctly yuppie feel with its pricey boutiques and eateries. People look good here and come to be seen. Densely packed with storefronts and kiosks, it's a lively place. And the neighboring streets, lined with well-maintained older homes, are lovely to walk.

Northwest 21st Avenue parallels its bigger sister, Northwest 23rd, but is not as flashy. It's also a bit younger. It does have some of the best restaurants in the city, though, as well as some popular pubs and coffeehouses.

North Portland
On a bluff overlooking the Willamette River, **St. Johns** was once its own city before it joined Portland many decades ago. The neighborhood has its own "Main Street" with bustling shops and restaurants. It is also close to the University of Portland. Its most distinguished landmark, though, is the St. Johns Bridge. A suspension bridge built in 1931 with 400-foot towers, it's arguably the most beautiful bridge in the city.

Albina, a community north of the Rose Garden Arena, is a cultural hub and flourishing urban neighborhood. A recent revival has resulted in the almost-overnight appearance of many new shops and restaurants.

Public Transportation

City Buses
Portland public transportation is run by its award-winning mass transit system, Tri-Met. Blue-and-white signs all over the city mark the bus stops. You can get schedules and transit maps for buses and MAX (Portland's

Metropolitan Area Express (MAX)

Tri-Met

light-rail train) at Pioneer Square. In general, buses run every few minutes in the city on common routes during peak hours, but on outlying routes they can run as seldom as every one or two hours on holidays, Sundays, or during off-peak times. So it's wise to be familiar with your route and to consider the hour. Buses don't run all night in Portland, but most go until after midnight, and after eight at night they will stop anywhere along the route at your request.

Bus travel in the immediate downtown area is free. Elsewhere you pay your fare and get a transfer when you board the bus. Be sure to have exact change (the buses do take dollar bills). Transfers are typically good for two hours and can be used on MAX trains as well as buses. Check for fares, which range slightly depending on how many zones you cross. Better yet, if you're planning to do a lot of bus travel during the day outside of the downtown "Fareless Square," then buy a day ticket for $3.50. Another good option is to buy a 10-ticket short-hopper book, especially if you're with a partner. You get a couple of free rides that way. Children under the age of six ride free. For information or tickets, go to the Tri-Met office downtown in Pioneer Courthouse Square or visit a Fred Meyer store. Alternatively, call 503/238-RIDE or go online to www.tri-met.org.

TRIVIA MAX's underground zoo station is the deepest light-rail station in North America. The three-mile-long tunnels enter the Washington Park Station 260 feet below the zoo parking lot. The tunnels' deepest point is 320 feet below the surface.

FARELESS SQUARE

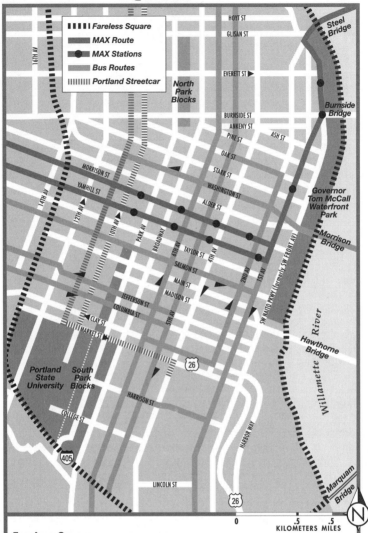

Fareless Square
■ ■ ■ ■ *Fareless Square*
■ ■ ■ ■ *MAX Route*
● *MAX Stations*
■ ■ ■ ■ *Bus Routes*
|||||||| *Portland Streetcar*

HOYT ST
GLISAN ST
Steel Bridge
16TH AV
EVERETT ST ▶
North Park Blocks
BURNSIDE ST
Burnside Bridge
ANKENY ST
PINE ST
ASH ST
OAK ST
STARK ST
MORRISON ST
WASHINGTON ST
YAMHILL ST
ALDER ST
14TH AV
12TH AV
10TH AV
PARK AV
BROADWAY
6TH AV
TAYLOR ST
4TH AV
Governor Tom McCall Waterfront Park
SALMON ST
Morrison Bridge
MAIN ST
2ND AV
1ST AV
MADISON ST
JEFFERSON ST
COLUMBIA ST
SW NAITO PKWY (formerly SW FRONT AV)
CLAY ST
MARKET ST
Hawthorne Bridge
26
Portland State University
South Park Blocks
Willamette River
HARRISON ST
COLLEGE ST
HARBOR WAY
405
Marquam Bridge
LINCOLN ST
26

0   .5   .5
KILOMETERS MILES
N

Fareless Square
All buses are free in the downtown area (bounded by the Willamette River, Northwest Irving Street, and Interstate 405). If you're in this area, just hop aboard. In the fall of 2001, this "Fareless Square" will extend into the Lloyd District on the Eastside.

Transit Mall
The Transit Mall, or Bus Mall, is downtown on Fifth and Sixth Avenues. From there, you can go anywhere Tri-Met goes. Covered stops over a several-block stretch, with computer displays, make finding your bus a breeze in any weather.

Return of the Streetcar to Portland

by Portland City Commissioner Charlie Hales

Portland is going back to the future as it prepares to return electric streetcars to its streets after an absence of nearly half a century. The city, which once boasted more than 200 miles of streetcar tracks, is growing excited about the opening of the modern Central City Streetcar in the summer of 2001. And indeed, it is a wonderful opportunity to undo the foolish mistakes made 50 years ago when Portland tore out its tracks and gave in to the domination of the automobile.

Portland will be the first city in the United States to introduce modern, European-style streetcars to its streets. The new air-conditioned streetcars, manufactured in the Czech Republic, will run 18 hours a day on a 2.5-mile line stretching from northwest Portland to the downtown campus of Portland State University. Along the route, visitors, shoppers, commuters, and residents will be able to hop off at such landmarks as Powell's City of Books, the Central Library, and the Portland Art Museum. The streetcars will be more than a mere way to move from here to there. Once again, as it did in its heyday at the turn of the 20th century, the streetcar line will shape the way the city grows and help lay the foundation for new neighborhoods.

We welcome you to Portland and urge you to take a ride on Portland's new streetcars. Our future looks a lot brighter thanks to the innovative thinking and public support that made this project possible. And if you really like it, go back to your hometown and tell your elected officials you want one, too!

City Light-Rail—MAX (Metropolitan Area Express)

Portland's MAX is a model light-rail system. Since opening in 1986, it has attracted transportation agents from cities all over the world seeking to emulate its success.

Buy your MAX ticket from the machine at the MAX station before boarding the train and hold it until you get off. Fares are the same as for buses.

Bridges Across the Willamette

Sellwood Bridge—connects Lake Oswego on the west to Sellwood on the east

Ross Island Bridge—connects John's Landing south of downtown to Southeast Powell Street on the Eastside

Marquam (I-5) Bridge—connects Interstate 5 to Interstate 84 East and Interstate 5 North

Hawthorne Bridge—connects Hawthorne Street on the Eastside to Southwest Madison and Southwest Main Streets downtown

Morrison Bridge—connects Belmont and Morrison Streets on the Eastside to Southwest Washington and Alder Streets downtown

Burnside Bridge—connects East Burnside and West Burnside

Steel Bridge—connects Northwest Glisan and Everett Streets with the Rose Quarter, Interstate 5, and Interstate 84 access

Broadway Bridge—connects West Broadway and East Broadway

Fremont (I-405) Bridge—connects the northwest and downtown with Interstate 5, Interstate 84, and north Portland

Any transfer slip from a bus is also good on the MAX train and vice versa. Ticket auditors do check tickets with some frequency. But remember, MAX is free in downtown Portland. The MAX runs through downtown between Gresham (east of Portland) and Hillsboro (west of Portland) and is a comfortable and fun way to ride into the city without hassle.

While the Eastside MAX has run successfully for years, Westside MAX is new. Look for the sculptures, sidewalk etchings, and art furniture that can be found at the new stops.

For information on MAX schedules and fares, contact Tri-Met at 503/238-RIDE or www.tri-met.org.

Driving in Portland

Driving in Portland is better than in many cities. In fact, many people consider it a treat, especially at night when the lights reflect on the Willamette. And while getting on and off freeways and bridges may take a little practice, for the most part streets are well marked. Just read your map carefully before you go.

Be aware that in downtown, in general, streets are one-way, alternating in direction each consecutive street. Odd avenues go south and even avenues go north. Avoid the Transit Mall downtown on Fifth and Sixth Avenues—through traffic is not permitted.

Parking can be difficult downtown. And when you do find a spot, it can cost you. Meters typically charge a dollar an hour, but long-term lots and garages are available. If you park in a SmartPark garage you can get your parking ticket validated (and the price of the ticket refunded) at many downtown stores and shops when you make a purchase.

Taxis are not readily available on street corners anywhere in Portland. Rather than wait for one, call ahead. Service is usually prompt.

Take your bike on MAX.

Portland Bureau of Traffic Management

Biking in Portland

Yes, the weather is rainy much of the year, but Portland's bike-friendly routes and accommodations more than compensate. In fact, 300 miles of bike lanes have been built in the past decade. That's why *Bicycling Magazine* named Portland the best city for bicycling in the United States. Whether you are a bike commuter, sightseer, or someone in search of great inner-city mountain biking, Portland delivers.

Bike racks can be found all over the city. All Tri-Met buses and MAX trains are equipped with bike racks. The fare is the same, but you need a permit ($5). Pick one up at the Tri-Met office downtown at Pioneer Courthouse Square (503/239-3044 or www.tri-met.org). Bike lockers are also available at some stations and can be rented overnight. For more information on bicycling in Portland, call Portland Bicycle Program, 503/823-7082.

Air Travel

Arriving in Portland by air is often trouble-free. Air-traffic delays are infrequent, and once on the ground getting baggage and exiting the airport is usually a quick process. Still, Portland International Airport (PDX) seems to be perpetually under construction. The resulting ground traffic can cause long-term parking and rental-car pick-up to be frustrating.

When driving to the airport, allow plenty of time for traffic delays, even though the airport is just 15 minutes from downtown. If at all possible take a shuttle. Many U.S. airlines service the Portland area, and international travel is available to Asia, Canada, and Mexico. PDX is a major stop on the West Coast between Mexico and Alaska.

Major Airlines Serving PDX

Air BC, Air Canada	800/776-3000
Alaska Airlines	800/252-7522
American Airlines	800/433-7300
America West	800/235-9292
Continental Airlines	800/523-3273
Delta Air Lines	800/523-3273
Horizon Airlines	800/547-9308
Northwest Airlines	800/225-2525
Southwest Airlines	800/435-9792
Trans World Airlines	800/221-2000
United Airlines	800/241-6522

Airport Parking/Shuttles

If possible, avoid long-term parking at the airport while it's under construction (through late 2002). Instead, use alternative transportation (such as public buses or free hotel shuttles) to get to the airport during peak traffic hours in the morning, midday, and afternoon. On the other hand, short-term parking has become more convenient with the completion of a new seven-story parking garage, which you can access from the terminal through a pedestrian tunnel. Rental-car services are available there as well. Some shuttle services include:

Portland International Airport shops

Portland International Airport

**T
I
P**

Starting in September 2001, you can pick up Portland's MAX
light-rail right from the airport terminal, thus avoiding delays to
and from the airport.

Eastside Airporter (503/249-1837): Door-to-door shuttles every 30 minutes
between the airport and Eastside locations. Call in advance.
Raja Tours (503/524-4386): Door-to-door shuttles 24 hours a day between
the airport, Westside locations, and downtown.
Valley Shuttle (503/885-8075): Shuttles between the airport and downtown daily 5:30 a.m. to 11 p.m.

Train Service

Train service is available from the downtown Union Station at 800
Northwest Sixth Avenue. For a mere $45 roundtrip you can take the new
and stylish Spanish-designed Talgo high-speed train between Portland
and Seattle. Plans are in the works to increase service between Portland
and Seattle to 14 trains a day. Amtrak (503/273-4865 or 800/872-7245)
provides daily service to San Francisco and cities east of Portland like
Spokane and Billings. Consider doing the overnight roundtrip to San
Francisco in a sleeper car for gorgeous Cascade scenery and an old-
fashioned rail experience.

Bus Service

Bus stations can often be grungy, but in Portland that's not the case. The
Greyhound Bus Terminal at 550 Northwest Sixth Avenue (503/243-2357) is
decent and clean, though simple. It is also conveniently located next to
the train station and near city bus and MAX light-rail lines. Greyhound
offers service to and from Portland to areas throughout the Pacific
Northwest and beyond. For more information, call 800/231-2222.

The Lion and the Rose Victorian Bed-and-Breakfast

3

WHERE TO STAY

Portland, having evolved from its historical status as an overnight "rest stop" for Indians and fur traders traveling between Fort Vancouver and Willamette Falls (Oregon City), has today become a destination for tourists and business travelers. The 1990s brought much renovation and restoration to some of Portland's wonderful historic hotels. Portland has also attracted some major luxury hotels in recent years, adding to the fine array of existing hotels, budget motels, and charming bed-and-breakfasts.

Most of the more expensive luxury hotels are downtown, while bed-and-breakfasts and budget accommodations are more readily found in the nearby suburbs or on the outskirts of town. Major chain hotels are scattered throughout the area but are clustered around the airport and Interstate 5 at the Columbia River. Farther from the city, you will find vacation resorts at Mount Hood, in the Columbia River Gorge, and along the coast. The following prices, for a double room per night, reflect an average. Actual prices vary.

Price-rating symbols:
$	**$55 and under**
$$	**$56 to $80**
$$$	**$81 to $125**
$$$$	**$126 and up**

DOWNTOWN PORTLAND

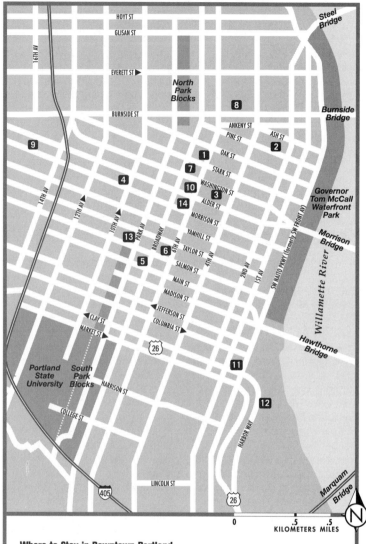

HOYT ST
GLISAN ST
16TH AV
EVERETT ST ▶
North Park Blocks
BURNSIDE ST
Steel Bridge
Burnside Bridge
ANKENY ST
PINE ST
ASH ST
OAK ST
STARK ST
WASHINGTON ST
ALDER ST
MORRISON ST
YAMHILL ST
TAYLOR ST
SALMON ST
MAIN ST
MADISON ST
JEFFERSON ST
COLUMBIA ST
CLAY ST
MARKET ST
HARRISON ST
COLLEGE ST
LINCOLN ST
14TH AV
12TH AV
10TH AV
PARK AV
BROADWAY
6TH AV
4TH AV
2ND AV
1ST AV
SW NAITO PKWY (formerly SW FRONT AV)
SW FRONT AV
HARBOR WAY

Governor Tom McCall Waterfront Park
Morrison Bridge
Willamette River
Hawthorne Bridge
Portland State University
South Park Blocks
Marquam Bridge

26
405
26

0   .5   .5
KILOMETERS MILES
N

Where to Stay in Downtown Portland

1. The Benson Hotel
2. Embassy Suites Hotel
3. Fifth Avenue Suites
4. Governor Hotel
5. Heathman Hotel
6. Hilton Hotel
7. Hotel Vintage Plaza

8. Macmaster House Bed-and-Breakfast
9. The Mallory Hotel
10. Marriott—Portland City Center
11. Marriott—Portland Downtown on the Waterfront

12. Riverplace Hotel
13. West Coast Paramount Hotel
14. The Westin Portland

DOWNTOWN

Hotels

THE BENSON HOTEL
309 SW Broadway
503/228-2000
$$$$
The Benson, established in 1912, is one of Portland's most elegant luxury hotels. The lobby, which hosts live jazz most nights, holds claim as Portland's first live jazz venue. The hotel underwent a beautiful $17 million restoration in 1990 and remains Portland's oldest operating hotel. Frequented by movie stars, the Benson has two restaurants, 24-hour room service, and on-site workout facilities. & (Downtown)

EMBASSY SUITES HOTEL
319 SW Pine
503/279-9000
$$$$
The Embassy Suites, previously known as the Multnomah Hotel and now a historic landmark, was restored several years ago. Today there are 276 guest rooms and a huge, comfortable lobby that often hosts live chamber music. The hotel houses Salon Nyla, known for its massages; a pool and fitness center; and the Portland Steak and Chophouse, which includes an extensive low-budget evening bar menu. Guests receive a cooked breakfast each morning and enjoy a manager's reception each evening as part of their stay. As with nearly all the downtown hotels, parking costs extra. & (Downtown)

FIFTH AVENUE SUITES
506 SW Washington at Fifth Ave.
503/222-0001 or 800/711-2971

$$$–$$$$
This four-star hotel is in a historic department store built in 1911 and completely remodeled in 1996. Guest rooms, all of which are suites, are spacious. Some of the corner suites on the upper floors include terrific views of Mount Hood and are perfect for entertaining small groups of people. A workout facility is available for guests 24 hours a day, and the Red Star Restaurant is on the premises. Valet parking costs extra. Pets are permitted. & (Downtown)

GOVERNOR HOTEL
SW 10th and Alder
503/224-3400 or 800/554-3456
$$$$
Recently restored, the Governor and everything in it seem big. Murals and a totem pole dominate the lobby, and yet the warm lighting maintains a homey ambience. Jake's restaurant and bar is a local landmark, famous for its seafood. The Princeton Athletic Club, also in the building, is open to guests for a fee. Valet parking is available. & (Downtown)

HEATHMAN HOTEL
1001 SW Broadway at Salmon
503/241-4100
$$$$
The elegant Heathman is an old luxury hotel in a historic building. Guests enjoy the Heathman as much for its four-star restaurant and sweeping lobby with grand staircase as for its rooms. Afternoon tea is served in the lobby, as is bistro fare. Live jazz is played evenings in the lobby's living room–like setting, and 24-hour room service is available. & (Downtown)

HILTON HOTEL
921 SW Sixth Ave.
503/226-1611
$$$–$$$$

This spacious downtown hotel is popular for meetings and conventions. The Hilton includes 455 guest rooms, a full-service athletic center with a pool, a bistro on the main floor, and a fine restaurant way up on the 23rd floor. Plans call for expansion on an adjacent block. & (Downtown)

HOTEL VINTAGE PLAZA
422 SW Broadway
503/228-1212 or 800/243-0555
$$$–$$$$

In a historic building and adjacent to a popular restaurant, Hotel Vintage Plaza is a great choice. Pazzo Ristorante serves breakfast, lunch, and dinner and provides room service until midnight. Because the hotel is relatively small, with just 107 rooms, it feels intimate. Try the complimentary wine tasting each evening in its comfortable lobby. & (Downtown)

THE MALLORY HOTEL
729 SW 15th Ave.
503/223-6311 or 800/228-8657
$$$

This old Portland hotel was built in 1912. Incredibly, and most welcome, it offers guests free parking. It also includes a restaurant and bar. Finally, for those who prefer public transportation, MAX, Portland's light-rail line, is right outside the door. Pets are permitted. & (Downtown)

MARRIOTT—PORTLAND CITY CENTER
520 SW Broadway
503/226-6300 or 800/228-9290

$$$$

The City Center Marriott is one of a handful of new hotels in downtown Portland. Opened in August 1999, this boutique-style establishment offers stunning views from the upper floors of its 20 stories. Because of its 3,300 square feet of meeting rooms, guests consider it a great choice for small gatherings. A fitness center with a whirlpool is great for unwinding after a long day of work or travel. The Chinook Grill and Lounge serves regional Northwest cuisine. Pets are permitted. & (Downtown)

MARRIOTT—PORTLAND DOWNTOWN WATERFRONT
1401 SW Naito Pkwy. (Front St.)
503/226-7600 or 800/228-9290
$$$–$$$$

This large Marriott near the Willamette waterfront has 503 rooms, plenty of space for large meetings and conventions, two restaurants, a bar and grill, athletic facilities, and a swimming pool. The upper rooms have breathtaking views of the river, Mount Hood, and Mount Saint Helens. Pets are permitted. & (Downtown)

THE RIVERPLACE HOTEL
1510 SW Harbor Way
503/228-3233
$$$$

This top-notch four-star establishment, near a cluster of shops and restaurants, is Portland's only riverfront hotel. You'll pay considerably more for the views from the Riverplace, but they're worth it. The Esplanade restaurant with French chef Pacal Sauton serves some of the finest cuisine in Portland and offers outdoor seating when the weather's nice.

Riverplace Hotel

THE WESTIN PORTLAND
750 SW Alder
503/294-9000 or 800/937-8461
$$$–$$$$
The Westin is yet another brand-new hotel to add to Portland's growing collection of luxury accommodations. Opened in 1999, the 19-story hotel in the heart of downtown houses 205 rooms, a health club, and a popular new restaurant, Oritalia. An elegantly appointed boardroom and a ballroom can be reserved for events. Parking is available but costs extra. Pets are permitted. ♿ (Downtown)

Another reason to consider the Riverplace is that it offers complimentary access to the Riverplace Athletic Club, one of the city's best gyms. ♿ (Downtown)

WEST COAST PARAMOUNT HOTEL
808 SW Taylor St.
503/223-9900
www.portlandparamount.com
$$$
This brand-new addition to the Portland hotel scene brings with it 154 rooms, a restaurant, a lounge, and a terrific central location near Pioneer Square and the arts and cultural district on the South Park Blocks. Parking costs $15 a day. ♿ (Downtown)

Bed-and-Breakfasts

MACMASTER HOUSE BED-AND-BREAKFAST
1041 SW Vista
503/223-7362
$$$
This 1895 historic home in a quiet neighborhood at the foot of Portland's West Hills offers a sweet retreat in the city. Guests find it perfectly situated for taking a short walk uphill to the Japanese and Rose Gardens or downhill to Portland's downtown and northwest districts. But book early. With only seven antique-filled rooms (some with fireplaces, two with private baths) and a wonderful chef, it fills up quickly. The same proprietor has run the place for 14 years. No

T I P

Don't be fooled. While there is no sales tax in Oregon, there is a hotel tax, and Portland's adds 9 percent to the cost of your room.

small children or pets are permitted. (Downtown)

NORTHWEST

Hotels

CYPRESS INN
809 SW King Ave.
503/226-6288
$–$$
You can't beat the location, especially for the price. This no-frills motel has the look and feel of countless places you'd find traveling across the country, only it is in an upscale neighborhood, a short walk from the pricey boutiques and outdoor cafés of Northwest 23rd Avenue. It's an ideal place to stay if you're on a budget and would rather spend your money on shopping or eating than on accommodations. The bargain gets better when you discover the free breakfast spread for guests: an array of doughnuts, muffins, fruit, coffee, juice, and Fruit Loops. (Northwest)

HAWTHORN INN AND SUITES
4319 NW Yeon
503/497-9044 or 800/527-1133
$$$
This hotel is on the far edge of northwest Portland, so you'll need a car. But it's a good place for families, with an indoor swimming pool, a spa, a sauna, a fitness center, and kitchenettes in the rooms. Some rooms even have spas. In addition, a hot buffet breakfast is included with each night's stay. &
(Northwest)

SILVER CLOUD INN
2426 NW Vaughn

503/242-2400
$$$
This chain hotel boasts easy access to both freeways and the bustling Northwest 23rd Avenue. Like other Silver Cloud Inns, it includes a hot tub. Private in-room Jacuzzis are available for a small additional fee. (Northwest)

Bed-and-Breakfasts

PITTOCK ACRES
BED-AND-BREAKFAST
103 NW Pittock Ave.
503/226-1163
www.bbhost.com/pittockacres
$$$
This small, little-known bed-and-breakfast nestles among the trees in the West Hills near Pittock Mansion, a historic Portland landmark. A romantic, contemporary place, it includes vintage linens, ruffles, a sitting room, a deck, and a garden arbor. Each of the three guest rooms has a private bath. This house has been decorated with French country wallpaper and wainscoting. Afternoon tea and refreshments are served daily, and breakfast takes place in a formal dining room with a view of the Hoyt Arboretum, one of several large, densely forested city parks in the West Hills. As with many B&Bs, this one is geared toward adults. (Northwest)

Campgrounds and Hostels

NORTHWEST PORTLAND
INTERNATIONAL HOSTEL
1818 NW Glisan
503/241-2783
$
This hostel has a few private rooms

GREATER PORTLAND

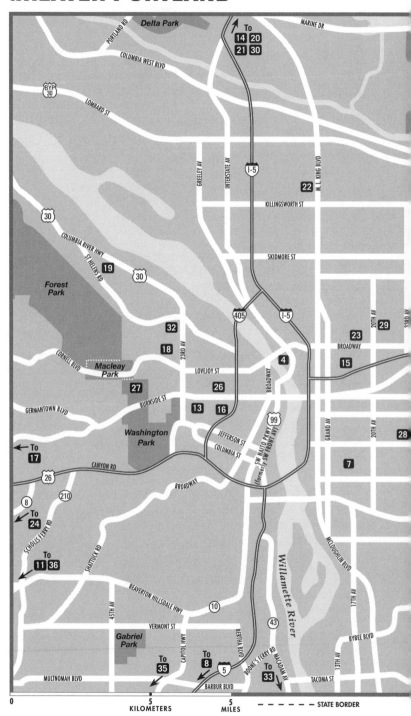

To
14 20
21 30

MARINE DR

Delta Park

PORTLAND RD

COLUMBIA WEST BLVD

BYP
30

LOMBARD ST

GREELEY AV

INTERSTATE AV

I-5

M.L. KING BLVD

22

KILLINGSWORTH ST

30

COLUMBIA RIVER HWY

ST HELENS RD

19

SKIDMORE ST

30

Forest
Park

405

I-5

20TH AV

33D AV

29

23

BROADWAY

15

32

18

23RD AV

CORNELL BLVD

Macleay
Park

LOVEJOY ST

4

BROADWAY

27

26

GERMANTOWN BLVD

BURNSIDE ST

13   16

GRAND AV

20TH AV

28

Washington
Park

JEFFERSON ST

SW NAITO PKWY
(formerly SW FRONT AV)

99

7

COLUMBIA ST

← To
17

CANYON RD

BROADWAY

26

8

210

← To
24

SCHOLLS FERRY RD

SHATTUCK RD

MCLOUGHLIN BLVD

Willamette River

To
11 36

BEAVERTON HILLSDALE HWY

45TH AV

17TH AV

10

VERMONT ST

CAPITOL HWY

BERTHA BLVD

43

BYBEE BLVD

Gabriel
Park

To
35

To
8

5

BOONE'S FERRY RD

MACADAM AV

13TH AV

To
33

TACOMA ST

MULTNOMAH BLVD

BARBUR BLVD

0

5
KILOMETERS

5
MILES

– – – – – STATE BORDER

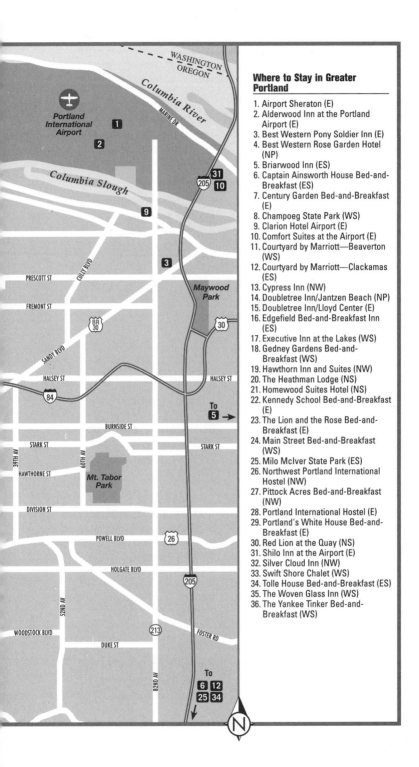

Where to Stay in Greater Portland

1. Airport Sheraton (E)
2. Alderwood Inn at the Portland Airport (E)
3. Best Western Pony Soldier Inn (E)
4. Best Western Rose Garden Hotel (NP)
5. Briarwood Inn (ES)
6. Captain Ainsworth House Bed-and-Breakfast (ES)
7. Century Garden Bed-and-Breakfast (E)
8. Champoeg State Park (WS)
9. Clarion Hotel Airport (E)
10. Comfort Suites at the Airport (E)
11. Courtyard by Marriott—Beaverton (WS)
12. Courtyard by Marriott—Clackamas (ES)
13. Cypress Inn (NW)
14. Doubletree Inn/Jantzen Beach (NP)
15. Doubletree Inn/Lloyd Center (E)
16. Edgefield Bed-and-Breakfast Inn (ES)
17. Executive Inn at the Lakes (WS)
18. Gedney Gardens Bed-and-Breakfast (WS)
19. Hawthorn Inn and Suites (NW)
20. The Heathman Lodge (NS)
21. Homewood Suites Hotel (NS)
22. Kennedy School Bed-and-Breakfast (E)
23. The Lion and the Rose Bed-and-Breakfast (E)
24. Main Street Bed-and-Breakfast (WS)
25. Milo McIver State Park (ES)
26. Northwest Portland International Hostel (NW)
27. Pittock Acres Bed-and-Breakfast (NW)
28. Portland International Hostel (E)
29. Portland's White House Bed-and-Breakfast (E)
30. Red Lion at the Quay (NS)
31. Shilo Inn at the Airport (E)
32. Silver Cloud Inn (NW)
33. Swift Shore Chalet (WS)
34. Tolle House Bed-and-Breakfast (ES)
35. The Woven Glass Inn (WS)
36. The Yankee Tinker Bed-and-Breakfast (WS)

($36 per night), but it's best known for its $15 dormitory-style beds. Bathroom and shower facilities are shared. A fully equipped kitchen and a washer and dryer are available for guests. (Northwest)

EASTSIDE

Hotels

AIRPORT SHERATON
8235 Airport Way
503/281-2500
$$$
The best part about the Airport Sheraton is its park-and-fly program. The program allows guests to park their cars at the hotel for up to 14 days. Other than that, it's more of the same: 213 guest rooms; large meeting facilities; a workout room, pool, spa, and sauna; a dining room; and a bar in the lobby. It's not centrally located but it is convenient for air travelers. &. (Eastside)

ALDERWOOD INN AT THE PORTLAND AIRPORT
7025 NE Alderwood Rd.
503/255-2700 or 888/987-2700
www.alderwoodinn.com
$$–$$$
Just five minutes from the airport, Alderwood has large rooms and includes an all-you-can-eat buffet breakfast with each night's stay. Also available are an indoor pool and Jacuzzi, a fitness room, a free airport shuttle, a park-and-fly package, and a restaurant and lounge. No pets are allowed. (Eastside)

BEST WESTERN PONY SOLDIER INN
9901 NE Sandy Blvd.

503/256-1504
www.ponysoldierinns.com
$$$
This hotel provides a free airport shuttle. Some rooms have Jacuzzis, and all come with a microwave and refrigerator. There is also a sauna and fitness room, an outdoor pool, and an open Jacuzzi. Complimentary breakfasts and a free *USA Today* come with each night's stay. No pets are allowed. &. (Eastside)

CLARION HOTEL AIRPORT
6233 NE 78th Court
503/251-2000 or 800/994-7878
www.clarionpdx.com
$$$
The Clarion Hotel is right on Colwood National Golf Course. The hotel's 24-hour airport shuttle service is free for guests. An indoor pool and sauna, a complimentary continental breakfast, a restaurant and lounge, meeting rooms, and a fitness facility round out the amenities. No pets are allowed. (Eastside)

COMFORT SUITES AT THE AIRPORT
12010 NE Airport Way
503/261-9000
$$
Conveniently located just 3.5 miles from the airport, this no-nonsense hotel offers complimentary continental breakfast and free airport shuttle service. It also offers a park-and-fly package that costs a bit more. An indoor pool and hot tub are on the premises, and each room has a microwave and refrigerator. Pets are not allowed. &. (Eastside)

DOUBLETREE INN/LLOYD CENTER
1000 E. Multnomah

503/281-6111 or 800/222-8733
$$$

Next to the Lloyd Center Mall and situated on Portland's MAX light-rail line, the Doubletree offers easy access to downtown and chain-hotel comfort at an affordable price. Plenty of meeting space is available to accommodate conventions and large gatherings. You'll find three restaurants, an exercise room, and an outdoor pool. 👤 (Eastside)

SHILO INN AT THE AIRPORT
Airport Way and I-205
503/252-7500
$$$

Here's one way to see Portland while avoiding the hassle of downtown. Conveniently located near the airport with free airport shuttles every 30 minutes, this hotel provides a comfortable stay at reasonable rates. Guests receive a full sit-down breakfast and two free drinks each evening. All rooms have mini wet bars. The indoor pool, sauna, spa, and fitness center are also a plus. What's more, the hotel offers a free shuttle, available on demand, for transportation to the nearest light-rail (MAX) station. MAX then whisks travelers into town in minutes. 👤 (Eastside)

Bed-and-Breakfasts

CENTURY GARDEN
BED-AND-BREAKFAST
1960 SE Larch
503/235-6846
$$

Nestled in the historic Eastside Ladd's Addition neighborhood, this quiet two-room bed-and-breakfast offers comfortable queen-size beds,

total privacy, and a made-to-order breakfast. Book at least a few weeks in advance. If you're traveling with friends, consider booking both rooms for a discount. (Eastside)

KENNEDY SCHOOL
BED-AND-BREAKFAST
5736 NE 33rd Ave.
503/249-3983
$$$

The Kennedy School doesn't really feel like a bed-and-breakfast. In fact, it's more like a small city. You'll find comfortable rooms set just down the street from a little movie theater, a pub, a bar, restaurants, a gymnasium, a library, and a pool. For a real treat, try the Japanese outdoor hot tub. Once an elementary school, the place was slated for demolition before Portland's McMenamin brothers rescued it. Free admission to the movie theater, which features first-run flicks, is included with your stay. 👤 (Eastside)

THE LION AND THE ROSE
BED-AND-BREAKFAST
1810 NE 15th Ave.
503/287-9245 or 800/955-1647
www.lionrose.com
$$$-$$$$

A Victorian bed-and-breakfast with a convenient Eastside location, the Lion and the Rose houses six unique rooms that tend to book months in advance for holidays. Some rooms have private baths; others share. (Eastside)

PORTLAND'S WHITE HOUSE
BED-AND-BREAKFAST
1914 NE 22nd Ave.
503/287-7131
www.portlandswhitehouse.com
$$$-$$$$

A charming bed-and-breakfast in a

quiet neighborhood near Lloyd Center, Portland's White House offers easy access to downtown. All nine guest rooms in this historic building have private baths. Gourmet breakfasts are served each morning. (Eastside)

Campgrounds and Hostels

PORTLAND INTERNATIONAL HOSTEL
3031 SE Hawthorne Blvd.
503/236-3380
$
Near Hawthorne shops, this old Victorian house has been configured to accommodate four dorms, two for males and two for females. Rock-bottom prices ($15 for members, $18 for nonmembers) get you a home away from home with laundry facilities, a full kitchen, and other common areas. Internet access is available, and the building is open 24 hours a day. Reservations are suggested, especially in the summer. (Eastside)

NORTH PORTLAND

Hotels

BEST WESTERN ROSE GARDEN HOTEL
10 N. Weidler St.
503/287-9900
$$$
Conveniently located near the MAX light-rail station and Lloyd Center and next to the Coliseum, Convention Center, and Rose Quarter, the Best Western Rose Garden offers free parking and a large indoor pool for its guests. A free shuttle is available to take guests to Emanuel Hospital and the Amtrak and Greyhound stations. No pets are allowed. ♿ (North Portland)

DOUBLETREE INN/JANTZEN BEACH
909 N. Hayden Island
503/283-4466 or 800/222-8733
$$$
Almost every room in this hotel on the Columbia River comes with a balcony, and many of those balconies offer excellent views of the water. Rooms are updated regularly so they remain "contemporary." Free airport shuttle service is available, and public buses into the city can be caught just outside the hotel. The Doubletree also includes a fine restaurant, a coffee shop and deli, a fitness center, an outdoor hot tub, and a swimming pool. Pets are permitted with a refundable $25 deposit. ♿ (North Portland)

WEST SUBURBS

Hotels

COURTYARD BY MARRIOTT
8500 SW Nimbus Ave.
(I-217/Progress exit)
Beaverton
503/641-3200 or 800/321-2211
$$–$$$
This hotel, amidst an array of high-tech companies, is just off Interstate 217 across from the massive Washington Square Mall. Most guests stay here because it's a convenient place from which to conduct business in the area. ♿ (West Suburbs)

Top Ten Places to Visit while in Portland

by Mike Rowland, concierge at the Benson Hotel

1. **Columbia Gorge and Hood River**—the windsurfing capital of the United States
2. **Mount Hood**—Timberline year-round ski area; Timberline Lodge, where *The Shining* was filmed
3. **Mount Saint Helens**—very scenic; great place to see herds of elk
4. **Washington Park**—Rose Test Gardens and the Japanese Gardens
5. **Pittock Mansion**—built by Henry Pittock, one of the founders of Portland
6. **Hood River, Columbia Gorge Hotel, and fruit orchards loop**—orchards and the Hood River Railroad
7. **Oregon City**—The End of the Oregon Trail Interpretive Center
8. **Forest Park**—one of the largest parks in the country, with endless trails for hiking and mountain biking
9. **OMSI**—a science museum including an OMNIMAX theater and the original Russian submarine from *The Hunt for Red October*
10. **The Old Highway**—beautiful scenic country drive along the Sandy River, past seven minor waterfalls (you have to hike a little to see some of them). The view from Crown Point is spectacular. You see the gorge, Mount Saint Helens, Mount Rainier, Mount Hood, and Multnomah Falls.

EXECUTIVE INN AT THE LAKES
18200 NW Cornell Rd.
Beaverton
503/645-2640 or 800/235-3932
$$-$$$

Geared for extended stays, this inn is near restaurants and a 24-hour grocery store. You can choose from one- and two-bedroom suites with washers and dryers, full kitchens, and in-room fireplaces. Complimentary continental breakfast is included, and an indoor pool and spa are available for use. It's near corporate giants Nike and Intel. (West Suburbs)

Bed-and-Breakfasts

GEDNEY GARDENS
BED-AND-BREAKFAST
2651 NW Cornell Rd.
503/226-6514
$$

This cozy bed-and-breakfast in a neighborhood at the edge of Forest Park has three rooms, all with shared baths and queen-size beds. Two rooms in the back of the house (where it's especially quiet) include fireplaces. The third room, up front, can be a little noisy during rush hours. (West Suburbs)

**MAIN STREET
BED-AND-BREAKFAST
1803 Main St.
Forest Grove
503/357-9812
$$**
This 1913 Craftsman bungalow has three guest rooms, all with shared baths. Choose from the Victorian Garden Room with a king-size bed, the Sweetheart Room with a queen, or the Sunshine Room with a full-size bed. Breakfast is made in the kitchen on the premises. (West Suburbs)

**SWIFT SHORE CHALET
1190 Swift Shore Circle
West Linn
503/650-3853
$$**
This B&B has a pretty view of Pete's Mountain and looks down on the Tualatin River. It has only two rooms, one with a queen-size bed and the other with extra-long twins, so book early. A family can reserve both rooms—basically the entire floor of the house with a common den and television. Breakfast is prepared by Nancy, the B&B's proprietor and cook. (West Suburbs)

**WOVEN GLASS INN
14645 SW Beef Bend Rd.
Tigard
503/590-6040**

$$
This little country inn is in a lovely rural neighborhood. The two guest rooms each have a private bath. One has a king-size, four-post bed with a private entrance. The other has a queen-size bed and a large sitting area. A full breakfast is served each morning. (West Suburbs)

**YANKEE TINKER
BED-AND-BREAKFAST
5480 SW 183rd
Beaverton
503/649-0932
$$**
This delightful 12-year-old bed-and-breakfast in a suburban neighborhood was the first B&B in Washington County. With just three rooms, it boasts loyal guests, warm hospitality, and great food. (West Suburbs)

Campgrounds and Hostels

**CHAMPOEG STATE PARK
7679 Champoeg Rd. NE
St. Paul
503/731-3411 or 800/452-5687
res.nw@state.or.us
$**
Originally the site of a Calapooya Indian village, Champoeg State Park also marks the establishment of the first American provisional government in the Pacific Northwest. Off Highway 99W, seven miles east of Newberg, facilities include six yurts, 48 electrical campsites, 58 tent campsites, two campsites for people with disabilities, three group camping areas, a group RV area, picnic and meeting areas, and rest room, shower, and waste

T I P

It's wise to reserve camping space in advance during peak times in the summer months. You can make a reservation for Oregon and Washington campgrounds by calling the Oregon State Parks and Recreation Department at 800/452-5687. For more information on Oregon State campgrounds, call 800/551-6949. For camping in Mount Hood National Forest, call 503/666-0700.

facilities. Maximum RV length is 32 feet. (West Suburbs)

EAST SUBURBS

Hotels

BRIARWOOD INN
2752 Hogan Rd.
Gresham
503/907-1777 or 877/907-1777
www.briarwoodinn.com
$$
The Briarwood, near Mount Hood Community College, claims to be Gresham's only full-service hotel. Some of those services include an airport shuttle, food and drinks from the City Grill Restaurant and Lounge, a complimentary breakfast buffet, an indoor pool and spa, in-room Jacuzzis, and a fitness room. Pets weighing under 10 pounds are permitted for an extra $10 per night. ♿ (East Suburbs)

COURTYARD BY MARRIOTT
9300 SE Sunnybrook St.
Clackamas
503/652-2900 or 800/321-2211
$$
It's a half-hour drive from downtown, but this Marriott offers good rates and an indoor pool and hot tub. If you like shopping at big malls

with ice-skating rinks and a movie theater, you'll be in heaven here, as the massive Clackamas Town Center is nearby. The kids will like the North Clackamas Aquatic Park down the road, a sensible place for family fun during foul weather. A restaurant and lounge are on the premises, too. ♿ (East Suburbs)

Bed-and-Breakfasts

CAPTAIN AINSWORTH HOUSE
BED-AND-BREAKFAST
19130 Lot Whitcomb
Oregon City
503/655-5172
$$–$$$
This lovely home, built in 1851, has been completely renovated in Greek Revival style, with big white columns in front and antique furnishings. The four guest rooms are large, and all have private baths. The least-expensive room is upstairs and has a bay window and sleigh bed. The Captain's Room has its own balcony and an antique wrought-iron bed. Some rooms downstairs include private entrances. All guests can enjoy the living and dining rooms. A gourmet breakfast is served each morning. The B&B's innkeeper lives in a separate cottage on the property. (East Suburbs)

EDGEFIELD BED-AND-BREAKFAST INN
2126 SW Halsey
Troutdale
503/669-8610 or 800/669-8610
$$$

This former farm, built in 1911, sits on 38 acres just 15 minutes from downtown Portland. Redeveloped by the McMenamin family, owner of several microbreweries and the Kennedy School complex, it has been converted to a European-style bed-and-breakfast. The Edgefield offers a country escape and has its own vineyard and brewery. The estate like grounds encompass a movie theater, ceramic and glass-blower shops, a golf course, several brewpubs, and an excellent restaurant known as the Black Rabbit. The 103 rooms in the main lodge are all nonsmoking. Bathrooms are in the hallway but are private. & (East Suburbs)

TOLLE HOUSE
BED-AND-BREAKFAST

15921 Hunter Ave.
Oregon City
503/655-4325
$$

This quiet three-room bed-and-breakfast is all on one level and is situated among trees. Enjoy a peaceful breakfast in the dining room while looking out at the woods. (East Suburbs)

Campgrounds and Hostels

MILO MCIVER STATE PARK
24101 S. Entrance Rd.
Estacada
503/731-3411 or 800/452-5687
(Reservations Northwest)
res.nw@state.or.us
$

Five miles northwest of Estacada, Milo McIver State Park, only 20 miles from Portland, is popular with picnickers from the metropolitan area. Camping facilities include 44 electrical sites, group camping areas, and 4 tent sites.

Edgefield Bed-and-Breakfast Inn

Hugh Ackroyd

Maximum RV length is 50 feet. The park comprises 937 acres of lawns and wooded areas on a series of natural terraces above the Clackamas River. From a memorial viewpoint near the entrance, the panorama includes three prominent peaks: Mount Hood, Mount Saint Helens, and Mount Adams. (East Suburbs)

NORTH SUBURBS

Hotels

THE HEATHMAN LODGE
7801 NE Greenwood Dr.
Vancouver, WA
888/475-3100
www.heathmanlodge.com
$$$
This wonderful hotel is affiliated with the long-established and elegant Heathman Hotel in downtown Portland. However, the lodge, opened just a few years ago, has a completely different character. This Heathman accommodation is designed as an alpine lodge with a rustic setting, and the atmosphere is more casual. An indoor pool, sauna, Jacuzzi, and exercise room are available for guests, and a restaurant is next door. One nice touch: Two robes are provided for guests in each room. ⅙ (North Suburbs)

HOMEWOOD SUITES HOTEL
701 SE Columbia Shores Blvd.
Vancouver, WA
360/750-1100

www.homewood-suites.com
$$$
This is a good place for families or travelers on extended stay. All rooms have kitchens, and some include views of the Columbia River. There is a 24-hour fitness room, an outdoor pool open seasonally, an outdoor hot tub open year-round, and an outdoor basketball court. A complimentary continental breakfast is included with each night's stay, as is an early-evening social with complimentary beer, wine, and hors d'oeuvres. While there is not a restaurant on the premises, several are nearby and within easy walking distance. Pets are permitted for a $25 nonrefundable deposit plus a $10 per-night fee. ⅙ (North Suburbs)

RED LION AT THE QUAY
100 Columbia St.
Vancouver, WA
503/285-0636 or 800/733-5466
$$$
This hotel on the Columbia River is within walking distance of downtown Vancouver, Washington, and just a 10-minute drive from downtown Portland. Some of the rooms have lovely river views, and all have been refurbished in contemporary styles. There's an outdoor pool open during summer months, and, while the hotel does not have its own exercise facilities, guests are given a free pass to Vancouver's Princeton Athletic Club, a short walk away. Free airport shuttle service is also available. ⅙ (North Suburbs)

Robin Klein

4

WHERE TO EAT

Portlanders love to dine out, which explains why restaurants keep popping up. Portland mayor Vera Katz boasts that the city has more restaurants and theaters per capita than any other city in the nation. And the dining in this city just keeps getting better. Portland is a mecca for vegetarians, Thai-food lovers, Italian-cuisine aficionados, and Spanish tapas fans—the city's progressive chefs and restaurateurs keep the competition and quality high. With so many great places in Portland to eat, a number of terrific spots did not make this guide. Still, those listed here ought to give you a rich array from which to choose, whether you're looking for a special night out or plan to grab a bite with the kids. Reservations are recommended at most restaurants for weekend nights, especially during prime times. Waits are noted when they can be expected at places that do not take reservations. Also, beware that parking can get tight during dinner hours on a Saturday night in restaurant districts such as Northwest 21st, which is sometimes referred to as Restaurant Alley. So that you're not disappointed, it's always a good idea to call ahead. All restaurants are wheelchair-accessible. The following price-rating symbols reflect the average cost of an appetizer, entrée, and dessert.

Price-rating symbols:
$ $11 and under
$$ $12 to $23
$$$ $24 to $32
$$$$ $33 and up

RESTAURANTS BY FOOD TYPE

Bagels/Bakeries
Bagel Land (E), p. 60
Beaverton Bakery (WS), p. 68
Empire Room (E), p. 63
JaCiva's Chocolates and Pastries (E), p. 64
Kornblatt's Delicatessen and Bagel Bakery (NW), p. 58
Marsee Bakery (NW), p. 59
Noah's Bagels (E), p. 65
Pearl Bakery (DT), p. 54

Breakfast
Beaterville Café (NP), p. 67
Besaw's Café (NW), p. 55
Bijou Café (DT), p. 50
Bread and Ink (E), p. 61
Bridges Café and Catering (NP), p. 68
Cup and Saucer Café (E), p. 62

Delis/Sandwiches
Dot's Café (E), p. 63
Elephant's Delicatessen (NW), p. 58
Goose Hollow Inn (DT), p. 51
Kornblatt's Delicatessen and Bagel Bakery (NW), p. 58
Little Wing Café (DT), p. 53
Main Street Deli (ES), p. 70

French
Couvron (DT), p. 50
L'Auberge (NW), p. 58
Le Bouchon (DT), p. 53
Paley's Place (NW), p. 59

Fusion
Caprial's Bistro (E), p. 61

Greek
Berbati Restaurant (DT), p. 48

Indian
India House (DT), p. 51
Swagat (WS), p. 70

Italian
Assaggio (E), p. 60
Caffe Mingo (NW), p. 58
Castagna (E), p. 61
Genoa (E), p. 64
Il Fornaio (NW), p. 58
Oritalia (DT), p. 53
Paparazzi Pastaficio (E), p. 65
Vista Springs (DT), p. 55

Japanese
Saburo's Sushi House (E), p. 66
Saucebox (DT), p. 54

Juice Bars/Smoothies
Bibo Juice and Crepes (DT, E), p. 50
Jamba Juice (WS, ES), p. 69

Late Night
Bistro Montage (E), p. 61
Caswell (E), p. 62

Latin American
Oba! (DT), p. 53

Mexican
Chez Jose (E), p. 62
Esparza's Tex-Mex (E), p. 63
La Cruda (E), p. 64
L'il Mexico (E), p. 65
Pollo Rey (Una Mas) (E), p. 66
Santa Fe (NW), p. 59
Taco Del Mar (DT), p. 55

Middle Eastern
Abou Karim (DT), p. 48

Seafood
Atwater's (DT), p. 48
Chart House (NS), p. 70
Heathman Restaurant (DT), p. 51
Jake's Famous Crawfish (DT), p. 51
McMenamin's Edgefield (ES), p. 70
Newport Bay (DT), p. 53
Southpark (DT), p. 54
Zefiro (Bluehour) (NW), p. 60

Southern
Bernie's Southern Bistro (NP), p. 68
Doris' Café (NP), p. 68

Spanish
Colosso (E), p. 62
La Catalana (E), p. 64
Tapeo (NW), p. 59

Steaks/Ribs
Buster's Texas-Style Barbecue (WS), p. 68
Red Star Tavern and Roast House (DT), p. 54

Teahouses
Pied Cow (E), p. 66
Tao of Tea (E), p. 67
Tea Zone (DT), p. 55

Thai/Vietnamese
Lemongrass (E), p. 64
Saigon Kitchen (E), p. 66
Thanh Thao (E), p. 67
Typhoon! (NW), p. 60

Vegetarian
Bijou Café (DT), p. 50
Higgins (DT), p. 51
Old Wives' Tales (E), p. 65
Sweetwater's Jam House (E), p. 67
Typhoon! (NW), p. 60

DOWNTOWN

ABOU KARIM
221 SW Pine
503/223-5058
$$
Authentic Middle Eastern food is served up in a tasteful little eatery tucked away in an old building downtown. This place will please both meat-eaters and vegetarians with scrumptious hummus, falafel, pita, and wines. While a great place for a discreet meeting, it is also kid-friendly, and the attentive owners assure good service. Lunch Mon–Thu, dinner daily except Sun. (Downtown)

ATWATER'S
111 SW Fifth Ave., 30th floor
503/205-9400
$$$$
Everything is a little dizzying at Atwater's. First, you dine on the 30th floor of Portland's tallest building. Second, the prices are high—you definitely pay for both the altitude and the attitude. But the food rarely disappoints, and the atmosphere is perfect for special occasions. The chefs here are some of the best in town, and the fare is American done with flair. Steaks, seafood, and the fine desserts make Atwater's menu as good as the view. The wine list is extensive and expensive. Enjoy the lights of Portland's growing skyline and toast your good fortunes. Dinner only. (Downtown)

BERBATI RESTAURANT
19 SW Second Ave.
503/226-2122
$$
For truly delicious Greek food in a warm environment with a buzz, try Berbati, an established traditional Greek restaurant named after a Greek town and run by friendly owner-brothers Ted and John. The place has also become a choice spot for hipsters and those making the music scene because a popular nightclub, The Pan, is adjacent. (The Pan, by the way, serves incredibly scrumptious fresh pita sandwiches and is the best healthy late-night fare in town.) Tzatziki, spanakopita, and flaming saganaki are worth coming back for, not to mention the calamari, the delectable fresh

DOWNTOWN PORTLAND

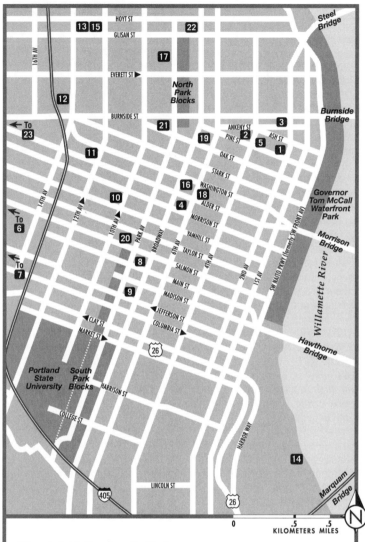

Where to Eat in Downtown Portland

1 Abou Karim
2 Atwater's
3 Berbati Restaurant
4 Bibo Juice and Crepes
5 Bijou Café
6 Couvron
7 Goose Hollow Inn
8 Heathman Restaurant
9 Higgins
10 India House
11 Jake's Famous Crawfish
12 Le Bouchon
13 Little Wing Café
14 Newport Bay
15 Oba!
16 Oritalia
17 Pearl Bakery
18 Red Star Tavern and
   Roast House
19 Saucebox
20 Southpark
21 Taco Del Mar
22 Tea Zone
23 Vista Springs

bread, and, if you're so inclined, the bitter Greek coffee. The baklava is simply the best in town. Plus, there's belly dancing on select nights. Lunch weekdays, dinner nightly except Sun and Mon. (Downtown)

BIBO JUICE AND CREPES
622 SW Broadway
503/227-2334
$
Delicious crepes and fresh juice concoctions are made to order. Some organic varieties are available, too. The Bibo at 1445 NE Weidler (503/288-5932; Eastside) is conveniently located inside Irvington Marketplace near Lloyd Center, adjacent to Torrefazione for Italian espresso and Irvington Market for fresh pastas, cheeses, primo produce, and other delectable (and pricey) grocery items. Open daily. (Downtown)

BIJOU CAFÉ
132 SW Third Ave.
503/222-3187
$–$$
The high ceilings, light fixtures, clanky bustle, and old bar bring to mind a restaurant in a Viennese train station. A simple, homey, no-frills ambience, along with low prices, good espresso, healthy fresh food, and warm waitpersons (who don't care how long you linger at the table while you work out the latest city plans) make this a very popular downtown lunch spot.

You are likely to see local fashion models, earth muffins, business suits, and city officials all dining on tofu scramble, delicious homemade soups, organic salads, and meatloaf. Breakfast and lunch daily. (Downtown)

Atwater's, p. 48

COUVRON
1126 SW 18th Ave.
503/225-1844
$$$$
Looking for a French dining experience to remember? You've got it at Couvron—not only because of the most sophisticated menu in Portland, but also because of the price. Yes, of course there are places in more happening locations: the Pearl district, Northwest 21st, and Northwest 23rd. But in those neighborhoods you would not find the kind of atmosphere that puts you in the mood to spend hours with somebody special, talking over excellently cooked and perfectly presented food, sipping the best choice of wine imaginable for the occasion. To compare this place to, let's say, Wildwood, one should think of the difference between symphony and chamber music. At Couvron, there are only six tables, configured so that all the guests have as much privacy as

possible. The subtle yet attentive service discourages patrons from leaving. Reservations are a must. Dinner Tue–Sat. (Downtown)

GOOSE HOLLOW INN
1927 SW Jefferson
503/228-7010
$
This neighborhood tavern is a great destination for summer lemonade or beer and a vegetarian Reuben sandwich to die for (a meat version is available, too). Sit at a picnic table outside on the deck and enjoy an escape from the claustrophobia of the inner city at this old restaurant and pub on the edge of downtown in the neighborhood referred to as Goose Hollow—an area at the base of the West Hills just west of town. Inside, funny paraphernalia and posters from another era adorn the smoky tavern walls. The place has been a favorite stomping ground of some of Portland's most colorful characters, including former mayor and co-owner Bud Clark. Lunch and dinner daily. (Downtown)

HEATHMAN RESTAURANT
1001 SW Broadway
503/790-7752
$$$
Surely one of Portland's finest restaurants, the Heathman is in the stately hotel of the same name. Its huge windows and high ceilings fill the place with light and a cosmopolitan feeling. Weekdays draw power-business types for lunch. Chef Philippe Boulot's acclaimed cuisine reflects both his classic French training and Northwest influences. The menu changes seasonally, but rack of lamb and delectable preparations of salmon

and duck frequently appear. Open daily for breakfast, lunch, and dinner. (Downtown)

HIGGINS
1239 SW Broadway
503/222-9070
$$$
Consistently a stellar dining experience, Higgins ranks among Portland's top restaurants. You'll enjoy a warmly elegant atmosphere and fine food with an emphasis on organic and locally grown produce and vegetarian entrées that rival the meat dishes. The chef-owner has an environmental activist's conscience to match his high culinary flair. The fare is often regional and the soups can be exceptional. Frequented by newspaper execs from the nearby *Oregonian,* Higgins makes for nice business meetings or a romantic evening. Lunch weekdays, dinner daily. (Downtown)

INDIA HOUSE
1038 SW Morrison
503/274-1017
$$
Right on the MAX line, this basic but elegant restaurant delivers the Indian food that you crave. You choose how mild or spicy you want your dish. The wonderful nan and the vegetarian paneer dishes are noteworthy. Be sure to enjoy an Indian beer and follow your meal with tasty seasoned anise seeds offered for breath enhancement. Dinner daily, lunch daily except Sun. (Downtown)

JAKE'S FAMOUS CRAWFISH
401 SW 12th Ave.
503/226-1419
$$$
A Portland landmark, Jake's has

PIZZA PARADISE

Here are some special places to get favorite pizza pies.

American Dream Pizza
4620 NE Glisan, 503/230-0699
$ (Eastside)

Escape from New York Pizza
622 NW 23rd Ave., 503/227-5423
$ (Northwest)

Flying Pie Pizzeria
7804 SE Stark St., 503/254-2016
$ (Eastside)

It's a Beautiful Pizza
3341 SE Belmont, 503/233-5444
$ (Eastside)

Pizzicato
505 NW 23rd Ave., 503/242-0023
$–$$ (Northwest)

Vista Springs
2440 SW Vista, 503/222-2811
$–$$ (Downtown)

served seafood for more than a hundred years. On the menu are bouillabaisse, crawfish, salmon, trout, halibut, bay scallops, lobster, oysters, mussels, and more. And Jake's does all its own smoking. It may seem incongruous that this top seafood restaurant with its dark wood and fine scotch selection has actually hatched a chain of McCormick & Schmick restaurants and products around the country, but a long history of consistently solid seafood dishes and desserts tells why. Lunch weekdays, dinner daily. (Downtown)

LE BOUCHON
517 NW 14th Ave.
503/248-2193
$$–$$$
In Old Town, this recent addition to the Portland restaurant scene looks solid. Typical French cuisine (though not really traditional, as it's more representative of today's rather than yesterday's fare *français*) is served. Casual but upscale, Le Bouchon is very French in every way. Tables are a little close together, but then that just adds to the small European restaurant-bistro feel. The wine list consists of reliably fine and affordable selections. If you blink, you may feel like you're on the Continent. Lunch Tue–Fri, dinner Tue–Sat. (Downtown)

LITTLE WING CAFÉ
529 NW 13th Ave.
503/228-3101
$
A little gem of a lunch place, this bakery in an Old Town warehouse has finally been discovered, and rightfully so. Great soups, hearty and healthful sandwiches, coffee in huge mugs, and treats so incredible and consistently good that they will keep you coming back have conspired to make this spot flourish as rapidly as the district has gone from artsy to yuppie chic. Sit on the loading dock on a warm summer day and enjoy a very good espresso with your soup—how Portland! Lunch Mon–Sat, dinner Tue–Sat. (Downtown)

NEWPORT BAY
425 SW Montgomery
River Place Marina
503/227-3474
$$

This popular chain restaurant can pack them in, especially at the prime Willamette waterfront location where you can have it all: seafood, kid-friendly atmosphere, outstanding views, and a great place to stroll after dinner along the riverfront and boat docks. For a real treat, come for Sunday brunch and ask to sit outside (as long as you're not prone to getting seasick), where you can watch the boats pull up and dock. Or better yet, approach the restaurant by small boat, dock, and debark to your lunch table. Open for lunch and dinner daily, brunch Sun. (Downtown)

OBA!
555 NW 12th Ave.
503/228-6161
$$$
Oba! is a pretty restaurant in Old Town. The lighting entices, from the fiery red sheen of the swanky bar to the cool crystal blue of the dining room, which unfortunately can get chilly in the winter. The dining room can also get a bit loud on busy bar evenings such as First Thursdays, when the place gets packed with gallery-goers. The food is Latin, but not really. It feels sort of made-up, but the creativity in menu design works well for the most part. Some people just love this place— *Willamette Week* rated it best restaurant of the year in 1998—but it leaves others unimpressed. The real draw here must be the unique ambience. Dinner served daily. (Downtown)

ORITALIA
750 SW Alder
503/295-0680
$$$$

One of the latest additions to Portland's thriving restaurant scene, Oritalia aspires to rank among Portland's top fine-dining establishments. Elegant and romantic, this restaurant off the lobby of the Westin Hotel does not really have an identity crisis, at least not a serious one. The name suggests a blend of Asian and Italian cuisine, adding yet one more trendy fusion restaurant to the city. Creativity extends beyond chopsticks and focaccia, however, to clever sauces in unusual combinations. In the end the food is tasty, and isn't that what really matters? Breakfast, lunch, and dinner daily. (Downtown)

PEARL BAKERY
102 NW Ninth Ave.
503/827-0910
$

Pearl Bakery artisan breads can be found all over the city these days. But the bakery also offers an interesting but limited selection of tasty sandwiches (like pear and gorgonzola on walnut levain) and soups that makes it a fit stop for lunch when in the Pearl district. Some pastries are available as well, and they are not as sweet as you find in typical American bakeries. Closed Sunday. (Downtown)

RED STAR TAVERN AND ROAST HOUSE
503 SW Alder
503/222-0005
$$$

Warm murals offset high ceilings in this restaurant and tavern on the bus mall in the heart of downtown Portland. Aside from a large selection of small-batch bourbons and scotches and a choice wine list,

the tavern boasts a lemon drop (martini) recipe that is the envy of Oregon and beyond. Executive chef Rob Pando keeps the rotisserie and wood-fired ovens busy with custom gourmet pizzas, spit-roasted pork loin, and other American regional cuisine creations. Enticing appetizers include smoked salmon and Dungeness crab cakes and a portobello mushroom tamale. Breakfast and lunch daily, brunch on weekends, dinner Mon–Sat. (Downtown)

SAUCEBOX
214 SW Broadway
503/241-3393
$$–$$$

This trendy upscale restaurant draws a hipster crowd. Dark, busy, and somewhat noisy, the Saucebox offers cuisine of distinctly Asian influence. You'll be served complimentary *edamame* (Japanese boiled soybeans—very tasty) for snacking while you peruse the extensive and unusual cocktail menu. The salad rolls are always a good bet. Fresh mint, mango, and lime seem to be staples here. Despite its trendsetter appeal, though, Saucebox has firmly established itself as one of Portland's finest, consistently pulling great reviews. At 10 p.m. the place morphs into a dance club as a deejay spins acid jazz or hip-hop. Be ready if you plan some late dining here, as Saucebox has been known to get down—right next to your table. Lunch and dinner Tue–Sat. (Downtown)

SOUTHPARK
901 SW Salmon
503/326-1300
$$$

The best part about Southpark is its gorgeous wine bar with its immense painted murals, where you can also order fabulous food, a martini, or cognac. You'd feel like you stepped back in time to the rich 1920s if only the customers were dressed in white jackets, bow ties, and red roses. Order the not-to-be-missed saffron-flavored shellfish soup or the salad with goat cheese and candied walnuts. It's a great place to dine or rendezvous before an event at the nearby Performing Arts Center. Lunch and dinner daily. (Downtown)

TACO DEL MAR
923 SW Oak
503/827-3040
$

This is a great place for cheap yet healthy Mexican food on the go. Fish tacos and fish burritos are the main things here. But good veggie tacos and other vegetarian items are noteworthy, and the standard chicken and beef items are served as well. There are few tables and the restaurant is cold in the winter, so consider getting your food to go. Other Taco Del Mar restaurants are on Hawthorne Street and on Southwest Martin Luther King Jr. Boulevard. Lunch and dinner daily. (Downtown)

TEA ZONE
510 NW 11th
503/221-2130
$

While the Tea Zone is relatively new on the Portland scene, the owners are from Australia and know their stuff. The tea menus are extensive and boast some rare varieties. While there is comfortable, pretty seating in a convenient

location in the heart of the artsy Pearl district, the place is small, and you may want to buy your tea in bulk to go or pick up some very scrumptious dainty miniature tea cookies—they have many varieties of the little gems. (Downtown)

VISTA SPRINGS
2440 SW Vista
503/222-2811
$–$$

This is a special pizza place situated in the West Hills, one that should come to mind on a cold rainy day in Portland (that's often enough). Huge wooden booths by windows, that Swiss chalet feeling, plenty of crayons and paper for the kids, and a nice selection of beer for the grownups make Vista Springs cozy enough to enjoy, rather than endure, what is often a long wait for pizza. Sit back, smell, and get ready for the freshly prepared mouthwatering gourmet pizza of your choice. Select from one of the many concoctions offered or design your own. Lunch and dinner daily. (Downtown)

NORTHWEST

BESAW'S CAFÉ
2301 NW Savier
503/228-2619
$$

Sunny and comfortable Besaw's, originally opened by loggers at the turn of the century, serves equally terrific breakfasts, lunches, and dinners. Breakfast at Besaw's on the weekend is sure to come with a wait. Large, dripping sandwiches and omelettes, incredible baked goods and desserts, and a certain historic seriousness mixed with a

GREATER PORTLAND

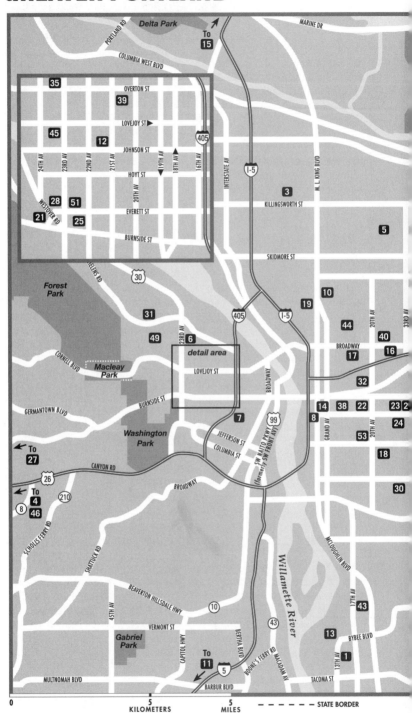

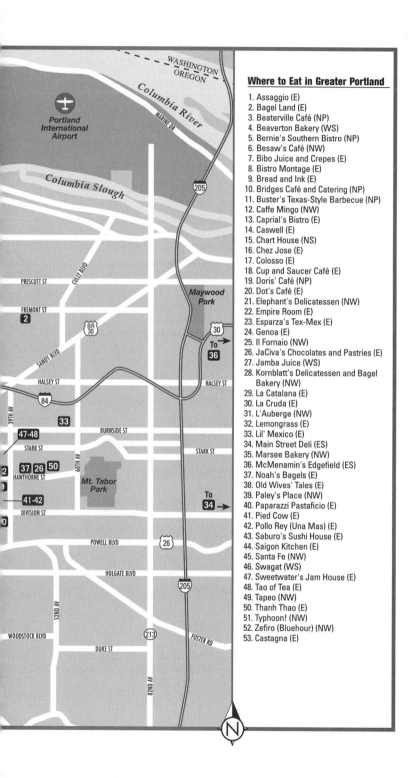

Where to Eat in Greater Portland

1. Assaggio (E)
2. Bagel Land (E)
3. Beaterville Café (NP)
4. Beaverton Bakery (WS)
5. Bernie's Southern Bistro (NP)
6. Besaw's Café (NW)
7. Bibo Juice and Crepes (E)
8. Bistro Montage (E)
9. Bread and Ink (E)
10. Bridges Café and Catering (NP)
11. Buster's Texas-Style Barbecue (NP)
12. Caffe Mingo (NW)
13. Caprial's Bistro (E)
14. Caswell (E)
15. Chart House (NS)
16. Chez Jose (E)
17. Colosso (E)
18. Cup and Saucer Café (E)
19. Doris' Café (NP)
20. Dot's Café (E)
21. Elephant's Delicatessen (NW)
22. Empire Room (E)
23. Esparza's Tex-Mex (E)
24. Genoa (E)
25. Il Fornaio (NW)
26. JaCiva's Chocolates and Pastries (E)
27. Jamba Juice (WS)
28. Kornblatt's Delicatessen and Bagel Bakery (NW)
29. La Catalana (E)
30. La Cruda (E)
31. L'Auberge (NW)
32. Lemongrass (E)
33. Lil' Mexico (E)
34. Main Street Deli (ES)
35. Marsee Bakery (NW)
36. McMenamin's Edgefield (ES)
37. Noah's Bagels (E)
38. Old Wives' Tales (E)
39. Paley's Place (NW)
40. Paparazzi Pastaficio (E)
41. Pied Cow (E)
42. Pollo Rey (Una Mas) (E)
43. Saburo's Sushi House (E)
44. Saigon Kitchen (E)
45. Santa Fe (NW)
46. Swagat (WS)
47. Sweetwater's Jam House (E)
48. Tao of Tea (E)
49. Tapeo (NW)
50. Thanh Thao (E)
51. Typhoon! (NW)
52. Zefiro (Bluehour) (NW)
53. Castagna (E)

down-home atmosphere make you feel like you are dining in a bed-and-breakfast hotel rather than in a restaurant. In the summer, sit on the patio for an extra treat. Breakfast, lunch, and dinner daily except Mon. (Northwest)

CAFFE MINGO
807 NW 21st Ave.
503/226-4646
$$

This small restaurant with an exposed kitchen and dim lighting gives you the sense of being in an Italian farmhouse getting ready for a scrumptious dinner. Everything is good. You can even make a light meal of salad, crusty Italian bread, and red wine. But the pastas and entrées are not shy; rather, they are hearty and flavorful. This place just feels like Tuscany! Blocks of Parmesan and cans of olive oil are everywhere. There's a tiramisu cheesecake to die for. Dinner daily. (Northwest)

ELEPHANT'S DELICATESSEN
13 NW 23rd Place
503/224-3955
$$

Elephant's is so much more than the best gourmet deli in town, with fresh baked breads like blueberry cardamom challah, imported cheeses and fine wine. It also carries four homemade soups each day, and at least one of them is vegetarian. And hot entrées like lasagna and a variety of meat dishes and salads make for special dinners when those unexpected guests catch you off guard. Specialty desserts include sugarplums at holiday time, tiramisu cakes, exquisite fruit tarts, and more. You can find gift items like table linens, candlesticks, and cookbooks as well. But, as with the food, you will pay the price, too. Open daily. (Northwest)

IL FORNAIO
115 NW 22nd Ave.
503/248-9400
$$–$$$

Unless you know the name, you wouldn't think this restaurant was part of a chain with locales in Del Mar and San Francisco, among others. But it is. Regardless, it is a class act all the way, especially the beautifully designed interior and the first-rate espresso. Tiles, wood, brass, and unique lighting (bright and natural during the day, warm library aesthetics at night) make up for any inconsistencies in food quality, which is generally quite high. Italian cuisine is served in the dining room, but consider taking home some wonderful not-too-sweet Italian cookies from the bakery just inside the entrance. Lunch and dinner daily. (Northwest)

KORNBLATT'S DELICATESSEN AND BAGEL BAKERY
623 NW 23rd Ave.
503/242-0055
$

Kornblatt's is your old-fashioned Jewish deli in Portland—a hard-to-find number. If you crave fried matzoh (matzoh Brie, served either savory or sweet) or blintzes, this is the place. There is often a wait on weekend mornings, so if you don't mind not having a seat, get in line and order your deli items to go. (Northwest)

L'AUBERGE
2601 NW Vaughn
503/223-3302

$$$

In a town arguably overpopulated with Italian and Asian restaurants, L'Auberge is a breath of Parisian fresh air on the outskirts of northwest Portland. Romantic and cozy almost to a fault with a fire burning in the hearth, L'Auberge will envelop you in its warmth. You can dine either in the downscale bistro or the country dining room. Start (or finish) with the fabulous fruit and cheese plate or a tantalizing slice of pâté. The entrées tend toward land meat, but seafood is also available. Wash everything down with fine French red wine and don't forget to order dessert. Lunch weekdays, dinner daily (in bistro only Sun). (Northwest)

MARSEE BAKERY
1323 NW 23rd Ave.
503/295-5900
$

Marsee is Portland's own bakery and bagel shop with delicious quality pastries, cakes, cookies, and breads. The original Northwest 23rd store was so popular that the bakery has expanded to other locations throughout the city. You can order at the counter and eat in the bakery, where homemade soups and fresh sandwiches are served. The coffee and espresso are quite good as well. (Northwest)

PALEY'S PLACE
1204 NW 21st Ave.
503/243-2403
$$$

This is one of Portland's finest, and maybe *the* finest. Paley's Place, in a quiet old Victorian house, serves French and regional Northwest cuisine in imaginative creations that always please. The place con-

sistently receives rave reviews, but its profile in Portland is understated, unlike its highly visible and well-known neighbors up the street (like Zefiro, for instance). Paley's superb and cozy dining experience is the creation of its chef- and hostess-owners Vitaly and Kimberly Paley. Dinner daily. (Northwest)

SANTA FE
831 NW 23rd Ave.
503/220-0406
$

Good and sloppy Mexican food with an enchilada sauce to remember makes Santa Fe a top choice on one of the most popular pedestrian streets in Portland. In warm weather, sit outside at one of the many tables, watch the pretty people and tourists go by, and enjoy a large glass of fresh lemonade or a margarita from the little adjacent bar. Lunch and dinner daily. (Northwest)

TAPEO
2764 NW Thurman
503/226-0409
$$$

This tapas place is a treasure. From the Spanish small plates to the prettily outfitted tiny restaurant to the quaint neighborhood location, Tapeo delivers an away-from-it-all experience. In the summer, sit outside on the street, if you can get a table, and order a glass of wine from the restaurant's wonderful selection. Cold and hot tapas are offered, among them a creative cheese plate, calamari, scallops with saffron, cannellini beans and sausage, and potato tapas. The tables are packed together, so don't plan on having any intimate conversations. Tapeo doesn't take reservations, so the wait can be long on busy nights. Call ahead to get an idea of the wait time. Dinner Tue–Sat. (Northwest)

TYPHOON!
2310 NW Everett
503/243-7557
$$

Fresh, fresh, fresh. Typhoon! dishes up "palace" Thai food alive with flavor and color. Coconut, ginger, curries, lime, chilies, peanuts, and garlic dance throughout the menu. As if that's not enough, to complement the variety of spices served an extensive tea menu offers more than 50 varieties. This restaurant is small and nearly always busy, so consider checking out the downtown location at 400 Southwest Broadway as an alternative, especially if you neglected to make a reservation. Lunch weekdays, dinner daily. (Northwest)

ZEFIRO (now Bluehour)
NW 13th Ave. and Everett
503/226-3394
$$$

Zefiro's name has been changed to Bluehour, but is still considered by many to be Portland's best restaurant. One thing is for sure: since this place arrived in the early '90s, dining has leapt to another level in Portland. Many other restaurants strive to surpass, or at least match, Zefiro's quality, but most fail. A changing menu that relies heavily on local and regional ingredients rarely disappoints. Salmon, winter squash, and marionberry presentations are common. But the chef experiments with a variety of world flavors as well. The buzzing cosmopolitan ambience is swank yet warm, European casual, and inviting. Knowledgeable waitpersons serve with energy and efficiency, and the adjacent bar offers a cozy place to sip a glass of wine or enjoy a delectable dessert. Dinner Tue–Sat. (Northwest)

EASTSIDE

ASSAGGIO
7742 SE 13th Ave.
503/232-6151
$$

You'll find some of the best Italian food in Portland at this cozy Eastside eatery. Begin your evening in Enoteca, the small wine bar adjacent to the restaurant where you will likely have to wait for your table. Bottles from Assaggio's extensive wine collection line the walls, and customers can choose a selection to carry into the dining room. The menu is simple but creative with a fine selection of pasta dishes, most without meat. *Assaggio* means "a sampling" or "a taste," so order a sample of the three daily pasta specials and enjoy them family style with your party. Assaggio changes its menu frequently and often features food from a particular Italian region for a month at a time. The atmosphere is warm and intimate, so you'll have to squeeze in close to your fellow customers. The tight space and warm din of conversation and clattering silverware help make dinner at Assaggio a truly wonderful experience. Dinner daily except Sun. (Eastside)

BAGEL LAND
4118 NE Fremont
503/249-2848

$

Bagel Land does not have any seating available in the small shop, but the bagels are the very best— warm, fresh, and not too heavy. Stop by and pick up a bag. (Eastside)

BISTRO MONTAGE
301 SE Morrison
503/234-1324
$$

Originally a young hipster hangout (open until four in the morning), Montage's cool, inexpensive, and tasty formula caught fire years ago. Now a popular restaurant and a teeming late-night nosh joint, this place is in a dark spot beneath the east side of the Morrison Bridge. But somehow this location is so fitting for Montage's character. The place buzzes, clanks, and oozes with life. It dishes hearty servings of macaroni and cheese, green eggs and ham, pecan pie, spicy jambalaya, and red wine in diner water glasses. Patrons sit Euro-style at big white-linen tables while wise-ass waiters do their thing in their white jackets. Oyster orders get screamed out to the back of the kitchen, so be ready. Dinner and late-night dining daily. (Eastside)

BREAD AND INK
3610 SE Hawthorne
503/239-4756
$$

Bread and Ink serves wonderful espresso, rich ricotta-cheese blintzes, and lox in a no-frills, white-linen, European-train-station atmosphere. While it serves respectable dinners, this bistro also offers some decidedly Jewish fare for breakfast, including chopped liver and smoked white fish, as well as pancakes, oatmeal, and omelettes. You'll feel comfortable ordering a coffee and light lunch next to the giant windows while watching colorful Hawthorne types whisk by. Bread and Ink is subdued, comfortable, and bright. Breakfast, lunch, and dinner daily. (Eastside)

CAPRIAL'S BISTRO
7015 SE Milwaukie Ave.
503/236-6457
$$–$$$

New Orleans has Paul Prudhomme, Los Angeles brags on Wolfgang Puck, and Portland has Caprial Pence. Famous for her cookbooks and her nationally syndicated television show, Pence serves the common man out of her small Sellwood storefront eatery. The food, of course, shows off her creative touch and spirit up and down the menu. The fusion dishes rarely fall short of perfect in either simplicity or taste. You can buy a bottle of wine in the shop next door and drink it with your meal for a three dollar corking charge. Pence rarely cooks here, but the menu (which changes monthly) still reflects her exquisite touch. Lunch and dinner Tue–Sat. (Eastside)

CASTAGNA
1752 SE Hawthorne
503/231-7373
$$$$

One of Portland's newest restaurants, Castagna is already one of its best. Co-owned by the founder of one of Portland's former premier restaurants, Zefiro, Castagna is simple, subtler, and just as good. The chef trained in Genoa, Italy, for four years, and the restaurant emphasizes French and Italian cuisine, featuring primarily local and organic ingredients. The menu matches the understated decor in its minimalist perfection. Castagna features fresh seafood, lamb, and rabbit, but the vegetarian risotto cakes should not be missed. Its wine list is extensive, consisting mostly of European vintages. Leave room for dessert. Dinner only Tues–Sat. (Eastside)

CASWELL
533 SE Grand
503/232-6512
$$

Want good, cheap, late-night eats? Well, Caswell is for you. Convenient to downtown (just go east over the Morrison Bridge), it's open until midnight. Caswell's atmosphere is unpretentious, and the food is consistently tasty. Start with bruschetta and then move on to crisp pizza or one of the half-dozen pasta selections. Caswell is known for the best espresso in town and wonderful cocktails. And the best news— you'll leave with a full belly and plenty of cash left in your wallet. Lunch weekdays, dinner Mon–Sat. (Eastside)

CHEZ JOSE
2220 NE Broadway
503/280-9888
$

This great family-friendly restaurant is conveniently located near Lloyd Center. Evenings between five and seven, younger children eat for free. As soon as you're seated the waitperson will bring the usual chips and salsa as well as a delicious mild dip unique to Chez Jose (and adored by children). The menu extends beyond the usual

Mexican fare of enchiladas, burritos, and the like. Dishes can be ordered à la carte or as small or large platters. The squash enchilada is so memorable you'll find yourself craving it long after you're done. Try the margaritas. Lunch daily except Sun, dinner daily. (Eastside)

COLOSSO
1932 NE Broadway
503/288-3333
$$

A newcomer to Northeast Broadway's restaurant row, Colosso is an eclectic gem. Owner Julie Colosso's distinctive style is in evidence from the cool cocktails in the tiny lounge to the bubble gum that accompanies the check. Colosso is a tapas restaurant, so expect small plates of traditional Spanish food. The selections are creative and inexpensive and focus primarily on seafood and vegetarian choices. Order a round of the little plates and share with your friends. The pace of the meal is up to you. Take your time, sip some wine, digest a bit, and then do it again. Colosso should not be missed. Dinner daily. (Eastside)

CUP AND SAUCER CAFÉ
3566 SE Hawthorne
503/236-6001
$

This no-frills home-style breakfast and lunch place has its following, and for good reason. Hearty pancakes and omelettes, mouthwatering daily specials, fresh juices, and baked goods served in generous portions bring 'em back despite long waits on weekends and a kitchen that's frequently slow. But your taste buds remember the smell of the coffee and that warm out-of-the-rain feeling you get at this popular Hawthorne spot. It's got a bit of that Birkenstock/pierced feeling, and tofu and sprouts are staples. Breakfast, lunch, and dinner daily. (Eastside)

DOT'S CAFÉ
2521 SE Clinton
503/235-0203
$

Do not be fooled by the dark and often smoky atmosphere of this hipster haunt. Monica and Jennifer Ransdell serve up some fresh and tasty vittles here for a good price. The enduring popularity of Dot's is evidenced by its successful reopening years ago after it was ravaged by fire. Their trademark sock monkeys, which were "killed" in the blaze, were replaced with dolls donated by dedicated customers. Burritos, spinach and broccoli quesadillas, spicy hummus, Greek salads, Middle Eastern plates, and the ever-popular turkey

Monterey are not to be outdone by Dot's American burgers and the like. A full bar is also on the premises. Lunch and dinner daily. (Eastside)

EMPIRE ROOM
4620 SE Hawthorne
503/231-9225
$

You may think you've stepped back in time to early-twentieth-century Paris. Dark and romantic in ambience, Empire Room is the perfect place to have a glass of port and dessert. Dinner Mon–Sat. (Eastside)

ESPARZA'S TEX-MEX
2725 SE Ankeny
503/234-7909
$$

Got buffalo? Esparza's does. And ostrich, too. This menu goes everywhere and anywhere with its own quirky style. You'll have fun tasting one of the 29 premium tequilas or just marveling at the dozens of marionettes suspended from the

One of the many fine dishes at Genoa, p. 64

John Rizzo

ceiling. Try a salmon enchilada with a side of mashed potatoes. Get the idea? This ain't Texas and you'll be too happy to care. Lunch and dinner Tue–Sat. (Eastside)

GENOA
2832 SE Belmont
503/238-1464
$$$$

Genoa is a Portland institution. You know the kind—every city has such a restaurant. Indeed, Portland can be proud of its icon, a tiny, formal, award-winning Northern Italian restaurant with a prix fixe menu that has served exquisite cuisine for more than 27 years. While Genoa's pasta dishes define its backbone, splendid preparations of fowl, meat, or fish and fresh, locally grown vegetables emerge throughout the dining experience. Portland's star of fine dining could easily go unnoticed from the outside, with its understated exterior and less than swanky neighborhood. But don't be fooled. Those in the know realize the gastronomical delights that lurk inside. Sixty dollars will buy you a complete and carefully orchestrated seven-course dinner. Vegetarians are graciously accommodated if they give advance notice. Dinner nightly except Sun. (Eastside)

JACIVA'S CHOCOLATES AND PASTRIES
4733 SE Hawthorne
503/234-8115
$

Sweet, sweet, sweet. And chocolate too. JaCiva's is a Portland institution with its popular fancy cakes and petit fours. Many are chocolate and white chocolate varieties, but other cakes and pastries can be found here as well. People come from all over the city to pick up these goods. While there is seating, service is primarily take-out. Cakes can be specially ordered, but many are on hand for last-minute buys. (Eastside)

LA CATALANA
2821 SE Stark
503/232-0948
$$–$$$

This low-key Eastside favorite offers romantic Spanish dining on tapas. Typical of Mediterranean cooking, garlic, shellfish, and paella abound. The restaurant's nice wine list features a strong selection of Spanish wines—of course. The creme catalana is memorable. Dinner nightly except Mon. (Eastside)

LA CRUDA
2500 SE Clinton
503/233-0745
$

Mexican food should be cheap, fast, and spicy. La Cruda delivers on all three counts. Cheap '50s-style kitchen furniture and low-budget beers let diners know La Cruda concentrates on food, not fancy atmosphere. The margaritas won't disappoint, and a salsa bar (orange, green, and red) is on hand for dressing up your enormous burritos. La Cruda also does a great brunch with an out-of-this-world breakfast burrito. This place is a great little taste of the barrio right in the heart of southeast Portland. Lunch and dinner daily, breakfast Sat–Sun. (Eastside)

LEMONGRASS
1705 NE Couch St.
503/231-5780
$$

This may be Portland's best Thai food. The long line out the door of this former residence testifies to the locals' love affair with Lemongrass. Owner Shelley Siripatrapa cooks the meals herself and you'll be thankful for it. The menu focuses on seafood and vegetables and leaves the red meat to McDonald's. Siripatrapa knows spicy and Lemongrass's heat scale ranges from 1 to 20. A word of caution: Eat anything above a 5 and you'll head straight into the stratosphere. Lunch and dinner daily except Wed. (Eastside)

L'IL MEXICO
5827 E. Burnside
503/231-6618
$–$$

This must surely be one of the most satisfying Mexican restaurants in town, despite the fact that the fare is largely Guatemalan. There is a bar adjacent, so you can get a margarita with your meal, and the friendly owners strive to please. If you're lucky, you just might be treated to an evening of magic by one of the family members, who wanders from table to table to perform really incredible close-up tricks. Lunch and dinner daily. (Eastside)

NOAH'S BAGELS
3535 SE Hawthorne
503/731-8855
$

Noah's Bagels is a one of a rapidly growing chain of bagel eateries from San Francisco. The smell when you enter the place is awesome, sure to prime your appetite for the tasty, heavy bagels. Deli items are available as well. (Eastside)

OLD WIVES' TALES
1300 E. Burnside
503/238-0470
$–$$

While the homemade soups alone are worth coming for (the Hungarian mushroom is a mainstay and legendary, but sample any other daily specials), the real reason to choose Old Wives' Tales is kids. In addition to serving wholesome food (as well as wine and beer), the restaurant provides a playroom just off the dining room—a wonderful idea that really works. Organic ingredients are used whenever possible, and many of the items are vegetarian. The extensive selection of entrées is a bit hit-and-miss in quality, but you can't go wrong ordering from the soup and salad bar. Children's menu items include peanut butter and jelly sandwiches, pasta, and burritos, and everything is cheap. All kids are given orange wedges to snack on as well as coloring supplies.

Thankfully, children here are not expected to sit still and behave like adults. Rather, they gleefully go back and forth between the table and playroom, thereby giving parents a welcome breather and a chance to really enjoy a meal out while perhaps even having an adult conversation or reading the paper. If you want to avoid the ruckus of the family dining room, ask to be seated in the separate, quiet, no-kids dining room. This restaurant should be cloned everywhere, if only for moms. Breakfast, lunch, and dinner daily. (Eastside)

PAPARAZZI PASTAFICIO
2015 NE Broadway
503/281-7701
$$

This small neighborhood trattoria used to serve only pizza but has now added a full menu of reasonably priced pasta dishes served without pretense or frills. The dozen or so pasta selections never fail to satisfy, and the menu includes several fine ravioli choices, such as wild mushroom and salmon. If you like seafood, don't miss the saffron pasta served with a curry cream sauce and scallops, prawns, and crab. The best bet is to order the full meal option, which includes a healthy salad and several dessert choices (try the gelato). The wine list is limited but affordable. There is nothing fancy about Paparazzi, but you'll walk away satisfied every time. Dinner daily except Mon. (Eastside)

PIED COW
3244 SE Belmont
503/230-4866
$

Come here for cozy ambience and a cup of tea—not necessarily the desserts, which are sometimes good and sometimes not. A popular gathering place for the younger set, the Pied Cow is especially enticing on summer eves when you can sit outside in the large garden (which can get packed) all festive with little lights. Closed Monday. (Eastside)

POLLO REY (now Una Mas)
3832 SE Hawthorne
503/236-5000
$

Here's fresh, fast Mexican food that doesn't leave you with that heavy, greasy feeling but still satisfies. While chicken items are a specialty at Pollo Rey (now called Una Mas), the menu is by no means

limited. Other selections, including vegetarian ones, are just as good. Child-size orders are a bargain. This chain restaurant with its colorful broken-tile decor does a respectable job of making you feel like you're nowhere near a Taco Bell. Lunch and dinner daily. (Eastside)

SABURO'S SUSHI HOUSE
1667 SE Bybee
503/236-4237
$

This very popular sushi place serves what some call the most consistently fresh raw fish in Portland. The food is plentiful, but so are waits, so be prepared. It's usually worth it. People cluster about the outside of this little box of a restaurant as reliably as the sushi is savory. Combination dinners can be an inexpensive way to sample a variety of sushi and sushi-esque items like teriyaki and gyoza. Dinner daily. (Eastside)

SAIGON KITCHEN
835 NE Broadway
503/281-3669
$

One of the better deals in town, and conveniently located near Lloyd Center, Saigon Kitchen serves inexpensive Thai and Vietnamese food. Spring rolls and pad thai are just a fraction of the offerings on the extensive menu, but they are worth ordering just the same. A fast kitchen, efficient wait staff, and roomy dining room with tables that can accommodate large groups make this stop an ideal family choice for a meal between shopping stops or before a Blazers basketball game. Lunch and dinner daily. (Eastside)

SWEETWATER'S JAM HOUSE
3350 SE Morrison
503/233-0333
$$

This is the place to eat the strangest, spiciest, and in some cases most delicious dishes in town. Curried goat, alligator, fried plantains with cream, and a *habañero* chili pepper that will keep you up all night are just a few of the standouts on the menu. But the best secret to ordering at Sweetwater's is to select a number of side dishes, most of which are small meals in themselves. Two superior choices are the curried avocado with jasmine rice (sometimes so hot that it's intolerable, but usually not—ask the waitperson what the heat level for the day is) and a hefty side order of cornbread. The food has Caribbean and old Southern roots with a large selection of creative vegetarian dishes. Desserts are not so memorable (go for the plantains instead), but there is a great selection of rums and Jamaican Red Stripe beer. The decor is casual-tropical with painted picnic tables. The popular adjacent bar attracts a younger alternative crowd. Dinner daily. (Eastside)

TAO OF TEA
3430 SE Belmont
503/736-0119
$

A find. Enter Tao of Tea and you feel like you've stepped off the boat onto some distant exotic island. A large tea menu offers varieties from common to unusual. Aromas from the brewing leaves combine with those from small food dishes, including curries. You can also order tasty little tea snacks like the almond cookies—a bargain at four for $1.50. (Eastside)

THANH THAO
4005 SE Hawthorne
503/238-6232
$

This neighborhood Thai restaurant right on Hawthorne Boulevard serves consistently tasty dishes and usually has a bit of a wait during peak times. Once you've had the tofu in black-bean sauce, you'll be hooked. Service is fast and the Chinese-restaurant-in-America ambience should be familiar. Other good choices are the spring rolls and the noodle dishes. Lunch and dinner daily except Tue. (Eastside)

NORTH PORTLAND

BEATERVILLE CAFÉ
2201 N. Killingsworth
503/735-4652
$

Big American breakfasts are Beaterville: omelettes and pancakes, loads of potatoes, big coffees, and total kitsch decor in a comfy joint that gets packed on weekends. Funky 1950s paraphernalia clutters the place, and tables are the old Formica-and-chrome variety (adding to the down-home feeling). The crowd is definitely '90s-alternative, though. Unless you like your latte tall with lots of milk, you might want to get your coffee here American-style—straight up. Breakfast and lunch daily except Mon. (North Portland)

BERNIE'S SOUTHERN BISTRO
2904 NE Alberta

503/282-9864
$$
This is serious Southern cooking way up North, complete with fried green tomatoes and crawfish. If it's okra, sweet potato, and pork chops you desire, you won't be disappointed with Bernie's. The bread pudding with bourbon sauce will take you right back to N'Orleans— just don't ask about calories. Although cheerful, the ambience is a bit dark, uncharacteristic of the bright and lively atmosphere you might expect from a Southern bistro. Dinner Tue–Sat. (North Portland)

BRIDGES CAFÉ AND CATERING
2716 NE Martin Luther King Jr. Blvd.
503/288-4169
$
For hearty fare, colorful atmosphere, and straightforward, friendly service, try Bridges Café. For the morning-impaired, the "All Day Slacker Breakfast" is available from seven in the morning till two in the afternoon on weekdays and eight till three on weekends. Various local artists' paintings can be viewed at this increasingly popular breakfast and lunch spot, named after both the proprietor, Bridget Bayer, and the numerous bridges over the Willamette, which separates the east and west sides of town. Call for information on upcoming evening music programs featuring local talent. Breakfast and lunch daily except Tue. (North Portland)

DORIS' CAFÉ
325 NE Russell St.
503/287-9249
$

Got a hankerin' for Dixie? Or maybe you're in the mood for soul food that sticks to your ribs while raising your cholesterol? Try the down-home cooking at Doris' Café. This is a rib and chicken joint (with slaw, yams, and cornbread on the side), and the bibs are for the adults as well as the kids. You'll need them unless you don't really want to wear that shirt again. Wash down your selection with a cold beer and, yes, a slice of Wonder Bread (something rarely seen in these parts). Lunch and dinner daily, breakfast Sun. (North Portland)

WEST SUBURBS

BEAVERTON BAKERY
12375 SW Broadway
Beaverton
503/646-7136
$
Not really a restaurant but more like an old-fashioned bakery, Beaverton Bakery produces loads of fresh breads, cookies, and cakes—great grandma-made birthday cakes and magnificent wedding cakes—every day. It delivers too. (West Suburbs)

BUSTER'S TEXAS-STYLE BARBECUE
17883 SE McLaughlin
Milwaukee
503/652-1076
$–$$
Buster's reeks of irresistible sweet barbecue sauce and wood smoke. Carnivores crave the place something awful—the ribs, chicken, and beef. Truer to Portland form, though, a garden burger is available, and a respectable selection of tasty side dishes, like those you remember from childhood picnics,

Top Ten Coffee Cafés

Listed here are 10 great coffee cafés. But in a city such as Portland, where coffee is king and Starbucks is considered too corporate (a virtual McDonald's of latte), where three separate Seattle's Best Coffee stores can be found on one street corner, it's worth seeking out Portland's finest joe. Indeed, some of the best coffee and espresso in town can be found in restaurants, bakeries, and markets, such as Bread and Ink, Bijou, Caswell, Pastaworks, City Markets, and Little Wing, in addition to the terrific cafés listed here.

1. **Ann Hughes' Kitchen Table,** 400 SE 12th Ave., 503/230-6977 (Eastside)
2. **Caffe Uno,** 4421 NE Sandy Blvd., 503/249-7926 (Eastside)
3. **Coffee Cellar,** 6031 SE Stark, 503/234-8665 (Eastside)
4. **Coffee People,** 737 SW Salmon, 503/227-1794 (Downtown)
5. **Coffee Time,** 710 NW 21st Ave., 503/497-1090 (Northwest)
6. **Common Ground,** 4321 SE Hawthorne Blvd., 503/236-4835 (Eastside)
7. **Fresh Pot,** Powell's Books on Hawthorne, 3723 SE Hawthorne Blvd., 503/232-8928 (Eastside)
8. **Morning Star Espresso,** 510 SW Third Ave., 503/241-2401 (Downtown)
9. **Peet's Coffee and Tea,** 1441 NE Broadway, 503/493-0192 (Eastside)
10. **Torrefazione Italia,** 838 NW 23rd, 503/228-1255 (Northwest) and NW Everett and 12th Ave., 503/224-9896 (Downtown)

keeps everyone satisfied. Beer and wine are also served. Lunch and dinner daily. (West Suburbs)

JAMBA JUICE
7515 SW Barnes
West Hills
503/296-9449
$
These yummy juices have become a rage. More like a frozen dessert than a healthy alternative to a milkshake. Made with fresh and frozen fruits and juices, these recipes are tried and true. You also get to choose a couple of scoops from the extensive optional extras list, which includes protein powder, yogurt, and yeast, to "boost" your vitality factor. Also at 11904 SE Division (503/760-7976; East Suburbs). (West Suburbs)

SWAGAT
4325 SW 109th Ave.
Beaverton
503/626-3000
$$

Who would have thought that this tiny house on a side street next to a Target superstore in the suburbs could create a legacy in Indian cooking for the Portland area? The lunch buffet offers so many great Indian courses to fill you up that you might have trouble focusing when you're through. Swagat has a solid history of wonderful southern Indian cuisine (which is typically spicier than northern Indian), but you'll find northern dishes as well. Lunch and dinner daily. (West Suburbs)

EAST SUBURBS

MAIN STREET DELI
56 NE Division
Gresham
$–$$

Step back in time to another era. Main Street Deli in Gresham is not an ordinary deli. Rather, it's a gourmet delicatessen and restaurant offering rich coffee, fresh-baked goods, special salads, and Italian sodas with cream. It's a real gem. (East Suburbs)

MCMENAMIN'S EDGEFIELD
2126 SW Halsey

Troutdale
503/492-3086
$$$

This fine restaurant in the Edgefield Hotel is acclaimed for its delectable Northwest cuisine and notable wine cellar. You'll find fresh seafood, vegetarian, and meat entrées. The restaurant's ambience is rustic, understated, and elegant—a romantic place to have a getaway dinner before retiring to one of the hotel's cozy rooms or heading back into the city. (East Suburbs)

NORTH SUBURBS

CHART HOUSE
101 SE Columbia Way
Vancouver, WA
360/693-9211
$$–$$$

The number one reason to visit this Chart House (one in a national chain) is the view of the Columbia River, especially during summertime when you can dine outside on the deck. Right on the water, it makes for a nice meeting place. Enjoy a drink in the lounge with its huge windows looking out over the river and across to Portland. Or come for dinner. The fare is primarily meat and seafood. Lunch and dinner Mon–Fri, dinner only Sat and Sun. (North Suburbs)

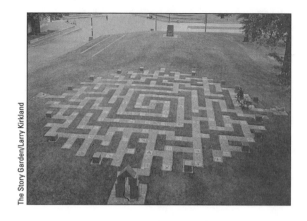

The Story Garden/Larry Kirkland

5

SIGHTS AND ATTRACTIONS.

It's hard sometimes to consider the sights of urban Portland when such spectacular landscapes surround the area, such as the dramatic Columbia River Gorge, the romantic windswept Oregon Coast, and striking Mount Hood. But, if you can get over the startling scenery and those get-aways that are a must, Portland has many wonderful sights large and small to explore. And what's more, the city is laid out so conveniently that it is a delight to indulge—consider a neighborhood by neighborhood approach to Portland's sights.

DOWNTOWN

ARLENE SCHNITZER
CONCERT HALL
SW Broadway and Main
503/248-4335
Known affectionately by locals as the "Schnitz," this beautifully reno-vated concert hall and historic landmark, now home of the Oregon Symphony, originally opened in 1928 as the Portland Publix Theater. The ornate Italian rococo palace was acquired by the city of Portland in 1983 as one of four des-ignated performance sites com-prising the Center for Performing

Arts. A huge restoration project commenced. Gold leaves on the walls and ceilings were refur-bished, and chandeliers were revamped with Austrian crystal donated by Zell Brothers, a local jewelry company. The end result is an elegant Portland showplace. (Downtown)

CITY HALL
1221 SW Fourth Ave.
503/823-4000
Built in 1895 and beautifully restored in 1998, Portland's City Hall is one of the grandest build-ings in the city. The $30 million

DOWNTOWN PORTLAND

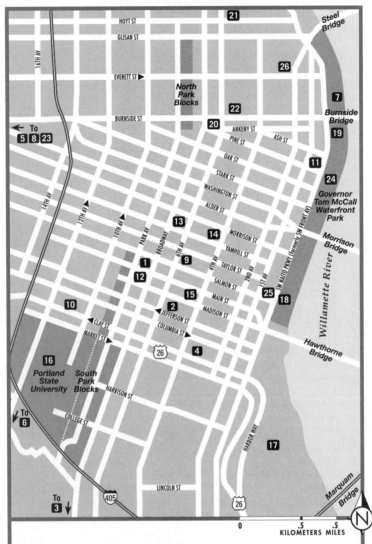

Sights and Attractions in Downtown Portland

1. Arlene Schnitzer Concert Hall
2. City Hall
3. Council Crest
4. Forecourt/Ira Keller Fountain
5. Hoyt Arboretum
6. International Rose Test Gardens
7. Japanese-American Historical Plaza
8. Japanese Gardens
9. Niketown
10. Old Church
11. Oregon Maritime Center and Museum
12. Performing Arts Theater District
13. Pioneer Courthouse Square
14. Pioneer Place I and II
15. Portland Building/*Portlandia*
16. Portland State University
17. Riverplace
18. Salmon Street Fountain
19. Saturday Market/Skidmore Fountain
20. 24-Hour Church of Elvis
21. Union Station
22. Vintage Trolley
23. Washington Park
24. Waterfront Park
25. World Trade Center
26. Classical Chinese Garden

restoration returned most of the original charm to the structure, much of which had been destroyed by haphazard changes over its lifetime. For example, two interior light courts now extend the entire height of four stories on both the north and south sides of the structure. They had been filled in for additional office space in the 1930s. The City Council's chambers have returned to their original layout. There, wood paneling has been removed from the main-floor windows, allowing natural light to flow into what is arguably one of the most intimate legislative chambers in the nation. The building sports Italian marble throughout and now includes the original decorative copper plating (discovered during the renovation) on the stairwells. Visitors frequent the building, and portions are rented out for weddings and other special events. Check out the quirky public art display outside the second-floor chambers or ask the guard to let you have a peek inside. On the ground floor, a video player displays more than a century of scenes from Portland's history. And in keeping with its zeal for ground-floor retail establishments, City Hall has its own bakery and coffee shop near the entrance. Open Mon–Fri 8–5. (Downtown)

CLASSICAL CHINESE GARDEN
NW Everett and Third Ave.
503/228-6688
Hailed as the largest authentic Chinese garden outside China, Portland's newest attraction opened in 2000 in collaboration with Portland's sister city Suzhou, China. The garden oasis, which spans a city block, contains water-ways, exotic tress, and numerous bridges, walkways, and pavilions, which are decorated with hundreds of thousands of tiles. Chinese artisans practicing centuries-old techniques were hired to create the garden and ensure authenticity. (Downtown)

COUNCIL CREST
SW Fairview
Looking for panoramic city views? Council Crest, the equivalent of San Francisco's Twin Peaks, delivers. A lovely park at the top of this peak in Portland's West Hills provides a great place to lie in the grass and stargaze on summer evenings or to park and watch the city lights on cooler nights. Council Crest also attracts droves of joggers, walkers, and their dogs. And watch out for the towering radio station transmitters. (Downtown)

FORECOURT/IRA KELLER FOUNTAIN
SW Third Ave. and SW Clay
Across from the Civic Auditorium, this fountain is really more like a series of terraces and cascading waterfalls linking pools that occupy a full city block. The fountain emits 13,000 gallons of water per minute. Kids are welcome to play in the shallow upper pools under parental supervision during warm weather. If you're looking for a place to steal a kiss, slip behind the waterfall. (Downtown)

HOYT ARBORETUM
4000 SW Fairview Blvd.
503/228-8733
Hoyt Arboretum, founded in 1928, contains an elaborate system of trails (10 miles on 175 acres) and 850 species of trees. It has one of

Pioneer Courthouse Square, p. 76

the largest collections of conifers of any arboretum in the United States. Formerly the Multnomah County Poor Farm, the site was abandoned by the county and turned over to the city of Portland in 1922. (Downtown)

INTERNATIONAL ROSE TEST GARDENS
400 SW Kingston Ave.
503/823-3636
This renowned rose garden, founded in 1917, harbors 8,000 rose bushes and 550 rose varieties. This picturesque location overlooking the city is featured in many postcards. The garden is on the edge of Washington Park and downtown. Most of the rose species tested here never get a name. For more information, see chapter 9, Parks, Gardens, and Recreation Areas. (Downtown)

JAPANESE-AMERICAN HISTORICAL PLAZA
Between Burnside and Steel Bridges, on the west side of the Willamette River
This waterfront plaza in Old Town is dedicated to Japanese-Americans forced into concentration camps during World War II. It includes a sculpture garden, plaques, and cherry trees. (Downtown)

JAPANESE GARDENS
611 SW Kingston Ave.
503/223-1321
Five traditional gardens and a ceremonial teahouse on a hillside provide an escape to a faraway land. Check out the Strolling Pond Garden, the Sand and Stone Garden, the Flat Garden, the Natural Garden, and the Tea Garden. Also see chapter 9, Parks, Gardens, and Recreation Areas. Open daily 10–7. (Downtown)

NIKETOWN
930 SW Sixth Ave.
503/221-6453
Nike, the athletic shoe giant, is headquartered in the west Portland

Portland's Tallest Buildings

Wells Fargo Tower, SW Fifth Ave. and Columbia: 546 feet, 40 stories
US Bancorp Tower, SW Sixth Ave. and Burnside: 536 feet, 40 stories
KOIN Tower, SW Second Ave. and Columbia: 509 feet, 35 stories

suburbs, and Niketown in downtown Portland is its signature store. Very cool and technological, the store glitters with sports-world icons, most notably Nike exec Michael Jordan (decked out, of course, in the uniform of his previous employer, the Chicago Bulls). Catwalks lead you from room to room past neon, an aquarium, and the ubiquitous video monitors. Chutes whisk your selected shoe, in the correct size, right to your feet from a stockroom somewhere in the belly of Niketown. Ask the clerk to demonstrate this. You might even be tempted to buy them, if it weren't for the fact that practically the same shoes can be purchased at better prices elsewhere around town—like the bargain Nike Factory Outlet on the other side of the river. Open Mon–Thu 10–7, Fri 10–8, Sat 10–7, Sun 11:30–6:30. (Downtown)

OLD CHURCH
SW 11th Ave. and Clay
503/222-2031
This historic landmark was completed in 1883 and restored in 1969. A striking example of Carpenter Gothic architecture, the church served Presbyterian and Baptist congregations until 1967. Ornate window traceries, archways, and buttresses blend happily with chimneys, spires, and more indigenous touches like the "wedding ring" nestled on the bell tower and the recently rebuilt porte cochere at the Clay Street entrance.

The architectural features and the acquired period furniture pieces attract the admiration of many. The Hook & Hastings tracker action pipe organ given to the church at its founding by the Ladd family is now a favorite. The Old Church Society presents free, weekly sack lunch recitals in the 350-seat auditorium every Wednesday at noon plus special concerts, exhibitions, meetings, and fairs throughout the year (a current calendar of events is available). Open Mon–Fri 11–3. (Downtown)

OREGON MARITIME CENTER AND MUSEUM
113 SW Naito Pkwy.
503/224-7724
This fascinating Old Town museum houses navigation and various other nautical instruments, ship models, and photographs relevant to Portland's maritime history. Be sure to check out the sternwheeler boat docked across the street in the Willamette River. Open Fri–Sun 11–4. (Downtown)

PERFORMING ARTS THEATER DISTRICT
SW Broadway between SW Salmon and SW Jefferson
The exquisite Arlene Schnitzer Concert Hall (see listing on page 71), the Newmark and Winningstad Theaters across the street, and the city's foremost art museum and ballet (the Portland Art Museum and the Oregon Ballet Theater) just across the park block to the north make this three-block stretch a rich one indeed. With busy Broadway and the elegant Heathman Hotel on one side of the complex and a graceful city park on the other, a stroll around the outside is a nice complement to a peek inside the buildings. The beautifully ornate Arlene Schnitzer Concert Hall contrasts dramatically with the newer, sleek Newmark Theater just across the brick-paved walkway. The Portland Youth Philharmonic and the Tygres Heart Shakespeare Company are based in the area as well. (Downtown)

PIONEER COURTHOUSE SQUARE
SW Broadway between SW Morrison and SW Yamhill
503/223-1613
Locals will tell you the square is the city's living room. The brick piazza teems with lunching professionals on the steps during weekdays and high school students after school. Formerly the site of Portland's first school, later a grand hotel, and then a parking lot, the square attracts vendors, musicians, and street performers. The city puts its Christmas tree and Hanukkah menorah here. Nearby coffee shops and department stores add to the bustle, which is further fed by coming and going passengers at the two MAX light-

Portlandia

rail stops at the square. Stop by at noon to see the weather machine. A sun comes out for sunny days, a dragon on stormy ones. A blue heron (the bird, not the local micro-brew) means light rain. (Downtown)

PIONEER PLACE I AND II
700 SW Fifth Ave.
503/228-5800
This four-block shopping mall is the centerpiece of downtown Portland. Pioneer Place I is easily the prettiest of Portland's malls and the most upscale, with shops like J. Crew, Anne Klein, Sharper Image, and Saks Fifth Avenue. Pioneer Place II made its debut in 2000 with a seven-screen movie-theater complex featuring independent films and operated by Sundance Cinemas of Robert Redford fame. Open Mon–Fri 9:30–9, Sat 9:30–7, Sun 11–6. (Downtown)

PORTLAND BUILDING
1120 SW Fifth Ave.
503/823-4000

This nationally recognized piece of architecture, designed by Michael Graves, has been heralded by some as a glimmering example of postmodern art deco and derided by others as oddly resembling a jukebox. Even Michael Graves's fans are disappointed when they visit the interior of the building, a drab, dark, and depressing tomb. But why go inside? Cross to the west of Fifth Avenue and hail the proud statue *Portlandia* (see next entry) on the portico. From there, notice the small ornamental windows, through which scant natural light can pass. The light-deprived workers inside labor for the city. Open Mon–Fri 8–5. (Downtown)

PORTLANDIA
Portland Building
1120 SW Fifth Ave.
503/823-4000
Erected in 1985, this looming statue of hammered copper is second in size only to the *Statue of Liberty* in New York. The powerful-looking windswept woman brandishes a trident from her place on the west side of the Portland Building. (Downtown)

PORTLAND STATE UNIVERSITY
724 SW Harrison
503/725-3000
www.pdx.edu
Oregon's only public urban university, PSU is at the southern end of the downtown South Park Blocks. The school dishes out more degrees than any other university

in Oregon. The Smith Center, on the east side of the South Park Blocks, houses the student union and cafeteria. PSU's impressive news library is on the north side of the South Park Blocks and is open daily to the public. (Downtown)

RIVERPLACE
SW Naito Pkwy.
This is a great place to stroll on a fine summer day or eve. With several outdoor cafés and a floating restaurant from which to choose, you'll find interesting places to eat, even if all you want is an ice-cream cone. Walk out on the boat piers or inspect the goods in the pricey shops lining the sidewalk. Nearby are the Riverplace Athletic Club and the luxurious Riverplace Esplanade Hotel. (Downtown)

SALMON STREET FOUNTAIN
SW Salmon at the Willamette River
Changing jet configurations offer a delightful water display. The Salmon Street Fountain makes for a pretty picture on the bank of the Willamette River. Come on one of Portland's occasional 100-degree days and you'll see people throwing themselves into the water as if their lives depended on it. Also see chapter 8, Kids' Stuff. (Downtown)

SATURDAY MARKET
SW Naito Pkwy. and the Burnside Bridge
503/222-6072
Arts and crafts, handmade ceramics

> **TRIVIA**
> The Willamette River, "the River of Life" that runs through the heart of Portland, is the longest north-flowing river in the continental United States.

and jewelry, uniquely Oregon items, street musicians and mimes, lots of ethnic food stands, loads of people . . . this is Portland's answer to the Kasbah bazaars of northern Africa and East Coast–style boardwalks. The open-air market in Old Town bustles, especially on nice summer days. Young skateboarders congregate on the green near

Willamette Riverfront

by Marc Zolton, transportation policy advisor, City of Portland

For decades, the east bank of the Willamette River, which slices the city in half south to north, has been inaccessible to locals and visitors alike. Dwarfed by the massive, elevated concrete of Interstate 5 and drowned by the deafening roar of cars and trucks, the east bank has attracted little human activity. But in keeping with Portlanders' intentions to return to the heart of their city, a public project to revitalize the east bank of the Willamette is now well underway.

By the summer of 2001, visitors and residents will be able to stroll unimpeded down the east bank of the Willamette along the East Bank Esplanade, from the Hawthorne Bridge on the south to the Steel Bridge on the north. The city is currently constructing a walkway over the river waters. The trail connects key locations such as the Oregon Museum of Science and Industry (OMSI) on the south side and the Rose Quarter—which contains Memorial Coliseum, a MAX station, and the Rose Garden Arena—on the north side. Better yet, thanks to a cantilevered walkway that will hang off the south side of the Steel Bridge, those in the mood for a longer walk can now hike a complete circle up both sides of the river and over it using the Steel and Hawthorne Bridges.

Plans also call for a new public boat dock on the east bank near the Rose Quarter and the development of additional public facilities on the water at the east end of the Hawthorne Bridge. The city has ambitious plans to redevelop several blocks adjacent to the east side of the Willamette and may try to locate a public market there.

the river, and tourists pile out of MAX trains. There is plenty to buy and see for everyone. The market runs weekends March through December and closes during winter. (Downtown)

SKIDMORE FOUNTAIN
West Burnside and Naito Pkwy.
Built in 1888, this fountain is in the heart of Old Town, the commercial core of historic Portland. Stephen Skidmore originally commissioned the fountain for use as a watering hole for dogs, horses, and people. He created it as a memorial for his mother. Made of bronze and granite, Portland's first drinking fountain has been praised as one of the finest fountains in American art. In fact, in 1888 the *New York Tribune* implied that the fountain was too fine an achievement for a western city. (Downtown)

24-HOUR CHURCH OF ELVIS
720 SW Ankeny
503/226-3671
Enter the religion of kitsch at the Church of Elvis. This place is just plain weird, but that doesn't mean you shouldn't show some respect. Loads of Elvis displays adorn the tiny room, jammed with trinkets and dorky memorabilia. Performance art, maybe. But a church for sure— you can get legally married here for $25. (Downtown)

UNION STATION
800 NW Sixth Ave.
503/273-4866
Union Station, in Old Town, underwent a lovely restoration consistent with the revived popularity of train travel. Amtrak trains run up and down the coast as well as eastward. There is a snack bar in the station if you're in a real hurry, but the established Wilf's Restaurant ought to be your choice for a rendezvous or farewell dining. The piano bar in Wilf's is a great place to meet, and the food is very good. (Downtown)

VINTAGE TROLLEY
115 NW First Ave.
503/323-7363
Historic streetcars shuttle passengers for free between Eastside and downtown. Catch one at any downtown MAX light-rail stop between Lloyd Center and the Central Library downtown. (Downtown)

WASHINGTON PARK
400 SW Kingston
503/823-3654
Washington Park's beautiful 330 acres contain some of Portland's favorite attractions: the Oregon Zoo, Hoyt Arboretum, the Japanese Gardens, the World Forestry Center, the International Rose Test Gardens, and the Vietnam Veterans Living Memorial. The memorial honors Oregonians who died or are still missing from the Vietnam war with its formal Garden of Solace. ♿ (Downtown)

WATERFRONT PARK
Portland's picturesque showplace park stretches for two miles along the Willamette River on the west side. An ideal place to stroll, in-line skate, bike, or skateboard, Waterfront Park is Portland's own boardwalk with a view. It provides the venue from spring through fall for several major Portland festivities: Blues Festival, the Brewers Festival, the Bite, Cinco de Mayo, the Rose Festival, and others. (Downtown)

GREATER PORTLAND

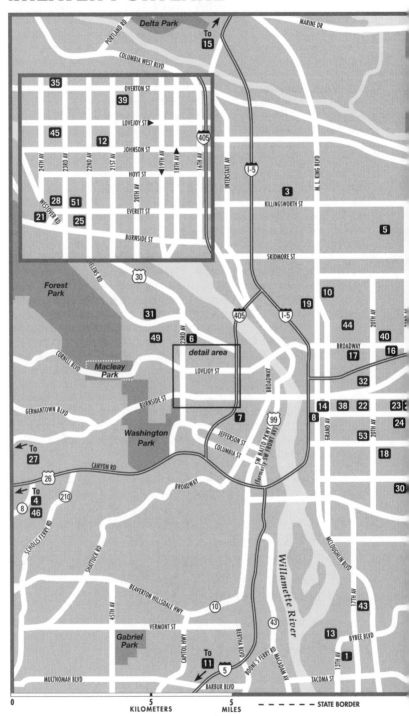

MARINE DR

PORTLAND RD
Delta Park
To
15
COLUMBIA WEST BLVD

35
OVERTON ST
39
LOVEJOY ST
405
45
12
JOHNSON ST
24TH AV
23RD AV
22ND AV
21ST AV
19TH AV
18TH AV
16TH AV
INTERSTATE AV
I-5
3
KILLINGSWORTH ST
M. L. KING BLVD
HOYT ST
20TH AV
28
51
EVERETT ST
21
25
5
BURNSISE ST
SKIDMORE ST

HELENS RD
30
Forest
Park
31
405
I-5
10
19
49
23RD AV
6
44
40
CORNELL BLVD
Macleay
Park
detail area
BROADWAY
17
16
LOVEJOY ST
Broadway
32
GERMANTOWN BLVD
BURNSIDE ST
14
38
22
23
8
24
7
99
GRAND AV
20TH AV
Washington
Park
JEFFERSON ST
53
To
27
COLUMBIA ST
SW NAITO PKWY
(formerly SW FRONT AV)
18
CANYON RD
26
BROADWAY
30
To
4
210
8
46
MCLOUGHLIN BLVD

SCHOLLS FERRY RD
SHATTUCK RD
BEAVERTON HILLSDALE HWY
10
17TH AV
45TH AV
VERMONT ST
43
Gabriel
Park
CAPITOL HWY
43
13
BYBEE BLVD
To
11
BERTHA BLVD
MULTNOMAH BLVD
5
BARBUR BLVD
BOONE'S FERRY RD
MACADAM AV
13TH AV
1
TACOMA ST

Willamette River

0   5
KILOMETERS   5
MILES   - - - - - STATE BORDER

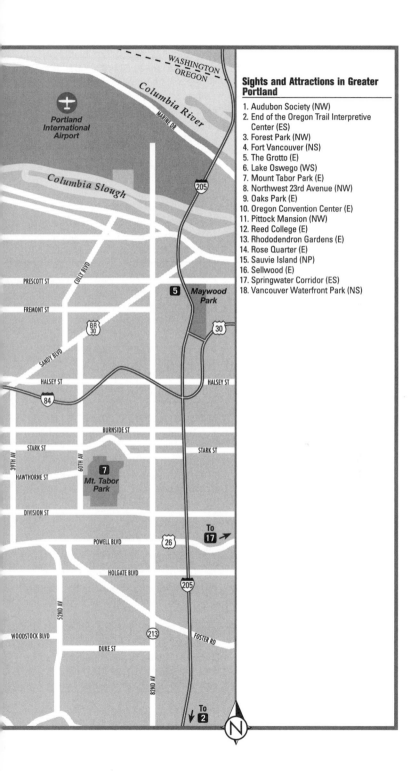

Sights and Attractions in Greater Portland

1. Audubon Society (NW)
2. End of the Oregon Trail Interpretive Center (ES)
3. Forest Park (NW)
4. Fort Vancouver (NS)
5. The Grotto (E)
6. Lake Oswego (WS)
7. Mount Tabor Park (E)
8. Northwest 23rd Avenue (NW)
9. Oaks Park (E)
10. Oregon Convention Center (E)
11. Pittock Mansion (NW)
12. Reed College (E)
13. Rhododendron Gardens (E)
14. Rose Quarter (E)
15. Sauvie Island (NP)
16. Sellwood (E)
17. Springwater Corridor (ES)
18. Vancouver Waterfront Park (NS)

WORLD TRADE CENTER
SW Salmon and SW Second Ave.
503/464-8888
Consider taking a walk through part of the World Trade Center if you're in the area. From outside, take the escalator up to the second level and walk into the sun-filled greenhouse of a café and enjoy a snack while gazing down at the changing Salmon Street Fountain and Willamette River. Afterward, treat yourself to a walk over Salmon Street through a glass-enclosed pedestrian walkway lined with flags from around the world. Open Mon–Fri 8–5. (Downtown)

NORTHWEST

AUDUBON SOCIETY
5151 NW Cornell Rd.
503/292-9453
The 120-acre bird sanctuary adjacent to Forest Park offers educational hiking. A terrific nature shop and a wildlife recuperation facility are also on hand. See also chapter 8, Kids' Stuff. Open Mon–Sat 10–5, Sun 10–6. (Northwest)

FOREST PARK
Forest Park, with nearly 5,000 acres and 50 miles of hiking trails, is the largest city park in the United States. Panoramic views and large fauna make this park an awesome treasure for Portland; elk and black bear are occasionally spotted. The park boundaries stretch north of West Burnside to Northwest Newberry Road and west of Northwest Saint Helens Road to Southwest Skyline Road. For more information see chapter 9, Parks, Gardens, and Recreation Areas. (Northwest)

NORTHWEST 23RD AVENUE
This neighborhood is worth a visit, if for no other reason than to check out some of Portland's upscale stores, chic boutiques, and outdoor cafés. Sit down, sip a latte, and watch the pretty people go by. See also chapter 10, Shopping. (Northwest)

PITTOCK MANSION
3229 NW Pittock Dr.
503/823-3624
Originally built by Henry Pittock, publisher and founder of the *Daily Oregonian,* Pittock Mansion sits on 46 acres overlooking the river commerce and the city, with panoramic views of Cascade mountain peaks including Hood, Saint Helens, Adams, and Rainier. This beautifully maintained former residence displays antique furnishings, fine art, and historic architecture including summer sleeping porches. For a special lunch or tea in a genteel setting, check out the Gate Lodge Restaurant on the property. Mansion open daily noon–4. $4.50 adults, $4 seniors, $2 ages 6–18. Gate Lodge open Tue–Sat with seatings at 11:30, noon, 1, and 1:30; reservations are suggested. (Northwest)

EASTSIDE

THE GROTTO
NE 85th Ave. and NE Sandy Blvd.
503/254-7371
This well-known Catholic sanctuary, built in 1925 on 62 acres, appeals to non-Catholics as well as devotees. You'll find extensive and beautiful gardens, peaceful walkways, streams, and ponds—all situated on a 110-foot north-facing

Pittock Mansion

cliff. You can access the cliff from the Grotto parking lot via a 10-story elevator. From the top, enjoy the panoramic view of the Columbia River and Cascade Mountains. Afterward, step inside the meditation chapel for another tranquil and breathtaking vista. Down below a rock grotto carved into the base of the cliff and a gift shop chock-full of religious items can also be explored. More than 100 statues are sprinkled throughout the property, including a marble replica of Michelangelo's *Pieta* in Our Lady's Grotto. Open daily 9–7:30. (Eastside)

MOUNT TABOR PARK
SE 69th Ave., south of Belmont
This park boasts the only volcano within city limits in the continental United States. From a distance, it has the shape of a large hill. Mount Tabor is graced with large fir trees, endless footpaths, and stunning views of downtown and Mount Hood. It's a popular place for dog

walkers, skateboarders, road lugers, picnickers, and couples. See also chapter 9, Parks, Gardens, and Recreation Areas. (Eastside)

OAKS PARK
East end of the Sellwood Bridge
503/233-5777
Opened in 1905, this historic amusement park does seem dated, yet it still delights with its roller coaster and other thrill rides. A huge attraction at the park is its indoor roller-skating rink. Situated serenely on the banks of the Willamette River, Oaks Park makes a fine place to picnic. The amusement park is open in summer only, but the roller-skating rink is open all year. See chapter 8, Kids' Stuff, for more information. (Eastside)

OREGON CONVENTION CENTER
777 NE Martin Luther
King Jr. Blvd.
800/791-2250 or 503/235-7575
The Convention Center site encompasses 17 acres near the

Commissioner Hales's Ten Coolest Corners in Portland

Portland City Commissioner Charlie Hales, who oversees Portland's transportation system, recommends the best places to see and be seen on the city's streets, boulevards, and avenues.

1. **Southwest Broadway and Morrison:** Welcome to Portland's living room—Pioneer Courthouse Square. The former department store parking garage has been transformed into Portland's favorite piazza. Well-heeled businessmen share the square with skateboarders and tourists. Don't miss the mechanical weather vane that forecasts each day at noon.

2. **Northwest 23rd Avenue and Kearney:** On Portland's most vibrant street, Northwest 23rd Avenue's shops and bistros attract tourists and locals alike. Window-shop or walk the street in search of a steaming espresso or a cold beer. You won't be disappointed!

3. **Southeast 26th Avenue and Clinton Street:** The epitome of cool, this intersection has something for everyone. Experience the punk sensibilities of a hamburger and fries at Dot's Café, catch an experimental film at the Clinton Street Theater, or settle in for a cheap burrito at La Cruda. Oh, and of course, there is coffee and beer, too.

4. **Southeast 34th Avenue and Belmont Street:** Welcome to Portland's poster child for new urbanism. The former Belmont Dairy building no longer does milk but has been transformed into housing, a grocery store, and numerous bars and restaurants at street level. Tired of eating and drinking? Then check out Portland's coolest furniture store—Sit Babe Stay!

Rose Garden Arena and the Memorial Coliseum and is right off the MAX line. With a half million square feet of enclosed space, the Convention Center is both huge and beautiful. Its two strikingly modern cathedral-esque glass spires can be spotted from just about anywhere in the city. The center is used for a wide variety of large business and industry conferences as well as trade shows and expositions, many of which are open to the public. Admission fees and building access depend on event. (Eastside)

REED COLLEGE
3203 SE Woodstock Blvd.
503/771-1112
"If you're a genuine intellectual, live the life of the mind, and want to learn for the sake of learning, the place most likely to empower

5. **Southeast 28th Avenue and Burnside Street:** More movies, more mochas, more health food. This Portland corner has been revitalized into a pedestrian's dream. Stroll about, but don't forget to duck into some of the city's newest haunts for food and drink.

6. **Southeast 37th Avenue and Hawthorne Boulevard:** The New Age meets the Old Age (as in the '60s, man) on one of Portland's most boisterous boulevards. Tattoos, piercings, candles, incense, pizza, beer, and, of course, more coffee. It's all here!

7. **Southeast Ninth Avenue and Sherrett Street:** There is no place in Portland quite like this one. An experiment in "intersection repair" by the nearby residents, the streetscape has been transformed into a tea stand, book-lending station, and an evolving art project (yes, right on the street itself). You'll have to see it to believe it!

8. **Southeast Milwaukie Avenue and Bybee Street:** The heart of Portland's Sellwood neighborhood features enough street-level activity for any age bracket. Good food and great antiques abound on one of Portland's best "main" streets.

9. **Southwest 35th Avenue and Multnomah Boulevard:** Southwest Portland's Multnomah Village offers a cool respite from the hustle and bustle of urban life. Take a trip back to when life was a little simpler and this part of town was farms and dairies.

10. **Northeast 15th Avenue and Weidler:** A giant tulip tree, the best espresso west of Italy, and fresh sushi. It's all here, plus fresh bread from the Grand Central Bakery.

you is not Harvard, Yale, Princeton, Chicago, or Stanford. It is the most intellectual college in the country —Reed, in Portland, Oregon," says Loren Pope, former education editor of *The New York Times,* in his book, *Colleges That Change Lives* (Penguin, 1996). Pope makes special note of the percentage of Reed alumni who go on to earn doctorates, especially in the sciences, as well as Reed's 30 Rhodes Scholars.

The setting is lovely as well: a quiet campus of rich green lawns and old brick buildings, all set in graceful Eastmoreland just 15 minutes from downtown Portland next to the Crystal Springs Rhododendron Gardens. (Eastside)

RHODODENDRON GARDENS
Crystal Springs
SE 28th Ave., one block north of Woodstock

503/823-3640

This garden is at its peak in the spring during April and May when the rhododendron are in full bloom. But don't miss the garden at other times, either. Nearly surrounded by water, the park is teeming with small, friendly fauna like ducks and squirrels. This must surely be one of the best parks for kissing. See also chapter 9, Parks, Gardens, and Recreation Areas. (Eastside)

ROSE QUARTER
1 Center Court, east side of
Willamette River
503/235-8771

Don't be confused by the name. There aren't any roses here, or greenery for that matter—unless you count the hefty salaries of the NBA stars who work here. This huge complex includes the massive 20,000-seat Rose Garden, Portland's premier concert venue and home to the Trail Blazers and an assortment of other teams, including hockey's Winterhawks, arena football's Forest Dragons, and the WNBA's Fire. Next to the Rose Quarter is the 12,000-seat Memorial Coliseum, and nearby is Rose Quarter Commons, which displays 500 high-intensity water jets and fiery pillars. Sometimes onlookers douse themselves, no matter how cold it is. (Eastside)

SELLWOOD
SE 13th and SE 17th Sts., south of
Woodstock

Sellwood's charm stems from its array of old-fashioned touches and antiques shops combined with quaint eateries and some of the best gourmet restaurants in town. It is an utterly civilized place reminiscent of provincial Portland. Even

Convention Center Towers

the nearby Oaks Amusement Park is a throwback to another era. Sellwood's business district is a must-stop for antiques lovers. (Eastside)

NORTH PORTLAND

SAUVIE ISLAND
Rte. 30 east of Portland (to the
Sauvie Island Bridge)

Lounge the day away on sandy beaches. Picnic in a pastoral setting. Bicycle through the countryside. You can do all of these things within 15 minutes of downtown. Sauvie Island, in the Columbia River, is a place to explore and relax. You can try everything from catching tiny frogs in the island's wildlife refuge to soaking up the rays at its nude beach. Amazingly undeveloped considering its proximity to the city, Sauvie Island can

The Mighty Columbia

The Columbia River, at 1,214 miles in length, is the fourth-largest river in the United States and the 18th-largest river in the world. It carries 10 times as much water as the Colorado and more than twice as much as the Nile. At one time, with annual salmon runs from 6 to 10 million, the Columbia was home to more salmon than any other place in the world. Today, however, the salmon numbers are declining because of logging, cattle grazing, and, most important, dams.

The Columbia rises in the Selkirk Mountains of British Columbia and wanders through eastern and central Washington, where it flows over and through numerous dams. It feeds hundreds of thousands of acres of cropland while also flowing past the nation's most contaminated nuclear site, Hanford. It cuts through the deep Columbia River Gorge, where it passes the last hurdle, Bonneville Dam, and then continues 146 miles to the Pacific Ocean.

The great dams were built from the 1930s to the 1970s to supply power to Hanford, Boeing, and aluminum companies. The last big dam, Lower Granite, is in southeast Washington on the Columbia's major tributary, the Snake River. The 1975 completion of Lower Granite marked not only the end of the dam-building era but also the possible beginning of the end for salmon. Immediately thereafter, salmon runs in the Snake took a sharp turn for the worse. In the 1990s salmon were added to the endangered species list. Today the federal government uses trucks and barges to move as many salmon as it can through the dams, rather than let them swim through the hazardous reservoirs and turbines.

Over the last two decades, government agencies have led a long, expensive, and abysmally unsuccessful effort to restore the salmon. Today the government is considering plans to destroy some of the dams, particularly four on the Snake River. Scientists say that is the only way to save the fish. But economic interests oppose dam removal. Ultimately, the controversy is likely to be decided in Congress.

be a very popular (crowded) spot on summer weekend days. Traffic, too, can be a problem because there is only one road onto the island. See also chapter 8, Kids' Stuff. (North Portland)

WEST SUBURBS

LAKE OSWEGO
503/636-3634 (Lake Oswego Chamber of Commerce)
Lake Oswego is just south of Portland, west of the Willamette River. This community, centered on a large and lovely lake southwest of downtown, has a reputation as an upscale suburban neighborhood lacking in ethnic diversity.

Loads of great shops and restaurants, private boats and lakefront properties, and bicycle paths make for a country-club atmosphere. Bruce Springsteen once owned one of the grander estates here with his former wife.
(West Suburbs)

EAST SUBURBS

END OF THE OREGON TRAIL INTERPRETIVE CENTER
1726 Washington St.
Oregon City
503/557-8542
Primarily an immigrant trail, the Oregon Trail was the route traveled by pioneers settling in the West in the mid-1800s—the pathway to the Pacific for fur traders, gold seekers, missionaries, and immigrants. Beginning in 1841 and continuing for more than 20 years, an estimated 300,000 immigrants followed this route from Missouri

to Oregon on a trip that took five months to complete. The trail starts in Independence, Missouri, and ends officially in Oregon City. Much remains on the trail for the modern visitor to experience, from the actual ruts left by the wagon trains to interpretive centers like the one at the trail's end in Oregon City.

The End of the Oregon Trail Interpretive Center is easy to find. Just go south of Portland on Interstate 5, go west on Interstate 205 to exit 10, and take Highway 213 to the Trail's End Highway. You can't miss the big wagons on your left. Visitors are welcome to browse or ask the staff for information and brochures for other attractions in the area. Mon–Sat 9–5, Sun 10–5. Free. (East Suburbs)

SPRINGWATER CORRIDOR
SE 136th Ave. and SE Jenne Rd.
(south of SE Powell Blvd.)
The Springwater Corridor is a former rail corridor that has been converted to an alternative transportation and recreational trail. It is the major southeast segment of the 40 Mile Loop, originally conceived in 1903 to form a nature trail encircling the city.

Today the loop is actually 140 miles long. The Springwater Corridor is 16.8 miles long, from Southeast McLoughlin in Portland to the town of Boring. The tracks have been replaced by a sidewalk to create a bicycling/inline skating/walking corridor through rolling countryside free of motor-vehicle traffic. The full loop takes you past ducks, goats, horses, Main Street in Gresham, parks, a creek, and terrific views of Mount Hood.
(East Suburbs)

NORTH SUBURBS

FORT VANCOUVER
Mill Plain exit off I-5, north of Portland
Vancouver, WA
306/696-7655 or 800/832-3599
Originally a fur-trading headquarters as well as a fort in the early 1800s, Fort Vancouver was the first settlement in the Oregon Territory. Step back in time and see people dressed in period clothing, browse various shops from the olden days, and hear tour guides tell the town's story. Afterward, visit nearby Officer's Row and see the beautifully reconstructed Victorian-era homes on a lovely green. A gift shop specializes in things Victorian, and period furniture is on display. (North Suburbs)

VANCOUVER WATERFRONT PARK
Columbia River, just east of I-5
Vancouver, WA

This well-designed park along the banks of the Columbia River just across from Portland is a great place to bike, walk, picnic, and play. Bogs, woodlands, and beaches can be found along the way, as can outstanding views of the Columbia River and Mount Hood. (North Suburbs)

CITY TOURS

Bicycle

CYCLE OREGON
8700 SW Nimbus
503/643-8064
Cycle Oregon is an annual seven-day bicycle tour that provides the opportunity to experience and explore rural Oregon. Each September 2,000 cyclists travel a different route on paved roads throughout the state. Cycle Oregon is a fully supported tour, including

Multnomah Falls

One of the tallest waterfalls in the world, Multnomah Falls plunges 620 feet in a dramatic ribbon on the south side of the Columbia River Gorge. Oregon's top tourist attraction awes hordes of visitors each year, no matter what the season. If you venture out into the gorge in nasty winter weather, you might have to deal with treacherous driving conditions, but you could also be rewarded with ice falls in parts of the gorge. To get there, take I-84 east of Portland to the Multnomah Falls exit (about 40 minutes). If you take the slightly longer scenic highway route, don't miss some of the other beautiful falls along the way.

all meals, food and beverages on course, hot showers, baggage transport, 24-hour medical support, seven SAG vans, bike repair on course and in camp, daily entertainment, and noncycling activities. Cost for the 2000 tour is $629.

Boat

CASCADE STERNWHEELER
1200 NW Front Ave.
503/223-3928
Excursions on the Columbia River run during the summer months. The rest of the year the sternwheeler makes shorter cruises up and down the tamer Willamette River. Columbia River cruises depart from Marine Park in Cascade Locks (about 45 minutes east of Portland on Interstate 84), while Willamette River cruises depart from downtown Portland. Columbia River excursions are $12.95 for adults, $7.95 for ages 4–11. Dinner cruises are $32.95 for adults, $20.95 for children. Brunch cruises are $28.95 for adults, $19.95 for children, and the Friday dinner dance goes for $37.95. Advance reservations are recommended.

PORTLAND SPIRIT
1200 NW Naito Pkwy.
503/226-2517
Dinner cruises up and down the Willamette River are a fine way to see the city and its lights at night. Daytime cruises are also offered with or without dining. Dinner cruises are two-and-one-half-hours long and cost $52 per person; lunch cruises are $28 and brunch cruises are $36. Daytime cruises take two hours and cost only $15 (without food). Some cruises depart from OMSI at 1945 Water Avenue.

WILLAMETTE JETBOAT EXCURSIONS
1945 SE Water Ave. (board at OMSI)
503/231-1532
www.jetboatpdx.com
For a different kind of boat tour, try this open-air high-speed jet boat on the Willamette River. The scenic tour takes passengers to dramatic Willamette Falls May through October 15. A special dinner tour includes a trip to a private park for a salmon bake for $45 per person. Scenic tours cost $22 for adults, and $14 for children ages 4–11.

Bus

GRAPE ESCAPE WINERY TOURS
4304 NE 22nd
503/283-3380
Grape Escape offers a personalized guided tour of Oregon wine country in a comfortable luxury van. A gourmet meal is included. Afternoon, full-day, or evening dinner escapes are available. For an overview of the Oregon wine country, see chapter 14, Day Trips from Portland.

GRAY LINE TOURS
4320 N. Suttle
503/224-8001
This company offers guided bus tours to popular sights and attractions in and around the Portland area. Gray Line of Portland claims to be Oregon's largest and most experienced motorcoach company. In operation since 1913, it offers sightseeing tours, convention and corporate shuttles, escorted vacations, custom itineraries, and charters in a variety of vehicles ranging from really large

buses to vans. Call Gray Line for itineraries and schedules.

Columbia River Gorge are also available.

Limo/Coach

RAZ TRANSPORTATION
11655 SW Pacific Hwy.
503/684-3322
Raz offers the following popular package tours: Portland City Highlights, Mt. Hood/Columbia Gorge Loop, North Oregon Coast, Mt. St. Helens, Central Oregon Coast, Oregon Wineries, End of the Oregon Trail, Spirit Mountain Casino and Wine Tasting, and Columbia River Gorge Cruise. Minibus city tours for five hours and up to 24 people cost $276.

VANGO TOURS
8150 SW Barnes Rd.
503/292-2085
VanGo offers standard and personalized minivan tours. Four-and-one-half-hour city tours cost $25. Tours to the coast, Mount Hood, and the

Walking/General

ECOTOURS
1906 SW Iowa
503/245-1428
www.ecotours-of-oregon.com
Ecotours offers sightseeing and nature tours both in and outside of the city. Whale-watching trips and hikes in the nearby mountains are among the offered options. An evening tour of Portland's micro-breweries costs $39.50. Call for details and arrangements.

PUBLIC ART WALKING TOUR
Portland Visitor's Association
26 SW Salmon St.
503/222-2223
Pick up a brochure at the Portland Visitor's Association for a self-guided walking tour of Portland's artwork, pedestrian sites, and parks and buildings.

Bridgeport Brewing Company

6

MICROBREWERIES

When you sit down to enjoy locally brewed ale in Portland, you are indeed seated at the epicenter of America's beer revolution. Since Portland's first microbrewery opened in 1984 in a former warehouse, nearly 30 breweries have begun operations in the metropolitan area. Portland now has the distinction of being home to the highest concentration of breweries of any city in the world.

Most of Portland's breweries are small, but several have outgrown that label and brew and ship enough beer to qualify as regional breweries. But size does matter. And in the brewing business, the smaller the brewery, the more likely your beers are handcrafted and drawn fresh within days of production.

Portland's beer is almost exclusively English-style ale. Ale varieties range from light golden to amber to hearty porters and stouts. Interestingly, Portland's favorite beer—Widmer Hefeweizen—comes from a German lager-style yeast strain but is brewed by the English-style ale method and is served unfiltered with a lemon wedge. It is not a stretch to say that on any given day in Portland, you could conceivably taste more than 100 different local beers.

The majority of Portland's breweries function as brewpubs, meaning the beer is brewed and then served in the same place. The kings of Portland's brewpub culture are the McMenamin brothers—Mike and Brian. From one small pub and restaurant opened in southeast Portland over 20 years ago, the brothers have built a food and beverage empire that now includes nearly three dozen restaurants, pubs, hotels, and cinemas in Oregon and Washington. The McMenamins' pubs are known for their enormous servings of french fries (that includes the "small" size), their laid-back service (in other words, relax, your beer will come eventually), and their willingness to allow you to taste any beer before you buy it.

Portland's beer scene fits perfectly with the city's often dark and dank weather, its vibrant neighborhoods, and its tendency to create rather than copy. Nothing says Portland more than a pint of fresh, local ale. So when you're here, do as the locals do—enjoy!

—*Marc Zolton*

BREWPUBS

ALAMEDA BREWHOUSE
4765 Fremont
503/460-9025
One of Portland's most creative brewpubs, Alameda has also filled a geographic hole in Portland's brewery landscape with its location on the northeast side of town. The pub is known for its wild beer creations, including brews made with juniper and desert sage. The brewery offers a full menu with suggested beers bound to complement the grub. The recent departure of its head brewer may signal the end of Alameda's creative character, but its signature brews are still among the tastiest in town. (Eastside)

BIG HORN BREWING COMPANY
320 Oswego Pointe Dr.
Lake Oswego
503/697-8818
One of the few brewpub alternatives in Portland's southern suburbs, Big Horn Brewing struggles to define itself as either a brewpub, a sports bar, or a restaurant. By trying to be all three, it has failed to distinctively capture any of them. The beer isn't exactly memorable. If you have only one chance to taste Portland microbrew, drive a

little farther north to do so. (West Suburbs)

LUCKY LABRADOR BREWPUB
915 SE Hawthorne Blvd.
503/236-3555
A southeast Portland gem, the Lab, as it's known to locals, has only been on the scene for a few years but has already built a loyal following. The pub usually features at least five of its own brews as well as one guest tap for another local microbrew. The small food selection includes sandwiches and excellent peanut curry bento. The atmosphere is a utilitarian beer hall with a great back deck for summer sipping at picnic tables. You will certainly see your fair share of local labs with their owners in tow, as this pub is a favorite with dog lovers. (Eastside)

OLD LOMPOC
1616 NW 23rd Ave.
503/225-1855
This is the grunge entry for the local brewpub scene. The Lompoc offers a fine lineup of seven house brews including creative seasonal selections. Guest taps include Bud Light, Guinness, and Pilsner Urquell. Purple felt pool tables, '90s music, and an outdoor beer garden give Old Lompoc its distinctive character. (Northwest)

OLD MARKET BREWERY AND PUB
6959 SW Multnomah Blvd.
503/244-0450
This suburban Superdome of a brewpub gives Portland's western neighborhoods a worthy alternative for fresh beer and pub grub. The former cannery is cavernous and includes a backroom pool hall where smoking is allowed and

GREATER PORTLAND

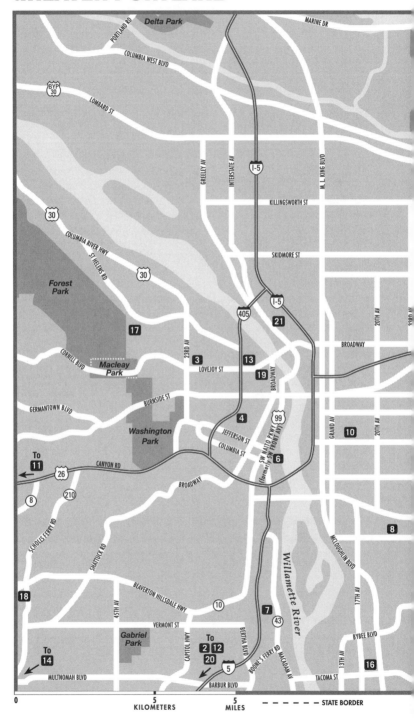

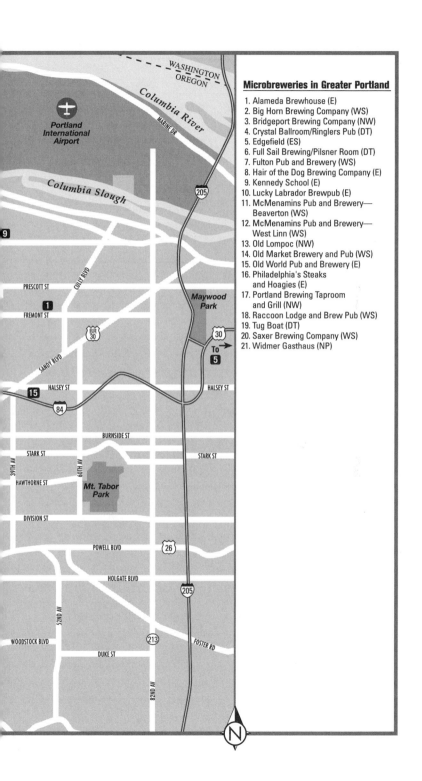

Microbreweries in Greater Portland

1. Alameda Brewhouse (E)
2. Big Horn Brewing Company (WS)
3. Bridgeport Brewing Company (NW)
4. Crystal Ballroom/Ringlers Pub (DT)
5. Edgefield (ES)
6. Full Sail Brewing/Pilsner Room (DT)
7. Fulton Pub and Brewery (WS)
8. Hair of the Dog Brewing Company (E)
9. Kennedy School (E)
10. Lucky Labrador Brewpub (E)
11. McMenamins Pub and Brewery—
    Beaverton (WS)
12. McMenamins Pub and Brewery—
    West Linn (WS)
13. Old Lompoc (NW)
14. Old Market Brewery and Pub (WS)
15. Old World Pub and Brewery (E)
16. Philadelphia's Steaks
    and Hoagies (E)
17. Portland Brewing Taproom
    and Grill (NW)
18. Raccoon Lodge and Brew Pub (WS)
19. Tug Boat (DT)
20. Saxer Brewing Company (WS)
21. Widmer Gasthaus (NP)

The McMenamins Empire

Nothing says Portland more than a cold glass of fresh McMenamin ale accompanied by a garden burger and fries. To really complete the experience, hum along to a Grateful Dead song as you chew. The McMenamin brothers, Mike and Brian, turned a single restaurant and pub (southeast Portland's Produce Row, now under different ownership) into a funky beer and burger empire stretching across Oregon north to Seattle. In 1985 the brothers began brewing their own beer (at the Hillsdale Pub and Brewery in southwest Portland) to serve on site and to supply other McMenamins restaurants in the area. The growth over the last 15 years has been nothing short of phenomenal. The McMenamins now employ more than 1,200, gross more than $50 million a year, and brew and serve more than 500 new beers each year at their 43 outlets.

But this is no Starbucks. The McMenamins may be mammoth, but they haven't lost their creativity or funky vibe. Hippies are still cool in Portland, and McMenamins celebrates the distinctly Pacific Northwest strain with original artwork, '60s-era music, and a laid-back atmosphere. They still take chances at McMenamins—with their beer, their help, and sometimes your meal. But don't worry, just lower those expectations, relax, and enjoy your beer.

A few practical tips for maximum enjoyment of the 33 Portland-area McMenamins: 1) Taste the beer before you order. (They don't mind if you do.) 2) Don't expect great service. McMenamins' service is famously spotty. While it's not always slow, you can definitely feel invisible at times. Relax and don't worry about it. 3) This is not fine dining. It is straight-up pub fare with eclectic names attached. 4) Don't order a large plate of fries unless you have at least eight people in your party. A small order is a meal for four by itself.

McMenamins brewpubs include the **Fulton, Crystal Ballroom/ Ringlers Pub, Edgefield**, and the **Kennedy School**. For information on any McMenamins pubs, call 503/223-0109, or visit their website at www.mcmenanims.com.

Bridgeport Brewing Company, p. 98

minors are forbidden. The beer selection is as big as the room with 20 tap handles and at least a dozen fresh beers available at any time. The food menu is extensive with sandwiches, pizza, pasta, and salads. It's a great place for large groups. (West Suburbs)

OLD WORLD PUB AND BREWERY
1728 NE 40th Ave.
503/335-9084
This new and worthy challenger to the brewpub scene is in the heart of Portland's Hollywood neighborhood and a short walk from the light-rail station. The high ceilings and sunken brewing facilities give an airy, spacious feel to the pub. There are half a dozen house beers on tap, including a seasonal brew, and the guest taps shine with stellar selections like Guinness, Pilsner Urquell, Spaten Munich, and the local Belgian-style delight, "Fred," from the Hair of the Dog brewery. The establishment serves a full menu of pub grub. Try the seafood chowder. (Eastside)

PHILADELPHIA'S STEAKS AND HOAGIES
6410 SE Milwaukie Ave.
503/239-8544
Longing for a little East Coast nostalgia? Then this is the brewpub for you. Modeled after a Philadelphia sub shop, the pub is complete with copies of the *Philadelphia Inquirer* and Tastykakes (including the author's favorite—butterscotch krimpets). The beer is plentiful and cheap with 10 selections on tap and happy-hour pints for 75¢. The food choices are pure Philly, including the requisite cheese steak, hoagies, and Italian sausage. (Eastside)

RACCOON LODGE AND BREW PUB
7424 SW Beaverton-Hillsdale Hwy.
503/296-0110
This recent addition to Portland's beer scene is the handiwork of Art Larrance, one of Portland's microbrew pioneers and the cofounder of Portland Brewing. Unfortunately, the half dozen beers on tap are tame by comparison to Larrance's previous efforts. The atmosphere combines a ski chalet with a hunting lodge (there are enough stuffed animal heads to make Noah wince). A full food menu is offered. (West Suburbs)

TUG BOAT
711 SW Ankeny
503/226-2508
This tiny, eclectic brewpub sits in the heart of downtown Portland and is a convenient walk from most major hotels. Nothing is fancy at Tugboat, and the numerous tap handles (I counted 19) are only partially in use. You'll find a slew of fresh brews on tap and a limited food menu. The cramped surroundings mean the house band (often

A Tour of Portland's Microbrew Styles

by Marc Zolton

Portland's local microbrews come in all tastes and colors. There is light and pale for those rare, hot summer days and dark and chewy ales to help chase those winter doldrums. Portland's pubs pride themselves on showing off their beer expertise, and you'll have no trouble finding sensational seasonal varieties on tap. Here is a quick guide to the wide variety of fresh ales available in the City of Roses.

Golden ale: A light, summer ale. This beer is usually available by late spring.

Pale ale: A more bitter or hoppy variety of ale. This beer has a higher alcohol content than others in its class.

Extra special bitter (ESB): A summer favorite, this ale packs a hoppy finish.

India pale ale (IPA): Named after the variety first brewed for British soldiers stationed in India, this is a favorite warm-weather ale with a bitter finish.

Brown ale: Brown ale is fuller in body and sweeter in taste than other ales.

jazz) can sometimes be a pain in the ears. (Downtown)

BREWERIES

Major Breweries with Attached Pubs

BRIDGEPORT BREWING COMPANY
1318 NW Northrup
503/241-7179
www.firkin.com

The original and, perhaps, the best brewpub in Portland, Bridgeport has stuck to its successful formula for 15 years. Hot, tasty pizza is the house food, but locals flock here for the fine ales.

The India Pale Ale may be the best beer in the city, especially on a warm summer day. The clientele is a mix of muddied soccer teams and downtown office workers. The atmosphere is dark wood-and-warehouse at its best with a small outdoor drinking area under the hop vines. This is a must-see on

Scottish ale: The maltier Scottish ale often has a smoky finish. The Portland Brewing Company offers up a fine example with its MacTarnahan's Scottish ale.

Wheat beer: You won't find many traditional German wheat beers in Portland, but you'll see plenty of folks sipping a Widmer Hefeweizen— Portland's most popular microbrew. This cloudy, unfiltered delight is usually served with a lemon wedge.

Porter: A winter favorite. Portland has a plethora of porters to enjoy. This is a dark, heavy ale great on a winter's day or in place of lunch.

Stout: When Portland's rainy gloom takes hold, the locals start reaching for a stout ale. These beers are black as night and offer up a nice, hoppy finish.

Winter ales: As the holidays approach, Portlanders receive a special gift from the local brewers—great tasting winter ales. Nearly every Oregon microbrewer features one for several months each winter. Be warned, however: they are usually heavy in both their taste and their alcohol content.

Barley wine: Watch out beer lovers—barley wine is truly an acquired taste. These incredible brews usually have twice the alcohol content (close to 12.5 percent in most cases) of normal ales. Sip them to fully appreciate their sweet, bitter taste.

any Portland beer tour. (Eastside and Downtown)

**FULL SAIL BREWING/
PILSNER ROOM**
307 SW Montgomery
503/222-5343
www.fullsailbrewing.com
This riverside brewpub is a great place to drink Oregon microbrews and enjoy fine dining at the same time. Full Sail Brewing hails from Hood River in the Columbia Gorge, but Portland head brewer John Harris (one of the best in Oregon)

delivers every one of the flagship brewery's beers, from Golden to Wassail Christmas. The only thing missing is the 45-mph gusts of wind. The McCormick and Schmick's restaurant attached to the brewery and pub offers top-notch seafood. On a summer day, grab a seat outside and enjoy the views of the Willamette River. It rarely gets better than this. (Downtown)

**PORTLAND BREWING TAPROOM
AND GRILL**
2730 NW 31st Ave.

503/226-7623
www.portlandbrew.com
One of the original Big Three in Portland's beer revolution, Portland Brewing recently built an expanded brewery complete with a fine restaurant and pub. Despite the gleaming copper beer kettles (imported from Germany), the sausages and schnitzel on the menu, and the beer steins hanging throughout, the Taproom serves English-style ales. MacTarnahan's is the company's signature brew and one of the most popular in the city. The pub's outdoor beer garden is open in the summer. (Northwest)

WIDMER GASTHAUS
929 N. Russell
503/281-2437
www.widmer.com
The Widmer Brothers are the biggest fish in Portland's brewing scene. Half owned by Anheuser Busch, Widmer Gasthaus produces more beer than any other micro-

brewery in the state, and their signature Widmer Hefeweizen is Oregon's best-selling craft beer. The Gasthaus, another taste of Germany, is in a historic brick building housing the company's offices and is directly across the street from its giant brewhouse. The pub boasts a fine menu complete with three different types of handmade sausage. While a glass of hefeweizen with a lemon wedge seems to appear at every table, breaking ranks and ordering an alt bierwill make you one happy customer indeed. (North Portland)

Major Breweries with Attached Pubs

HAIR OF THE DOG BREWING COMPANY
4509 SE 23rd Ave.
503/232-6585
www.hairofthedog.com
This may be the best brewery in Portland. Brewers Alan Sprints and

Brewing kettle at Hair of the Dog Brewing Company

Hair of the Dog Brewing Company

Doug Henderson have been brewing their high-alcohol, Belgian-style brew for a little more than five years. Mostly available in bottles (the brewers recommend you let the beer age in the bottle for years in some cases), Hair of the Dog offers four draft varieties—Adam, Golden Rose, Fred, and Ed—at several local pubs around town (check their Web site for a list). Some of the toughest beer critics in the world have been left speechless by this brewery's distinctively flavored, high-octane ale. This is beer for a true beer lover or a very ambitious beer taster. (Eastside)

SAXER BREWING COMPANY
5875 SW Lakeview Blvd.
Lake Oswego
503/699-9524
www.saxerbeer.com
Saxer Brewing (now owned by Portland Brewing) represents two lines of beer—Saxer and Norwester. The Bavarian-style brewery is unique in Oregon, as it is the only one that exclusively produces lager-style beer. Lager beer is German and Czech in its origins. The brewery's beer is available in many states, and its Lemon Lager garnered much praise and press several years ago. Look for it in local grocery stores as well as in area pubs and restaurants. (West Suburbs)

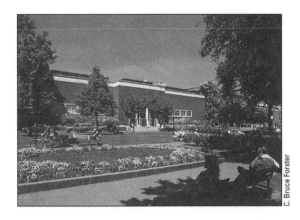

C. Bruce Forster

7

MUSEUMS AND GALLERIES

The last decade has placed Portland museums on the map, so to speak. Some, like the Portland Art Museum, the Advertising Museum, and Oregon Museum of Science and Industry (OMSI), have gained national recognition, expanding and boosting the city's offerings. Indicative of Portland's simultaneous appreciation of education, art, and culture, these renowned institutions span the sciences, art, and pop. And that extrapolates to the lesser venues, as art-loving crowds can be witnessed cruising Portland's art galleries the first Thursday evening of every month.

ART MUSEUMS

PORTLAND ART MUSEUM
1219 SW Park Ave.
503/226-2811
www.pam.org
The Portland Art Museum, the oldest art museum in the Northwest, carries an impressive permanent collection including works of Renoir, Cézanne, and Monet. The European Galleries hold some impressionist masterpieces. The museum also maintains terrific collections of Native American art as well as West African and Asian collections, and it houses the Gilkey Center for Graphic Arts. In recent years, major world-class exhibits like *The Splendors of Ancient Egypt,* Monet collections, a Rodin collection, and *Tombs of China* have come to PAM largely due to the fund-raising efforts of executive director John Buchanan and his wife, Lucy. In 2000 the exhibition *Stroganoff: Palace and Collections of a Russian Noble Family* makes its international debut here. Check with the museum for current exhibitions. Tue–Sun 10–5, first Thu every

month 10–9. $7.50 adults, $6 seniors and students, $4 children 5–18. &

SCIENCE AND HISTORY MUSEUMS

END OF THE OREGON TRAIL INTERPRETIVE CENTER
1726 Washington
Oregon City
503/657-9336

Look for the large covered wagons. Step into the first wagon and back to 1840 as a guide presents a history of pioneering adventure along the famous Oregon Trail. Next, climb aboard another wagon to see and hear real accounts of life along the trail as recorded in three diaries and presented on screen. Finally, enjoy the hands-on exhibits where children and adults alike can experience what it was like for the pioneers to make food and wash clothes, among other routine chores. To add to the authenticity, the museum is located where the trail ended, 20 minutes from downtown on Interstate 205 (exit 10). Mon–Sat 9–5, Sun 10–5; call for show times. $5.50 adults, $4.50 seniors, $3 children 6–12. & (East Suburbs)

OREGON HISTORY CENTER
1200 SW Park Ave.
503/222-1741
www.ohs.org/exhibitions

If you want to learn more about Portland history, take the time to visit the Oregon History Center, which also serves as headquarters of the Oregon Historical Society. It's a great way to get acquainted with the city. The museum houses

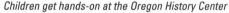

Children get hands-on at the Oregon History Center

Oregon Historical Society

interesting exhibits that tell the story of Oregon and the Pacific Northwest. Marvel at the *Historic Vehicles in Miniature* exhibit featuring 63 little horse-drawn wagons. Also browse *Portland: A History of the City* and the new *Willamette Valley: Visions of Eden,* as well as displays of Native American baskets and Benson automobiles. When you're through, visit the museum's store and the Historical Society's library. Tue–Wed and Fri–Sat 10–5, Thu 10–8, Sun noon–5. $6 adults, $3 students, $1.50 children 6–12. ♿ (Downtown)

OREGON MARITIME CENTER AND MUSEUM
113 SW Naito Pkwy.
503/224-7724
Located in Old Town, this intriguing museum is packed with remnants of Portland's interesting maritime

Oregon History Center

Robin Klein

past. Navigational and nautical instruments, ship models, and various old-time photographs make this museum a treat for seafaring buffs. Make time to see the sternwheeler docked across the street from the museum in Willamette River. Museum open Fri–Sun 11–4. (Downtown)

OREGON MUSEUM OF SCIENCE AND INDUSTRY
1945 SE Water Ave.
503/797-4000
www.omsi.edu
OMSI is the fifth-largest science museum in the country. On the east bank of the Willamette across from downtown, it has both permanent and changing exhibits, most of which are interactive and designed for people of all ages. Two of the most popular exhibits are a space capsule and a chemistry lab. The museum's OMNIMAX Theater includes a five-story wraparound screen and promises, among other things, to take viewers to the top of Mount Everest, into a herd of stampeding African elephants, or surfing across a 30-foot Hawaiian wave. The shows are so realistic that some people get motion sickness. The museum also has a planetarium called the Murdock Sky Theater (check out its laser show). Outside the main building is the USS *Blueback,* a retired Navy submarine docked in the Willamette River. Regular tours of the submarine are offered daily, but you can book a "technical" tour if you're so inclined. Tue–Sun 9:30–5:30, as well as Monday public school holidays. General admission $6.50 adults, $4.50 seniors and children 4–13.

Admissions package for all major exhibits and shows $15, $11.50 seniors and children 4–13. Call for individual exhibit prices. ♿ (Eastside)

WORLD FORESTRY CENTER
4033 SW Canyon Rd.
503/228-1367
www.worldforest.org
The World Forestry Center is a great place to learn about tropical and temperate rainforests, forest fires, logging, and wood products. Conveniently located next to the Oregon Zoo and Hoyt Arboretum, the center also houses an extensive collection of petrified woods and hosts special shows and changing exhibits. Visitors, who are greeted by a huge, "talking" tree, are encouraged to take a walk

through the arboretum when they're through exploring the museum. Daily 10–5. $4.50 adults, $3.50 seniors and children 6–18. ♿ (West Suburbs)

OTHER MUSEUMS

AMERICAN ADVERTISING MUSEUM
5035 SE 24th Ave., near Holgate
503/226-0000
This unusual museum is one of only four media-related museums in the country and the only one that archives print, radio, and television advertising in the same place. Founded in 1996 with the support of local ad agencies, the museum now receives a broader range of contributors that extends beyond

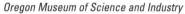
Oregon Museum of Science and Industry

Portland Oregon Visitors Association

Public Art in Portland

Portland has embraced public art: animal fountains in Pioneer Courthouse Square, the controversial Portlandia *sculpture (Portland's own statue of liberty) hovering outside the Portland Building, and light-rail station art. In 1980, both Multnomah County and the City of Portland passed a 1 percent-for-art building ordinance and then in 1988 adopted the Bonus Program for Private Developers. It provides bonus floor area ratios in return for public art contributions as an incentive for ensuring art incorporation in new constructions. Tri-Met also passed a Public Art Policy in 1997, which sets aside 1.5 percent of certain capital projects for public art. Consequently, you can find interesting artwork throughout the city, whether at MAX light-rail stops, in Pioneer Square, on city buildings, or in numerous less likely spots.*

The Regional Arts and Culture Council, a nonprofit regional arts agency, fosters and oversees Portland's public art projects. For a list of public art works and descriptions, as well as more information about the Percent for Art program, view the council's website at www.racc.org.

Portland. Portland may be far from the world's media center, but it is home to the world-famous Weiden & Kennedy agency, creator of Nike's "Just Do It" campaign. The museum presents advertisements in their historical context, displaying collections of works grouped to show advertising's influence on society over time.

On display is a collection of award-winning print media ads, among other permanent and changing exhibits. This intriguing museum is open Sat noon–5, Mon–Fri by appointment. $3. (Eastside)

STATE OF OREGON SPORTS HALL OF FAME
321 SW Salmon
503/227-7466
This is a museum for sports fans or, for that matter, anyone who ever wanted to catch a major league baseball game or see a Heisman Trophy (Terry Baker's is here). You can also view video programs of

First Thursday

On the first Thursday evening of every month, galleries across Portland stay open late (from six to nine) as evening crowds linger and pass through. Many of the galleries serve hors d'oeuvres and offer wine for sale by the glass. Art experts and novices alike fill the streets, and the crowds seem undaunted even by the rain.

While First Thursday is a citywide happening, the heart of this event is definitely in the Pearl district and centered at Northwest 13th and Glisan. If you unknowingly stumbled upon this intersection on a warm Thursday evening at the start of the month you might not believe you were in Portland.

The Pearl district galleries are clustered in old buildings that formerly served as warehouses. Upscale artist lofts, trendy shops, good restaurants, and coffeehouses have moved in, and now the district bursts with life. First Thursdays go year-round regardless of the weather, so come with an umbrella. Summer and fall months attract the largest crowds.

For a Gallery Guide, *which describes special exhibits and includes a map showing gallery locations, stop by Art Media, 902 Southwest Yamhill, downtown.*

If you plan to dine in the Pearl district on First Thursday, be sure to make a reservation well in advance. All the local bars and restaurants will be packed.

---

sports highlights or see what it's like to be a wheelchair athlete. Sports enthusiasts will find an interesting history of Oregon sports with profiles of homegrown stars like distance runner Steve Prefontaine. Consider combining your visit to the Hall of Fame with a trip to Niketown, just a few blocks away. There is a gift shop on the premises. Tue–Sun 10–6. $4 adults, $3 seniors and youth 8–21. ♿ (Downtown)

GALLERIES

AUGEN GALLERY
817 SW Second Ave.
503/224-8182
Augen Gallery features works by contemporary Northwest artists

After Hours at the Portland Art Museum

Check out the live music at the Portland Art Museum on Wednesday evenings. Various musical artists booked by the museum may come from Portland, San Francisco, Seattle, or elsewhere. The museum stays open "after hours" from 5:30 to 7:30 and converts to a festive venue where guests can sip wine, enjoy music, and even dance. And when the urge to view some great art comes along, they can just take a stroll through the galleries. $6 nonmembers, $3 members. Contact the museum for more information: 503/226-2811.

as well as prints and works on paper by internationally recognized artists. Mon–Sat 10:30–5:30. (Downtown)

BUTTERS GALLERY, LTD.
520 NW Davis
503/248-9378
www.teleport.com/-bgl
This is a contemporary art source for both private and corporate collectors. Tue–Fri 10–5:30, Sat 11–5. (Downtown)

ELIZABETH LEACH GALLERY
207 SW Pine St.
503/224-0521
This gallery represents contemporary fine art by Northwest and national artists. Tue–Sat 10:30–5:30. (Downtown)

PHOTOGRAPHIC IMAGE GALLERY
240 SW First Ave.
503/224-3543
This Old Town photographic gallery includes works by Robert Ketchum, the nature photographer famous for his remote landscapes. You'll also find traditional nudes by

nationally known artists. The gallery offers up the West Coast's largest selection of fine photography posters, as well as changing exhibits. Mon–Sat 10–5:30. (Downtown)

THE REAL MOTHER GOOSE GALLERY
901 SW Yamhill St.
503/223-9510
This gallery showcases American arts and crafts including ceramics, glass, woodwork, furniture, paintings, and custom-made jewelry. Mon–Thu 10–5:30, Fri–Sat 10–6. (Downtown)

SHADES OF COLOR GALLERY
1438 NE Alberta St.
503/288-3779
This unique gallery and gift shop in northeast Portland specializes in African American prints, sculpture, and other works. Tue–Sat 10–4. (North Portland)

TWIST
30 NW 23rd Place
503/224-0334

This gallery is really a retail shop featuring a funky and diverse collection of handcrafted American art, jewelry, furniture, and metal work. Mon–Sat 10–7, Sun 11–6. (Northwest)

WATERSTONE GALLERY
733 NW Everett St.
503/226-6196
This artist-owned gallery features a diverse collection of Northwest contemporary artwork. Tue–Sat noon–6. (Northwest)

WENTZ GALLERY
1219 SW Park Ave.
503/226-4391
At the Pacific Northwest College of Art, the Wentz Gallery exhibits contemporary work by regional and national artists as well as PNCA faculty. Daily 9 a.m.–10 p.m. (Downtown)

Oaks Amusement Park

8

KIDS' STUFF

Portland must be one of the kid-friendliest towns in America. Loads of parks and playgrounds, terrific educational activities and museums that target young ones, a clean downtown full of water fountains for both drinking and playing, small city blocks for little legs, boats galore, and nearby ocean and mountain recreation conspire to make this city a family destination.

Many young families moved to the Portland area in the 1980s and '90s, seeking its affordable housing, sense of community, good public schools, clean streets, and fun atmosphere for raising children. Today Portland continues to attract families as it grows.

ANIMALS AND THE GREAT OUTDOORS

AUDUBON SOCIETY OF PORTLAND
5151 NW Cornell Rd.
503/292-9453
The Portland Audubon Society, nestled in an old-growth forest west of downtown, gives children and adults who love nature a glimpse of wildlife in the Northwest. The society shelters and cares for injured birds, orphaned animal babies, and other wild animals found in distress or jeopardy. You never know what creatures will be on hand in the cages outside. Inside, you'll find a variety of stuffed animals and an engaging gift shop full of books, birdhouses, games, and nature toys. After browsing the store, be sure to take a walk along Audubon's nature trails through a dense forest behind the building. Audubon also offers an extensive selection of guided nature tours for everyone. Mon–Sat 10–6, Sun 10–5. Free. & (Northwest)

BONNEVILLE DAM
I-84, exit 40
541/374-8820

The dam's huge ship locks are a treat for kids of all ages, especially those who are lucky enough to witness a boat passing through. Peer through windows at fish ladders to see powerful salmon in spring and summer struggle to climb upriver to their spawning grounds. Or, if the salmon aren't running, check out the interesting movies and displays at the visitors centers, which educate the curious about electricity generation. Tours can be booked in advance at no charge. Visitors centers and powerhouses are on both sides of the dam, in Oregon and in Washington. Daily 9–5. Also plan to explore the nearby Bonneville Fish Hatcheries to see rainbow trout and sturgeon in rearing ponds. If you visit in October you can see how the eggs are extracted from the adult fish. There is a gift shop. No entry fee. Daily 9 a.m. to dusk. ᕦ (East Suburbs)

CAMP NAMANU
Sandy
503/224-7800
www.portlandcampfire.com/campnamanu

A favorite coed camp for schools and individuals, Camp Namanu, just outside Portland near the town of Sandy, runs through summer and promises to keep kids ages 7 to 17 engaged in a variety of sports, games, and crafts during one- or two-seek sessions. Campers enjoy boating, fishing, drama, horseback riding, and other activities. Prices range from about $275 to $375. (East Suburbs)

OREGON ZOO
4001 SW Canyon Rd.
503/226-1561
www.zooregon.org

The award-winning Oregon Zoo has African grassland and rainforest exhibits, a renowned Asian elephant breeding program, and one of the largest chimpanzee exhibits in the United States. The zoo just opened a *Great Northwest* exhibit that features white mountain goats and Steller's sea lions. Summer daily 9–5, winter daily 9–4. Visitors may stay for up to one hour after the gates close. ᕦ (Downtown)

If your kids love to hike, leave your car at Lower Macleay Park (part of Forest Park, accessible by car at Northwest Upshur) then hike up to the Audubon Society building on a one-mile path along a winding creek in an old-growth forest grove. The last part of the hike is uphill, so plan on resting every once in a while and bring water. The path is dirt and follows a creek. When you reach the Audubon Society at the top, you'll find cages outside holding some live rescued birds. At the top of the hill the kids can explore the Audubon's gift shop and check out the interesting animals.

Oregon Zoo

Portland Oregon Visitors Association

SALMON STREET FOUNTAIN
Salmon Street and the Willamette River

Consider this treat on a hot summer day after dragging the kids around town shopping or visiting museums. The 185 fountains on Salmon Street, set against a beautiful backdrop of boats on the Willamette River, provide a great way to cool off. Bring a change of clothes, a lunch or snack, and a towel. ♿ (Downtown)

SAUVIE ISLAND

Bored with the mainland? You'll find berry-picking, frog-hunting, picnicking, pumpkin-gathering, beaches, and boating on this quiet island in the Columbia River only 10 minutes from downtown. The island holds 12,000 acres of wildlife habitat including roosts for 35 bald eagles. In late fall the island comes alive as thousands of ducks and geese pass through on their migration south from Canada on the Pacific Flyway. To get to the island, take Route 30 west and over the Sauvie Island Bridge. (North Portland)

MUSEUMS AND LIBRARIES

BEVERLY CLEARY CHILDREN'S LIBRARY
Central Library
801 SW 10th Ave.
503/248-5123

Oregon's largest library, the Central Library, recently underwent a major renovation, and the results are impressive. The library's splendid children's room is called the Beverly Cleary Children's Library, and it is sure to delight.

An impressive bronze tree with castings of animals supports the librarian's desk; it weighs more than a ton. Shadow boxes make up three large bookends, each displaying a mesmerizing array of miniatures in three scenes. There are also 16 computers and a collection of 50,000 books. Library is

Beverly Cleary, the author of many popular children's books, grew up in northeast Portland and once worked in the Children's Library.

open Mon–Thu 9–9, Fri–Sat 9–6, Sun 1–5. ♿ (Downtown)

FORT VANCOUVER
Mill Plain, exit I-5 North from Portland
Vancouver, WA

Step back in time to see people dressed in period clothing, browse various shops from the olden days, and hear tour guides tell the site's story. Then, visit nearby Officer's Row and see the beautifully reconstructed Victorian-era homes on a lovely green. Fort Vancouver was the first settlement in the Oregon Territory. Originally a fur-trading headquarters as well as a fort in the early 1800s, the site has been authentically restored. A gift shop specializes in things Victorian, and period furniture is on display. (North Suburbs)

OREGON MUSEUM OF SCIENCE AND INDUSTRY
1945 SE Water Ave.
503/797-4000

The Oregon Museum of Science and Industry's five large halls, each dedicated to a different scientific discipline, provide loads of interactive learning for kids of all ages. You'll find everything from the Discovery Station, designed for very small children (6 and under), to chemistry, physics, and computer labs, which are geared for the older set. There is even a real submarine, the USS *Blueback,* docked

Salmon Street Fountain

Robin Klein

outside in the Willamette River and open for tours. OMSI also offers many educational programs, including camps and overnighters. Check out what's showing at OMSI's popular OMNIMAX Theater. Or view the stars from a seat in the Murdock Sky Theater. You'll also find treasures in the gift shop, with its interesting science and nature toys. Tue–Sun 9:30–5:30. Admissions package covering all exhibits: $15 adults, $11.50 seniors and children 4–13. Call for individual exhibit prices and special offers. ♿ (Eastside)

THE PORTLAND CHILDREN'S MUSEUM
3037 SW Second Ave.
503/823-2227
The Portland Children's Museum, where kids can pretend to "work" in a child-size bistro as chefs, waiters, or cashiers, is full of hands-on fun for children age 10 and under. Kids can go grocery shopping in a play store, fill their carts with play food, and check out at registers run by other young museum visitors. The museum's brick building feels like a comfortable old house, but here each room holds a fantasy. Smaller children especially enjoy the water play station, where they can get as messy as they want without getting in trouble with the adults. Learning isn't supposed to be so much fun! Another room allows Lego-lovers and other young construction workers to build to their hearts' content. Themes change in certain rooms from time to time. A gift shop with educational fun toys is on the premises, and there's a great playground just outside—a perfect place to break for a sack lunch.

Plans are underway to open a brand-new Children's Museum in March 2001. Tue–Sun 9–5, as well as Monday public school holidays. $4. ♿ (Downtown)

PUPPETS AND THEATER

DO JUMP! EXTREMELY PHYSICAL THEATER
Echo Theater
1515 SE 37th Ave.
503/231-6605
Echo Theater is the home of Do Jump! Extremely Physical Theater, a troupe of acrobats, trapeze artists, and dancers. Echo also is experienced in teaching kids in the trapeze techniques of Do Jump. This unusual theater blends acting, acrobatics, and dance together into movement that fascinates and delights. Shows sell out, so purchase your tickets in advance. Call for show times and ticket prices. ♿ (Eastside)

IMAGO
17 SE Eighth
503/231-9581
IMAGO's creators blend clay, papier-mâché, wood, wire, foam, electronics, films, slides, lighting, and music with movement and mime to create strange creatures that provoke the imagination, like an acrobatic larval insect or a magical ball that transforms from eggplant to boulder to circus performer. Performances delight children, especially the signature *Frogs, Lizards, Orbs and Slinkys*. The acclaimed troupe has toured internationally and appeared on national television programs. Call for upcoming shows, tickets, and prices. ♿ (Eastside)

Top Ten Places to Go in Portland
by Lenna Bortnick, 10-year-old Portlander

1. OMSI (Oregon Museum of Science and Industry)
2. Oaks Amusement Park and Roller Rink
3. Clackamas Aquatic Park
4. Oregon Zoo
5. Sauvie Island
6. Lloyd Center Mall/Ice Chalet
7. Mount Hood for snowboarding or skiing
8. Audubon Society
9. Oregon Children's Theater
10. Malibu Grand Prix

LADYBUG THEATER
SE Spokane St. and the
Willamette River
503/232-2346
This little gem of a theater company, in Oaks Park at the foot of the Sellwood Bridge, is a great introduction to theater for young children. Professional actors improvise and involve the audience in every play, and children really get into the shows, which are usually quite funny and clever. The audience sits on the floor in a small building adjacent to the Oaks Amusement Park. Here, you are never too young. Weekday morning shows target preschool children. The weekend shows target older children. Weekday shows $2.50, weekend shows $3 ages 3 and up. Call for show times and reservations. ௬ (Eastside)

NORTHWEST CHILDREN'S
THEATER
1819 NW Everett

503/222-2190
The Northwest Children's Theater is *the* children's theater and acting school in Portland. Performances are first-rate and always include some child actors. The theater typically runs classics such as *The Miracle Worker, Jungle Book,* and *Winnie-the-Pooh.* Call for performance dates, times, and prices. ௬ (Northwest)

OREGON CHILDREN'S THEATER
600 SW 10th Ave., Ste. 543
503/228-9571
Portland's largest professional theater company for children ages 4 and up stages shows like *Miracle on 34th Street, Treasure Island,* and *Charlotte's Web* at various venues around town. Call for show information, location, times, and ticket prices. ௬ (Downtown)

TEARS OF JOY PUPPET THEATER
1109 SE Fifth Ave.
Vancouver, WA

503/248-0557

Finger puppets or dainty marionettes these puppets and masks are not. Rather, they're impressive works of art that come to life in creative performances that frequently tell stories from a range of cultures. Call for show information, times, theater locations, and ticket prices (and to determine which performances are specifically for children and which are for adults). & (Downtown, North Suburbs)

STORES KIDS LOVE

CAL'S PHARMACY SKATEBOARDS AND SNOWBOARDS
1644 E. Burnside
503/233-1237
This is skateboarder heaven. Strangely enough, Cal's skateboard business was born out of a pharmacy. The owner-pharmacist, Marvin, knew the drugstore business, and his son knew skateboards. Over the years they cleared away pharmaceutical sundries (nearly down to the prescription room) to make more skateboard retail space. Cal's adopted as its logo the Russian acronym for the former Soviet Union, CCCP (but in Cal's case it stands for Corporate Coercion of Cal's Pharmacy). Your skateboarder will appreciate the helpful clerks who know their stuff. The shop sells snowboards, too. & (Eastside)

CHILD'S PLAY
907 NW 23rd Ave.
503/224-5586
A quality children's toy store, filled to the brim with special toys for babies and older children, Child's Play has dress-up clothes, doll houses, loads of animal figurines,

puppets, wooden toys, and uncommon items that keep kids busy for quite a while. & (Uptown)

COMPUSA
1780 N. Jantzen Beach Center
503/240-4900
This place draws more than just computer geeks. If your child loves computer games, then this megastore is guaranteed to please. There are countless aisles of games and educational software. The store even allows shoppers to try the software on its in-house computers before purchasing. & (North Portland)

THE DISCOVERY CHANNEL STORE
700 SW Fifth Ave. (Pioneer Place Mall)
503/222-0015
Formerly a nature store, the Discovery Channel Store maintains a good selection of intriguing nature items. Themes focus on animals and faraway places with learning in mind. It is conveniently located at the heart of Pioneer Place shopping downtown. & (Downtown)

FINNEGAN'S TOYS AND GIFTS
922 SW Yamhill
503/221-0306
This large toy store is a great place to find that unique gift or certain stuffed animal you could never find in a chain store. Finnegan's holds a large selection of educational toys, as well as classic toys such as dolls, trucks, marbles, beads, and little candies that you can buy singly for a dime or a quarter. The store is also stocked with great travel toys and booklets. & (Downtown)

IMAGINARIUM
Clackamas Town Center Mall
503/786-9640

This mall toy store is a favorite stop for young children. Games, building toys, and wooden train sets abound, and kids are encouraged to try out everything. A good selection of books and music is available in the rear of the store, and sales clerks are crafty at assisting with that purchase-the-gift-while-the-child-isn't-looking maneuver. 点 (East Suburbs)

KIDS AT HEART II
1736 SE Hawthorne
503/232-5927

This store carries selected toys and games of higher-than-usual quality. It's a great place to buy a unique gift for kids between the ages of 8 and 18. Also check out Kids at Heart I (for ages 8 and under), just up the street on Hawthorne. 点 (Eastside)

Kids enjoying a Portland park

Michael O. Schmitt

OPB'S STORE OF KNOWLEDGE
Clackamas Town Center
503/654-6960

The store run by Oregon Public Broadcasting is as interesting for adults as it is for children. It's a store of wonder where you can find clever toys, educational games, and creativity-stimulating products on subjects ranging from rockets, minerals, and wild animals to golf, basket-weaving, and mega-3D puzzles. Be careful in here—it's easy to get lost (cerebrally speaking, that is). 点 (East Suburbs)

THINGS FROM ANOTHER WORLD
4133 NE Sandy
503/284-4693
www.tfaw.com

This comic store has a great selection of fantasy and science fiction games and toys. You name it, they've got it: comic books, collecting cards, figurines, science fiction and computer game character dolls, not to mention Spiderman, Star Wars, X-men, and Dungeons theme toys. In fact, the store claims to have the largest selection of back issues in Oregon. It even has a 24-hour comic hotline: 503/644-7036. 点 (Eastside)

THEME PARKS/OUTINGS

COSMIC BOWLING AT GRAND CENTRAL BOWL
808 SE Morrison
503/232-5166

Cosmic bowling is more like disco bowling, with darkened alleys and disco lights, a party atmosphere, a deejay spinning music, and glow-in-the-dark pins and bowling balls. Automatic computer scorekeeping makes tracking points easy for kids.

Buy a soda and pizza and enjoy bowling's groovy revival. Open 24 hours a day Sept–May; call for summer hours. $13 per person or $60 per lane for two hours (includes shoe rental). Reservations recommended. (Eastside)

LASERPORT LASER TAG ARENA
10975 SW Canyon
Beaverton
503/526-9501
If there's a futuristic warrior in your family, send her into battle with a harmless laser gun in a dark, obstacle-filled room. Players wear chest sensors that detect and count each laser "hit" as it is made. Laser tag is great for groups and parties, but individuals can play, too. Laserport organizes all players into teams for loads of fun. Open Mon–Thu noon–9, Fri noon–midnight, Sat 10 a.m.–midnight, Sun 10–9. $7 per person for first game, $5 per person for each additional game. ♿ (West Suburbs)

MALIBU GRAND PRIX
9405 SW Cascade Ave. (off Hwy. 217 at Scholl's Ferry exit)
Beaverton
503/641-8122
If you (or your kids) ever wanted to drive a racecar, this is your chance. Children can drive one of two machines—a Slick car or a Sprint car. The only requirement is they must be at least four feet, six inches tall. The Sprint cars are smaller and slower, designed for those who don't crave the speed. A third type of car, a two-seater known as the Grand Barrage, is for licensed drivers older than 18 and can accommodate young passengers at least three feet, six inches tall (a nice chance for the little ones to join in the fun).

A variety of packages are available—the more laps, the better the deal. There can be waits for the cars, especially evenings and on weekends, but kids can stay busy in Malibu's large game room or get a bite at the snack bar. Sun–Thu 11–9, Fri–Sat 11–11. Sprint cars stop running at eight. Call for prices, and beware—things can get quite expensive.
(West Suburbs)

MOUNT HOOD SKIBOWL
Mount Hood
503/272-3206
For a summertime thrill, ride a toboggan-type sled down a half-mile cement chute on Mount Hood. You control the brakes and the speed through a half mile of mountain meadows on the Northwest's only Alpine Slide. A ski resort in the winter, SkiBowl offers great fun for mountain bikers and would-be luge alpinists on its slopes during the summer months. Other summer activities geared for kids include Indy karts, a scenic sky chair, 18-hole miniature golf, and a mountain bike park. Memorial Day–October 1 (weather permitting) Mon–Fri 11–6, Sat–Sun 10–7. To get there, take

TRIVIA

A new skatepark planned to open in 2001 in Old Town at the base of the Steel Bridge will be the city's first official park for skateboarders, as well as the largest of its kind in the area.

Highway 26 west for about 45 minutes to Mount Hood. (East Suburbs)

NORTH CLACKAMAS AQUATIC PARK
7300 SE Harmony Rd.
Milwaukie
503/557-SURF
This water wonderland is really a huge indoor swimming pool. Actually, there are five pools, as well as giant slides (including one tunnel slide), diving boards, a large whirlpool for adults, a wave pool, and sprinkling fountains. It's great for a rainy winter day. $9.50 adults, $6.50 seniors, $6.50 ages 9–17, $4.50 ages 3–8. Family rates are also available. Call for public open hours as they vary depending on season and other uses. & (East Suburbs)

OAKS AMUSEMENT PARK AND ROLLER RINK
SE Spokane at the Willamette River
503/236-5722
On the banks of the Willamette River, Oaks Amusement Park is a good old-fashioned amusement park that has delighted children for years. The rides are closed during winter, but the large popular indoor roller-skating rink is open all year. Traditional amusement park rides include a roller coaster, carousel, and rides for small children. Call for times—schedules are seasonal. & (Eastside)

VANCOUVER WATER WORKS PARK
Fourth Plain and Fort Vancouver Way
Vancouver, WA
360/696-8171
This sunny spot provides kids with a great place to practice their skateboarding or rollerblading while other family members picnic, play, or stroll. The ramps and rails are considered among Portland's best and the skating can get aggressive, depending on the crowd that day. Conveniently located near Officer's Row just across the river from Portland, the setting at Water Works Park offers a gentler alternative to the very urban Burnside Skatepark. The park is just 15 minutes from downtown Portland near Fort Vancouver. To get there, take Interstate 5 north to the Fourth Plain exit, then drive east for about one mile. (North Suburbs)

Oregon Tourism Commission

9

PARKS, GARDENS, AND RECREATION AREAS

Portland's more than 700 parks provide space, and plenty of it, for nearly any outdoor activity in nearly every neighborhood.

Metro Greenspaces was created in 1989 to create and preserve a carefully linked system of natural areas throughout the city. The system allows wildlife and hikers to travel uninterrupted in a 40-mile loop.

Portland cherishes its parks. Early city developers had the foresight to set aside plenty of land for posterity. Coined the Rose City, Portland is also garden crazy. With its abundance of public and private gardens, the city has been rated again and again by top garden magazines as one of the country's great garden cities.

COUCH PARK
NW 20th Ave. and NW Glisan
This park has an inviting play structure, beneath a great chestnut tree, guaranteed to keep children busy for hours. Not large enough for hiking but delightful for sitting, Couch Park offers a welcome break from shopping and strolling on nearby Northwest 23rd and 21st Avenues. Consider picking up some bread, cheese, and fruit at City Market on Northwest 21st and Johnson for a picnic. The park is behind the Metropolitan Learning Center and fills with schoolchildren during their recess times. (Northwest)

FOREST PARK
End of NW Thurman or Upshur St.
Feel like taking a hike in the beautiful Northwest woods? You don't have to get in your car and drive for an hour. In Portland you can hike through a forest all day without seeing a trace of city life, yet all the while be no more than five minutes from the nearest latte.

Forest Park is the granddaddy of parks, but it's unlike any other. In fact, it's a true wilderness reserve in the city. Forest Park is the largest city park in the United States, with 5,000 acres and 60 miles of trails through old-growth forest. Much of the land would be prime development property if it wasn't preserved. The park is home to wildlife such as trout, elk, and black bear and includes dramatic views of the city, the Columbia River, and the Cascade Mountains. The park boundaries stretch north of West Burnside to Northwest Newberry Road and west of Northwest Saint Helens Road to Southwest Skyline Road.

Even though trails are well signed, it is possible to get lost in Forest Park, so be careful and inspect the maps along its boundary. A good first hike begins at the end of Northwest Thurman Street. Park your car, walk a short distance on an access road to the Wild Cherry Trail, then continue to the Wildwood Trail. From there, continue to the Aspen Trail, which eventually leads back to Thurman Street and your car. For an even easier hike, park in the lot at the end of Northwest Upshur Street (Lower Macleay) and walk along the easy trail amidst ancient trees. When you've had enough, turn back. (Northwest)

HOYT ARBORETUM
4000 SW Fairview Blvd.
503/228-8733
Hoyt Arboretum is not only a botanist's delight, it's also a joy for anyone who loves trees. Ten miles of trails wind through 175 acres of gentle woods that harbor the nation's largest collection of conifers. Many of the 850 species of trees in the arboretum are identified with plaques at their bases. For a special treat in the fall, go to the arboretum on a sunny day to see it dripping in buttery golds and reds after the leaves have turned color. (Downtown)

INTERNATIONAL ROSE TEST GARDENS
Washington Park
400 SW Kingston Ave.

Portland's Forests

The forests in the nearby Coast and Cascade Mountains constitute some of the last and finest remnants of North American coastal temperate rain forests. The region's special combination of mild temperatures, loads of rainfall, limited snowfall, and fertile marine wetlands produces, according to Ecotrust of Portland, the "highest standing bio-mass of any terrestrial ecosystem." For more information on Portland's forests, contact Ecotrust, 503/227-6225; the Oregon Forest Resources Institute, 503/229-6718; or the World Forestry Center, 503/228-1367.

Oregon's Ancient Forests

When Lewis and Clark arrived in Portland nearly 200 years ago, they found a landscape covered with 1,000-year-old grand Douglas firs, 300 feet tall and 10 feet in diameter. Today 95 percent of these old-growth trees are gone.

Years ago, the timber industry viewed the old forests as wasteland. It thought the forests would be more valuable if the slow-growing old trees were converted to young, fast-growing plantations that could be harvested every 40 years. Companies began clear-cutting the land and, at the same time, driving species like the northern spotted owl, the chinook salmon, and the grizzly bear, as well as mosses, lichens, and invertebrates, toward extinction. Together, these species form an ecosystem that once lost will be impossible to replace.

In the last 10 years, political and legal victories have preserved some of the old forests, but many others remain scheduled for harvest. Conservation groups, government agencies, and the timber industry will continue to clash over their fate.

Years ago, the government thought it would be enough to preserve "representative samples" of the old-growth forests. Today, the conservation movement is spreading the message that the forests—and all the creatures in them—cannot survive unless large, connected ecosystems are protected. Ultimately, it may turn out that protecting the trees is better for the economy. For example, tourists have already indicated that they prefer dense forests to unsightly clear-cuts. Could it be that a tree left standing is worth more than one cut down?

503/823-3636
The International Rose Test Gardens boast more than 8,000 rose bushes in 550 varieties terraced prominently in Washington Park above the city. Familiar photographs of the city and Mount Hood are taken from these gardens, leaving no doubt that Portland is truly the City of Roses. Portland is home of the oldest rose society in the United States, the

Portland Rose Society, started in 1887. The best way to get to the gardens is via the little train from the Oregon Zoo. Just be sure to check the times for return trains. Admission is free. (Downtown)

JAPANESE GARDEN
611 SW Kingston
503/223-1321

Recognized as one of the most beautiful Japanese gardens outside of Japan, this downtown sight is a peaceful place to explore. A shuttle offers rides from the parking lot to the main entrance gate at regular intervals. From there you will find five gardens on more than five acres with ponds and bridges. In addition to a sand garden, there's a ceremonial Japanese teahouse, a meeting center, and several shelters. Almost 70 percent of the area is wheelchair accessible. Daily 10–4. $6 adults, $4 seniors, $3.50 students, children under 5 free. (Downtown)

LAURELHURST PARK
West of SE 39th Ave., between SE Stark and Burnside

Laurelhurst is a beautiful city park with acres of large Douglas firs and hemlocks and a lake full of ducks.

Forest Park, p. 120

Rich Iwasaki

Japanese Garden, p. 123

You'll find plenty of park benches and picnic tables scattered around manicured greens. The trails are mostly paved and perfect for biking, and on the edge of the park is an outdoor basketball court and playground. (Eastside)

MOUNT TABOR
SE 69th Ave., south of Belmont

Mount Tabor, set high above the city's east end, rises almost 600 feet over nearby streets. On a clear day, the mountain's west side offers stunning views of the West Hills and west of downtown. The east side includes sweeping vistas of Mount Hood. An active volcano more than a million years ago, Mount Tabor is now a huge forested park with loads of hiking trails winding up and down through firs. The park is frequented by a wide array of users, from dogs to lovers, joggers to skateboard junkies. Look out for the skateboarders and street lugers who tend to hurl down the streets at frightening speeds,

especially on Wednesdays when the park is closed to automobile traffic. For a special treat, picnic above the reservoir on the west side and stay long enough to watch the sun set over the city. Near the top you'll find a basketball court and amphitheater in the remnant volcanic crater and, nearby, a playground and tennis courts. The steep stone staircase that climbs to the top of the mountain from Southeast 69th Avenue is a popular spot for fitness buffs. (Eastside)

PARK BLOCKS
Ninth and Park Aves.

These urban city blocks in the heart of downtown and the theater district offer a welcome oasis and walking opportunity amidst the bustle of the city. Professionals, students, street people, and pigeons sit on park benches and stroll the paths among gardens and statues. One block wide, the park stretches nearly the full length of downtown. The blocks north of

Burnside are called North Park Blocks; those south of Burnside pass museums, theaters, a ballet school, and Portland State University and are known as South Park Blocks. (Downtown)

RHODODENDRON GARDENS
Crystal Springs
SE 28th, one block north of Woodstock
503/823-3640 or 503/771-8386
The Hoyt Arboretum may be the place to visit in fall, but the Rhododendron Garden is definitely the place to go in the springtime, when the colorful azaleas and rhododendrons—900 species in nearly every hue on seven acres—are blooming. Also in the spring, look among the reeds along the water for ducklings. If you can't make it in the spring, however, come anytime. The garden is beautiful and tranquil all year with its duck ponds, bridges, and easy pathways sprinkled with benches. This is a nice place to stroll with young children—they love spotting all the small animals. Call for hours, as they change each season. (Eastside)

VANCOUVER WATERFRONT PARK
East of I-5 on the Columbia River
Vancouver, WA
This riverfront park allows visitors to bicycle, walk, and picnic along a lengthy and lovely corridor on the banks of the Columbia River, just across from Portland. Bogs, woodlands, and beaches can be found along the way, not to mention some outstanding views of the Columbia River and Mount Hood. (North Suburbs)

Pioneer Place

10

SHOPPING

Much like the city's neighborhoods, Portland's shopping districts have flavors all their own. The Hawthorne/Belmont area is laid-back hippie. Downtown Pioneer Place is full of high-end department stores and specialty shops. Uptown is swarming with boutiques. Old Town is funky while the Pearl is artsy and practically bursting at the seams with new (and interesting) shops. And Lloyd is the place for malls and boutiques. Portland also harbors a clothing and shoe "garment district" with everything from small manufacturers of hemp sportswear to the home bases of commercial giants Columbia Sportswear, Adidas, and Nike. Finally, there are lots of secondhand stores, garden supply shops, and great bookstores. What to do with all this variety? Browse and explore. A vast array of stores awaits you.

SHOPPING DISTRICTS

Northwest 23rd Avenue

Pricey boutiques, one-of-a-kind clothing stores, music stores, gourmet delis, specialty gift and jewelry shops, and expensive linen stores abound in Portland's northwest district. Mix these shops, densely packed in a six-block stretch of Northwest 23rd Avenue,

with lots of sidewalk cafés and pretty people, and you have Portland's version of San Francisco's Union Street (only more affordable)—a wonderful place to stroll and people-watch and a lovely, walkable neighborhood.

ELEPHANT'S DELICATESSEN
13 NW 23rd Place
503/224-3955
Fresh breads and desserts (the best challah in town each Friday), wines

and cheeses, homemade soups, and great gourmet deli salads are at Elephant's. Be prepared to pay, however, as the prices are high. Still, Elephant's is a perfect place to pick up last-minute meals, tasteful gift items, chocolates, and sauces, or the ingredients for a perfect picnic. (Northwest)

JANE'S OBSESSION
728 NW 23rd Ave.
503/221-1490
Ooh la la. For the finest imported lingerie, check out Jane's. Jane expanded from her original store—Jane's Vanity, still on Broadway downtown—to add this newer uptown shop with more affordable pieces. If you enjoy beautiful fine European lingerie, you might also want to stop by Jane's Vanity. (Northwest)

MUSIC MILLENNIUM
801 NW 23rd Ave.
503/248-0163
This is *the* place to buy CDs, tapes, and more. Music Millennium has a huge selection of music and a knowledgeable staff. If you can sing a little bit of the song, the staff can almost surely identify the artist. You can preview choices with a headset before purchase. The store frequently hosts free mini-appearances of big-name artists on tour. (Northwest)

RESTORATION HARDWARE
315 NW 23rd Ave.
503/228-6226
Not really a hardware store, Restoration is more of an upscale furnishings store and a pleasure to visit. A few choice sofas, chairs, and a very nice selection of lamps recall an understated elegance of another time. The products are all new, but designs are from yesteryear. This might be just the place to pick up that perfect missing piece or accent. (Northwest)

RETRO VIVA
816 NW 23rd Ave.
503/227-5105
This funky women's clothing boutique carries an array of styles from the 1960s, '70s, and beyond. It's a great place to find that unique something to wear. (Northwest)

RICH'S CIGAR STORE AND NEWSSTAND
706 NW 23rd Ave.
503/227-6907
Want to read *Vogue en Français*? Or in Italian? Rich's is the place to pick up foreign magazines and newspapers, as well as the *New York Times,* a few other major city newspapers, from the United States and just about every American magazine you could want. The shop is small and can feel claustrophobic when more than six people stop to browse, but it's definitely worth a look. Rich's also offers a fine selection of cigars and tobacco. A larger outlet downtown at 820 Southwest Alder has even more cigar offerings. (Northwest)

SMITH & HAWKEN
26 NW 23rd Place
503/274-9561
Smith & Hawken is designed for the gardener who has everything. The store sells expensive garden touches like arbors, fountains, plants, and ornaments. It's not really a practical garden shop, more of a designer's selection of garden enhancements for the outdoors and for the home. (Northwest)

THREE MONKEYS
803 NW 23rd Ave.
503/222-5802
This trendy women's clothing boutique is aimed at a younger set. There are actually three stores in a one-block stretch on Northwest 23rd Avenue. One store sells hip, cheap, trendy young women's clothing. Upscale furniture and chandeliers are sold in an adjacent shop, while a few doors down Three Monkeys sells funky and fun gifts, souvenirs, and novelty items. (Northwest)

URBAN OUTFITTERS
2320 NW Westover
503/248-0020
This huge store and retail chain member is popular with teenagers as well as adults seeking fashion-of-the-moment casual wear. While most of the goods are new, some decent secondhand clothing is available. Upstairs you'll find men's clothing, while the larger space on the main floor sports women's wear, jewelry, and trendy household items. In the winter, the warehouse-like store can become uncomfortably chilly. (Northwest)

WILD WEST
740 NW 23rd Ave.
503/222-6666
A wonderful selection of women's clothing at—gasp!—reasonable prices makes Wild West a refreshing find on this yuppie street. Despite the name, the clothing has nothing to do with cowboys or cowgirls. Stylish gowns, sweaters, and wispy summer dresses can be found among other items. Look for the frequent sale signs and racks on the sidewalk in front of the store. (Northwest)

The Pearl

The lines between Old Town and the Pearl district can get blurred. But in general, Old Town is in a busy and established business area clustered around the Burnside Bridge. It is loaded with retro and vintage shops. The Pearl, however, has undergone major gentrification in the past few years and has exploded with new stores to become the city's art-gallery and specialty-furniture hub.

CAL SKATE SKATEBOARDS
210 NW Sixth Ave.
503/248-0495
This hardcore skateboard shop is conveniently located near the popular paved waterfront park—and the site of the new skateboard park planned at the base of the Steel Bridge—and ramps below the Burnside Bridge, hot spots for skateboarders. The store has everything a skateboarder could ever want. (Downtown)

COREEN SALOME
404 NW 10th Ave.
503/827-8693
This is an apothecary with catalog ordering available. It also carries specialty hair and spa products from around the world. (Downtown)

DIECI SOLI
304 NW 11th Ave.
503/222-4221
It's hard to say what's more beautiful at Dieci Soli—the hand-painted Italian ceramics or the exquisite imported table and bed linens. Sunlight fills this spacious and bright store, located on a corner in the Pearl and reminiscent of Tuscany. (Downtown)

Saturday Market

Old Town comes alive every weekend March through December with merchants, street performers, tourists, and craftspeople as more than 300 vendors offer their goods at the Saturday Market open-air bazaar beneath the west end of the Burnside Bridge. The lively marketplace feels like an Eastern Kasbah with the aroma of international food stands and the chatter of busy artisans. You'll find imported fabrics and clothing, tie-dyed shirts, handmade jewelry, hemp goods, and ceramics. A portion of the market area is covered so that even when it rains the shopping may continue. Still, Saturday Market, which takes place Sunday as well as Saturday, is at its best on hot summer days when the crowds appear.

EXIT REAL WORLD
820 NW Glisan
503/226-3948
This relatively new store sells skateboards and the latest in snowboarding fashion, with an emphasis on girl items—beanies, pullovers, bags, baggie pants, and the like—but not the serious gear or outerwear for the sport. (Try U.S. Outdoor or the Mountain Shop for that stuff.) Cute summer wear—like little Ts, shorts, and swimsuits—is available as well. This is the second Exit for proprietors Jake and Missy of Salem. (Downtown)

HANNA ANDERSSON
1010 NW Flanders
503/321-5275
The famous Swedish maker of quality children's clothing has a retail store in Portland. The bold bright colors that are the signature of Hanna Andersson bring life to even the dreariest of days. (Downtown)

MADE IN OREGON
10 NW First Ave.
503/273-8354
www.madeinoregon.com
Made is Oregon is absolutely the place to stop to get your Oregon gifts before you travel home. Smoked salmon, marionberry jam, filberts, and canned slugs (yes, a joke), not to mention pretty picture books, calendars, and anything else that might have Oregon's name on it, can be purchased here. (Downtown)

PH REED CONTEMPORARY LIGHTING AND FURNITURE
1100 NW Glisan
503/274-7080
If you're looking for that special sofa or light fixture, this may be your find. Beautiful pieces crowd this small space. The place aims to please; you can places special orders for a wide variety of fabrics and materials to suit your tastes. (Downtown)

POKERFACE
128 SW Third Ave.
503/294-0445

Pokerface is a popular and fashionable clothing store for hipster and trendy looks. Sleek slacks, creative fabrics, and unique shoes appeal to a stylish (and well-off) young set. (Downtown)

THE WHOLE 9 YARDS
1033 NW Glisan
503/223-2880

This is one of the best fabric stores around—a designer's treasure. Whether you're looking for inspiration or a hard-to-find material, this shop will have what you need. (Downtown)

Pioneer Square Area

The Pioneer Square Area comprises Portland's largest department stores and most upscale shopping in a densely packed district surrounding Pioneer Courthouse Square. It includes Pioneer Place, Saks Fifth Avenue, Anne Klein, J. Crew, Meier and Frank, Nordstrom, Sharper Image, Columbia Sportswear, Niketown, and Jane's Vanity. All are within a short walk and near great places to lunch, such as the Heathman and Southpark. Or go cheap and grab an espresso and snack and sit in the square and watch the world go by.

COLUMBIA SPORTSWEAR
911 SW Broadway
503/226-6800
www.columbia.com

This flagship store of Portland's homegrown outdoor clothing manufacturer sells everything from ski parkas and expedition wear to hiking boots and rain gear. Look for grandmotherly owner Gert Boyle, made famous in Columbia Sportswear's national advertisements. (Downtown)

KATHLEEN'S OF DUBLIN
860 SW Broadway
503/224-4869

This is the place to rent a kilt in Portland. The Irish boutique offers fine bone China and Waterford crystal as well as specialty foods, coffees, teas, bread mixes, and jellies. You'll also find sweaters for men and women, jewelry, and pottery. (Downtown)

NIKETOWN
930 SW Sixth Ave.
503/221-6453

Nike's showplace store is almost a museum of shoes and athletic wear, with each room specializing in a different sport: basketball, tennis, running, cycling, cross-training, water sports, you name it. As slick as can be, Niketown's cool architecture and gadgetry add to the "shopping" experience and make it feel as though you've wandered onto the set of *Bladerunner* or *The Matrix* instead of into a shoe store. It's well worth the visit if only for the selection, but you won't find any bargains. (Downtown)

OSU GIFT STORE
240 SW Yamhill
503/725-5765

Beaver souvenirs from Oregon State University's first football bowl game in three decades are on sale at this campus outlet downtown. The Oregon State University Gift Store also sells team athletic wear and other nice memorabilia sporting the university's logos. (Downtown)

Fred Meyer, the Portland Superstore

Fred Meyer stores are a Portland institution. These are no ordinary grocery stores. Rather, Fred Meyer stores are the original superstores, where you can buy everything from food (each store has a natural-foods section) to bed linens, electronics, hardware, toys, clothes, gardening supplies, and pharmaceuticals. You can buy a new toilet in the same checkout line that you buy your dinner groceries. Really. And, as much as you may fight the commercial superstore captive-audience thing, the extreme convenience of such one-stop shopping is hard to turn down. Food prices admittedly are very reasonable, and fashionable everyday clothing can be had for cheap. There's no denying that Fred Meyer has a near monopoly going on in Portland. The Safeways and the like hang on, but how can they compete? Some of the Fred Meyer stores are super-superstores, almost like mini-malls but with the added convenience that you can pay for all your goods at the same register. So go ahead—be like everybody else in Portland. Pick up a roast chicken or birthday cake while you have that can of paint mixed to color and check out a diamond ring.

PORTLAND PENDLETON SHOP
SW Fourth and Salmon
503/242-0037
www.pendleton-usa.com
The Pendleton brand is renowned for its fine woolen blankets and clothing. Pendleton wool products, priced a little high but of superb quality, are an Oregon tradition dating back 100 years. Styles are typical of the Pacific Northwest and often include forest greens, plaids, and Native American patterns. (Downtown)

UNIVERSITY OF OREGON
DUCK SHOP
SW Second and Yamhill
503/725-3057

www.uobookstore.com
Come here for sportswear and gifts from the University of Oregon, Eugene. Next to a MAX light-rail stop, the Duck Shop is a branch of the University of Oregon Bookstore. (Downtown)

U.S. OUTDOOR
219 SW Broadway
503/223-5937
www.usoutdoor.com
This sports shop carries a huge selection of snowboard and ski equipment and outerwear. The three-level store is packed with snow and rain parkas, gloves, and the like, with name brands like The North Face, Patagonia, and Helly-

Hanson. The lower floor is dedicated to snowboards, including racing boards by Burton and Rossignol, and surfing gear. The main floor serves skiers and includes a good selection of children's products. Upstairs you'll find camping and climbing gear. (Downtown)

Lloyd/East Broadway

Don't limit your Lloyd district shopping to the mall. If you do, you'll miss some of the best stores in the area. The Lloyd district has lots of great shops on Broadway and Weidler. Stores are not as densely packed as in other Portland areas, and Broadway is practically a major thoroughfare, but the area still manages to thrive and grow.

THE FRENCH QUARTER
1444 NE Broadway
503/282-8200
www.eurolinens.com
This lovely shop sells beautiful European linens for the bedroom, bath, and table, as well as traditional French gift items for the house. A second store is in the heart of Pearl district at 536 Northwest 14th Avenue. (Eastside)

IRVINGTON STREET MARKET
NE Weidler and 16th Ave.
Irvington Street Market is a fine addition to the Lloyd district gentrification effort. A short walk from the Lloyd Mall and movie theaters, it is a welcome oasis from those mega-complexes. Two of the market's highlights are the Italian Torrefazione coffee bistro (no sweet lattes here, just the real Italian espresso drinks) and the Bibo Juice and Crepes Bar. This is also the place to find some of the best produce and cheeses in town. (Eastside)

THE MOUNTAIN SHOP
628 NE Broadway
503/288-6768
www.mountainshop.com
The Mountain Shop has an excellent selection of ski, snowboard, and climbing equipment and outerwear. Rental equipment is available at reasonable prices, and staff members are really helpful. The store's snowboard department, called Castle Snowboard Shop, is in a little house attached to the main building. Quality tuning jobs and repairs are done here as well. (Eastside)

VERGOTIS
1713 NE 15th Ave.
503/284-4065
This small upscale boutique is home to unique and fine women's apparel and is one of several fashionable clothing shops in the area. The nearby Lloyd Center Mall has your usual mall department stores and boutiques, like The Limited, Nordstrom, Wet Seal, Victoria's Secret, etc. Other interesting women's shops in the area (on Broadway) include: Byrkit, Sheba's House of Elegance, Matisse, Naira, and Kobo African Imports. (Eastside)

Hawthorne/Belmont

Hawthorne is the Haight-Ashbury of Portland, an old hippie street that has been "adopted" by a younger alternative set. The result is a delightful collection of import, secondhand, and funky pet supply stores; gift shops; and, yes, head shops. There are also plenty of coffee shops, inexpensive eateries, theaters, and pubs. Not as slick and clean as Northwest 23rd, Hawthorne nevertheless has plenty of colorful character. The main business district goes from Southeast 33rd to Southeast 39th on Hawthorne. Nearby Belmont, between Southeast 33rd and Southeast 35th, is similar if a little younger and, for the purposes of this chapter, is considered a part of the same shopping district.

BEADS FOREVER
3522 SE Hawthorne
503/230-2323

Beads ... everywhere. When you walk into this shop you'll be handed a little organizer box, a piece of paper, and a pencil—and you'll need it all to help you sort whatever beads you decide to buy. Beads range from the common 10¢ varieties to specialty ones costing up to several dollars. Beware—even if you don't make beaded jewelry or handbags, you might just decide to take up stringing beads after a visit here. (Eastside)

BLUE BUTTERFLY
3646 SE Hawthorne
503/238-6639

You'll find pretty sarongs and other Indonesian imports in a variety of colors and patterns in this corner shop. The aroma of incense and faraway places engulfs you upon entering. Children's clothing and jewelry items are on hand as well. (Eastside)

BUFFALO EXCHANGE
1420 SE 37th Ave.
503/234-1302

This secondhand store works well not just as a place to find that one-time vintage piece, but as *the* source

Zupan's in the Belmont shopping district

for fashionable clothes at bargain prices. The Exchange, which began as a small shop in Tucson, Arizona, will recycle your used goods, too, but just try to get them to pay for something. The buyers/recyclers have a sharp and selective eye for trendy styles that sell. This is a great last-minute stop for that special dress or shirt when your wallet's feeling a little thin. (Eastside)

CAT'S MEOW
3538 SE Hawthorne
503/231-1341

What does your cat want? This supply store is for the kitty who has everything. It's a virtual catpourri of blankets, bowls, books, umbrellas, aprons, whatever the cat lover dreams of, and more. (Eastside)

IMELDA'S DESIGNER SHOES
1431 SE 37th Ave.
503/233-7476

This store may not have as many

shoes as the ousted Philippine monarch, Imelda Marcos, but it certainly comes close. Imelda's Designer Shoes has a terrific selection of fashionable urban footwear, including boots, shoes, and sandals. (Eastside)

KITTY PRINCESS BOUTIQUE
3356 SE Belmont
503/233-2567
This secondhand store is filled with things from the '50s and '60s ranging in price from $5 to $30. The dressing rooms have that overdone boudoir feeling and give Kitty's added charm. (Eastside)

MAN'S BEST FRIEND
3425 SE Yamhill
503/230-0237
Appropriately located down the street from the kitty store, this dog store offers serious supplies for the pup in your life. You'll find bones, biscuits, bowls, beds, and more, all designed with care for the pampered pet. (Eastside)

PASTAWORKS
3735 SE Hawthorne
503/232-1010
Ravioli di Zucca, potato gnocchi, Barberesco wine, *Parmesan Reggiano* ... this is the place for fresh pasta, fine Italian wines, and imported cheeses. Add wonderfully fresh produce, beautiful flowers, homemade bread, and arguably the best espresso in Portland, and you have to ask, Why go anywhere else? Everything you need to prepare a wonderful dinner for any occasion can be found at Pastaworks. (Eastside)

PRESENTS OF MIND
3633 SE Hawthorne
503/230-7740
This card and gift shop includes an extensive selection of greeting cards, special wrapping paper and ribbons, candles, and trendy jewelry. You'll also find an array of unique gift items, such as kits for casting spells and novel little boxes. (Eastside)

The General Store

The General Store

Powell's City of Books, p. 136

ZUPAN'S
3301 SE Belmont
503/239-3720
This upscale 24-hour grocery store is one of several in the Portland area. You'll find gourmet items such as cheeses, meats, and baked goods; a great selection of olives; and organic produce. The dessert case carries a variety of baked goods from some of Portland's finest bakeries and may be reason alone to stop in. Open all night, Zupan's is a great place to go if you're looking for a delectable breakfast sweet for the next morning or a dessert to bring to a late-night party. (Eastside)

Sellwood

Quaint is the word that comes to mind when describing Sellwood. You'll find wonderful gourmet restaurants in small Victorian houses, interesting novelty shops, and a plethora of antique shops (Sellwood's claim to notoriety in Portland). While there are notable antique stores throughout Portland, nowhere else in the city will you find such a high concentration. Visit Sellwood on either of the two streets that serve as the area's business district: Southeast 13th and Southeast Milwaukie.

1874 HOUSE
8070 SE 13th Ave.
503/233-1874
Old plumbing and stained glass, moldings, and other trimmings for the house make the 1874 House a good place to visit when restoring your historic home. (Eastside)

GENERAL STORE
7987 SE 13th Ave.
503/233-1321
This Sellwood antique store, with its early American pieces and wooden furniture, is easy to find.

It's right next to an old red caboose. (Eastside)

THE RAVEN
7927 SE 13th Ave.
503/233-8075
This antique shop specializes in wartime collectibles like lead soldiers. (Eastside)

SELLWOOD PEDDLER ATTIC GOODIES
8065 SE 13th Ave.
503/235-0946
www.sellwoodpeddler.com
Antique knickknacks fill this place to the brim. You'll find the huge space chock-full of old jewelry, vintage glassware and silverware, aging photos, sewing machines, dolls, and musty armoires. (Eastside)

STARS, AN ANTIQUE MALL
7027 SE Milwaukie
503/239-0346
Stars claims to be the largest antiques mall in Portland. And there's little doubt that they're right. Row after row, room after room, you'll find goods from 300 dealers. If you haven't found what you want elsewhere, check out Stars. A visit to Sellwood would not be complete without a stop here. (Eastside)

NOTABLE BOOKSTORES AND NEWSSTANDS

BORDERS BOOKS, MUSIC, AND CAFÉ
708 SW Third Ave.
503/220-5911
This large chain store conveniently located near the MAX light rail sells over 200,000 titles in addition to music CDs and tapes. A comfortable place to browse, Borders has a large children's section designed to be attractive to kids. Feel free to grab a magazine or book and peruse while sipping an espresso in the in-store cafe near the travel section. The music store in the back affords the opportunity to hear a tape or CD before you buy. Borders regularly hosts free literary events—call for information. (Downtown)

POWELL'S CITY OF BOOKS
1001 W. Burnside, between 10th and 11th
800/878-7323
www.powells.com
Powell's, a Portland landmark for years, is known for its laid-back attitude and social conscience, late hours, extensive selection, and coffee shop. A frequent host of speakers and book readings, it's also the largest independent bookstore in the city. The main store occupies an entire city block on three levels. Still, despite the fact that it was recently remodeled and expanded, the store feels more like an old library than a Barnes and Noble. It's not at all slick, and that's part of the appeal. (Downtown)

OTHER NOTABLE STORES

CATFISH MOON
7780-B SW Capitol Hwy.
Multnomah
503/245-4124
Unique items from around the world (and a proprietor with a social conscience, Lisa Kendall) make this little gift shop worth a visit. The store teems with unusual books, novelties, jewelry, candles, baby items, greeting cards, and other stuff found only once in a Catfish Moon. (West Suburbs)

Portland Saturday Market

NATURE'S FRESH NORTHWEST
2825 E. Burnside
503/232-6601

This is the supernova of natural-foods stores, at least in Oregon. The newest edition of a chain of several in the Portland area, Nature's is the place to buy fresh and organic produce, imported cheeses, fine meat and deli items, baked goods, wines, and novelty gifts. (Eastside)

MAJOR DEPARTMENT STORES

FRED MEYER
SUPER-SUPERSTORE
3030 NE Weidler
503/280-1300

Buy groceries, clothes, toys, hardware, office or gardening supplies at this Fred Meyer, one of a chain of Portland superstores (see sidebar) that has become a city institution. Inside you'll find a bank and electronic shop as well. You can even check in your small child at the play-room while you shop for up to two hours. And, if you need to purchase a Tri-Met bus pass, this is the place. A Starbuck's and a Hollywood Video are adjacent. (Eastside)

MEIER AND FRANK
621 SW Fifth Ave.
503/223-0512 or 503/241-5118

Meier and Frank is Portland's Macy's, similar in both content and price. This huge department store carries a wide selection of women's and men's apparel, linens, towels, gifts, housewares, and children's clothing. (Downtown)

NORDSTROM
710 SW Broadway
503/224-6666

This upscale and often pricey department store from Seattle is largely dedicated to stylish clothing (especially shoes) for men, women, and children. Nordstrom also has a large cosmetics and accessories department. A beautiful grand piano graces the entrance to the lower escalator and is often played by a local pianist during store hours. Nordstrom is known for its impeccable service, with clerks who are always nice and helpful. Park in the nearby lot across the street on Park Avenue—it's free if you purchase something at the store. Just be sure to get your ticket validated. (Downtown)

SAKS FIFTH AVENUE
850 Fifth Ave.
503/226-3200
Saks Fifth Avenue is synonymous with elegance and expense. The Portland department store is no exception. Access the store from Pioneer Place via the enclosed pedestrian walkway over the dividing street, Southwest Yamhill. (Downtown)

MAJOR MALLS

CLACKAMAS TOWN CENTER
12000 SE 82nd Ave.
Clackamas
503/653-6913
www.clackamastowncenter.com
This giant on the southeast side is one of the best Portland-area malls for kids. Two levels include department stores Meier and Frank, Nordstrom, JCPenney, Sears, and Wards; a video arcade; fast-food places; an indoor ice-skating rink; and an adjacent movie theater. Large trees and skylights help on dreary days when mall strolling is one of the few entertainment options in town. (East Suburbs)

JANTZEN BEACH
Hayden Island exit off I-5, north of Portland
503/247-1327
The best part about this mall is the

historic merry-go-round in its parking lot. Stores of note include the camping- and climbing-gear store REI, Toys 'R' Us, and Copeland's Sportswear. (North Suburbs)

LLOYD CENTER
2201 Lloyd Center
503/282-2511
The biggest mall in Portland, Lloyd Center carries chain stores found in malls across the country, as well as Nordstrom and Meier and Frank department stores and Toys 'R' Us. At the center of the 2.5-level mall, on the lower floor, is a popular ice-skating rink. A food court is above on the third level next to Lloyd Mall Movies. More movies can be found outside at the Lloyd Cinemas. (Eastside)

PIONEER PLACE
700 SW Fifth Ave.
503/228-5800
Pioneer Place, with huge skylights that flood the multilevel structure with sunshine, is Portland's prettiest mall. It also harbors some of the city's most popular designer stores, including J. Crew, Anne Klein, Sharper Image, Banana Republic, and Eddie Bauer. At basement level you'll find an array of eateries and an information booth with free city maps, brochures for various attractions and tours, and very helpful information clerks who can point you in the right direction if you don't know where to go. Pioneer Place II, which is being built just across the street, will add more shopping, a parking garage, and a movie-theater complex. (Downtown)

WASHINGTON SQUARE
Hwy. 217 and Progress Rd.
Tigard
503/639-8860

This huge, dark, sprawling, single-level mall has five department stores: Nordstrom, Meier and Frank, Sears, JCPenney, and Mervyns. It also has Eddie Bauer and J. Crew stores and many smaller shops. (West Suburbs)

WESTFIELD SHOPPING TOWN
(formerly Vancouver Mall)
8700 NE Vancouver Mall Dr.
Vancouver, WA
360/892-6255
Westfield Shopping Town's 140 retail stores include A Children's Place and Colonial Gift Gallery plus five major department stores: JCPenney, Meier and Frank, Sears, Nordstrom, and Mervyns. Free strollers and wheelchairs are available. There is also a train ride for children on the lower level. (North Suburbs)

FACTORY OUTLET CENTERS

COLUMBIA GORGE PREMIUM
OUTLETS
450 NW 257th Ave.
Troutdale (exit 17 off I-84 East
from Portland)
503/669-8060
Levi's, Norm Thompson, Adidas, Carters, Calvin Klein, Gap, and Samsonite are among the 44 factory outlet stores in this complex just 20 minutes from downtown. (East Suburbs)

HANNA ANDERSSON FACTORY
OUTLET
7 Monroe Pkwy.
Lake Oswego
503/697-1953

Come here for bold and brightly colored children's clothes at wholesale prices. (West Suburbs)

JANTZEN, THE STORE
921 SW Morrison
503/221-1443
A Portland original, Jantzen offers swimsuits at this retail outlet. (Downtown)

KUTTERS OUTLET STORE
SE Hawthorne St. at 43rd Ave.
503/228-4858
This Portland original (around for 15 years) carries men's designer shirts and ties and ladies' blouses and sportswear at bargain prices. A variety of labels are carried: factory overruns and some irregulars from makers including Lands' End, Nordstrom, Eddie Bauer, J. Crew, L.L. Bean, Betsey Johnson, and much more. The owner claims she has the cheapest white shirt in town and has been shirting Portland's waiters for years. (Eastside)

NIKE FACTORY OUTLET
3044 NE Martin Luther King Jr.
Blvd.
503/281-5901
This recently redone outlet is the place to buy Nike clothes and shoes at discounted prices. (North Portland)

NORDSTROM RACK
401 SW Morrison
503/299-1815
Items not sold in the main Nordstrom's store end up here at a discount. (Downtown)

11

SPORTS AND RECREATION

The explosion in professional sports has all but bypassed Portland. Though the city has a successful men's pro basketball franchise, the Trail Blazers, and a new WNBA team, the Portland Fire, there's no place here for a major-league baseball or NFL team to play. While other cities have been erecting mammoth stadiums costing up to half a billion dollars, Portland aspires to do no more than modestly upgrade its undersized downtown ballpark for minor league baseball and soccer. The last time the city's voters considered spending money to build a big domed stadium was 1964, and they turned it down.

Theories about why Portland isn't a major-league sports town abound. One says the city feels strongly inferior to its major-league neighbor to the north, Seattle. But in fact, Portlanders have taken to rooting for the Seattle Seahawks and Mariners. Weekend roundtrips via Amtrak to Seattle have become a tradition among many Portland fans. Another theory suggests Portlanders would just as soon spend their summer weekends and mild winters hiking, fishing, boating, or skiing. These days, Seattleites, with their fabled traffic jams and sprawling population, are more likely to be envying Portland.

There's a chance Paul Allen, the Microsoft cofounder, will decide to buy a pro hockey team, and an assortment of off-brand teams (arena football, indoor soccer) no doubt will pass through. But as the price of joining professional sports leagues continues to skyrocket, and small-market cities find it tough to compete, Portlanders won't feel like they're missing out.

PROFESSIONAL SPORTS

Auto Racing

PORTLAND INTERNATIONAL RACEWAY
1940 N. Victory Blvd.
503/823-7223
Every June, the Rose Festival Indy Car race attracts huge crowds for world-class racing with internationally renowned drivers and crews competing. Prices for the popular event range from $15 to $82. Sports car, bicycle, motorcycle, go-kart, and drag-racing events are hosted at the Portland raceway throughout the year. (North Portland)

PORTLAND SPEEDWAY
9727 N. Martin Luther King Jr. Blvd.
503/285-2883
The Portland Speedway hosts NASCAR stock-car racing every Friday April through September. The speedway, a half-mile clay oval track with an inner quarter-mile oval, is one of the oldest continuously operated automobile racing tracks in the United States. It has hosted the oldest West Coast stock-car racing circuit, the NASCAR Winston West Series, since 1954. In 1984, the lease for Portland Speedway was acquired by Western Speedways, Inc., and a sanctioning agreement with NASCAR was granted. (North Portland)

Good News for Baseball Fans

Portlanders are still waiting for the arrival of major league baseball, but there will be a new game in town in the summer of 2001. The single-A minor league Portland Rockies have left, and the Rose City will soon be the home base of the Los Angeles Dodgers' triple-A team, currently known as the Albuquerque Dukes.

The team arrives on the heels of $30-plus-million, publicly financed facelift of the old Civic Stadium downtown (1844 SW Morrison). Now called the PGE Park—after its corporate sponsor, the local electric company—the stadium features luxury boxes, additional seating, and new restrooms. PGE Park will also host concerts, high school sporting events, and soccer games.

As if a new team and a better park aren't enough, fans will be getting a great deal with public transportation. Event tickets will be honored as passes for free round-trips aboard the Tri-Met buses and the MAX train on game days. Free shuttle buses to the park will also be available from downtown.

Basketball

PORTLAND FIRE
Rose Quarter
One Center Court
503/797-9601
Owned by the NBA's Portland Trail Blazers organization, the WNBA's Portland Fire play a 32-game schedule between June and September. This is Portland's second foray into women's professional basketball. The first team, the Portland Power, was a genuine success drawing fans, but it died when the American Basketball League folded midway through its third season. The new franchise sold the required 5,500 season tickets by late 1999 and became one of four expansion franchises to join the WNBA for its 2000 season. The new team plays on the Blazers' home court, the Rose Garden Arena in Rose Quarter. (Eastside)

PORTLAND TRAIL BLAZERS
Rose Quarter
One Center Court
503/797-9600
One of the National Basketball Association's most successful franchises, the Blazers are Portland's favorite professional sports team. While they have won only one championship (in 1977), the Blazers are perennial playoff participants and made two trips to the NBA finals in the early 1990s. In the past, when the Blazers played at cozy Memorial Coliseum, it was nearly impossible to get a ticket without becoming a season-ticket holder. But the opening of the Rose Garden Arena several years ago expanded seating capacity (and ticket prices) significantly and resulted in the possibility of last-minute seats. Blazers owner Paul Allen spared no expense in building his $240 million behemoth, and he can often be found courtside at games. Blazermania is peaking again thanks to the recent and expensive acquisition of several big-name NBA stars, including Scottie Pippen, formerly of the Chicago Bulls. One of the nicest things about the new arena is its downtown location. Its excellent transit service includes a light-rail station only a few steps from the front door. Tickets for Blazers games can be purchased at several downtown locations and at the Rose Garden ticket office near the arena. (Eastside)

Dog Racing

MULTNOMAH GREYHOUND PARK
NE 223rd at Glisan
Wood Village
503/667-7700
Greyhound racing takes place at Multnomah Greyhound Park May through October. Simulcast Racing Center (not live), on the park's second floor, remains open all winter long, however, offering wagering signals from many of the nation's top horse and greyhound parks. (East Suburbs)

Hockey

PORTLAND WINTER HAWKS
300 N. Winning Way
503/238-6366 or 503/236-4295
The Portland Winterhawks are the city's best-kept secret. Drawing nearly 10,000 fans a night to the Memorial Coliseum, the Winter Hawks are a true minor-league

Blazermania

The Portland Trail Blazers are the only game in town, literally. As the only top-level professional sports franchise in the city, the Blazers dominate Portland's sports scene. Several rumored attempts to bring a National Hockey League franchise to Portland have sputtered, and talk of a major-league baseball franchise has never moved beyond mere dreaming. As a result, Portlanders are just a little crazy about their beloved Blazers, and few residents, if any, have escaped the clutches of Blazermania.

The Blazers reflected Portland's sleepy, small-town image in the 1970s, when they were owned by local sports promoter Harry Glickman. The city erupted in spontaneous joy in 1977 when the Bill Walton–led Blazers defeated the Philadelphia 76ers for the NBA title. A huge victory parade the next day is still cherished as one of the biggest parties ever seen downtown. But as the city grew up, so did the Blazers, and they are now owned by one of the world's richest men: Paul Allen, the cofounder of the Microsoft. Allen has pumped hundreds of millions of dollars into a new arena and an expensive lineup of free-agent players in his quest to win a second NBA title. Trail Blazers games are now some of the most expensive in the nation, and a family outing to see the Blazers will take a serious bite out of your wallet. Because of these high ticket prices, the Blazers do not regularly sell out the Rose Garden, even though they always field a highly competitive team. That means visitors can probably grab last-minute tickets if they are willing to fork over a significant amount of cash.

As members of the only big-time pro team in town, Blazers players suffer from intense media scrutiny of both their good and questionable natures. Local television sportscasts are dominated by the latest goings-on in the locker room or antics off the court. On the court, the Blazers are considered one of the most consistently successful franchises in the NBA. But Portlanders and Paul Allen won't be satisfied until the Blazers capture another championship.

hockey success story. Fans travel from throughout the metro area and southwest Washington to cheer on their baby-faced favorites, many of whom have moved on to star in the National Hockey League. The team is usually made up of young Canadians in their late teens, and Portland fans have been known to serve as surrogate families for the young men. The Hawks play in the Western Hockey League against Canadian teams with strange names like Red Deer, Moose Jaw, Medicine Hat, and Kamloops. The players endure grueling bus rides across the Pacific Northwest and western Canada, but they play with a zest unmatched at any other level. The games are far more affordable than those of the millionaire Blazers, and as a result families flock to the arena. (North Portland)

Horse Racing

PORTLAND MEADOWS
1001 N. Schmeer Rd.
503/285-9144
Live horse racing takes place at Portland Meadows October through April. Spread over more than 100 acres at Delta Park, the one-mile oval track ranks among the best in the country for wet-weather racing. To get there from downtown, take the Delta Park exit (#306-B) off of Interstate 5 and follow the signs to the racetrack. Visitors and gamblers can view the horse races from a glass-enclosed facility with wagering windows, color TV monitors, bars, and food service offer a wide variety of fare ranging from small snacks to fine dining. Parking is free. (North Portland)

AMATEUR SPORTS

Basketball

PORTLAND STATE UNIVERSITY
Peter Stott Center
SW 10th and Hall
888/VIK-TIKS
www.GoViks.com
The Division I-A women's and men's basketball squads play at the Peter Stott Center on campus or at either the Memorial Coliseum or Rose Garden in the Lloyd District. Call for game times and ticket prices. The women's team has caught on in Portland, attracting crowds as large as 6,000 to its home games. The men's program was shut down from 1981 to 1996. Since reviving the program in 1996–97, the men have improved every year. (Downtown)

UNIVERSITY OF PORTLAND
Chiles Center
5000 N. Willamette Blvd.
503/943-7525
The Pilots play at the Division I level in the West Coast Athletic Conference, along with such schools as Gonzaga, Pepperdine, and the University of San Francisco. Games are held at the Chiles Center on campus and tickets range from $4 to $10. The women's team is a powerhouse in the West Coast Athletic Conference, making almost yearly trips to postseason play. While the Pilots have not been a major force in their league, they do play strong teams in their conference. Among them is Gonzaga, which any college basketball fan would recognize as one of the best teams in the country. (North Portland)

Football

PORTLAND STATE UNIVERSITY
Civic Stadium
SW 18th and Morrison
888/VIK-TIKS
www.GoViks.com
The Vikings play in the Big Sky
Conference against the likes of
Montana, Northern Arizona, and
Sacramento State. The Division I-
AA football team plays at Civic
Stadium. Call for game times and
ticket prices. In 1999, the Vikings
were ranked No. 20 in the nation.
They feature an explosive passing
offense that's fun to watch. PSU
has sent numerous players to the
NFL, including passing great Neil
Lomax. (Downtown)

Soccer

UNIVERSITY OF PORTLAND
Merlo Stadium
5000 N. Willamette Blvd.
503/943-7525
The women's soccer team has
made it to four Women's College
Cup semifinals in the last five
years. The men's team has made
seven NCAA appearances in the
last eight years. Tickets to games
at Merlo Stadium range from $4 to
$10. (North Portland)

RECREATION

Basketball Courts

THE HOOP
9685 SW Harvest Court
Beaverton
503/644-2191

With loads of courts, as well as
other workout facilities (including
weights and aerobic equipment),
The Hoop is a bargain at $25 per
person for a one-week pass. Six
full courts are often busy with an
average to above-average level of
competitive skill. Call first for times
and cost. (West Suburbs)

LAURELHURST PARK
SE 39th Ave. and Stark
Look for a pickup game at this pretty Eastside park. This is friendly
street basketball and can get lively
and aggressive when busy. Best
chances to find a game are nice
weekend days and after school or
work. (Eastside)

METROPOLITAN LEARNING
CENTER
NW Hoyt and 20th Ave.
The Metropolitan Learning Center—or MLC, as it is commonly
known—is an alternative public
school. If you're in the mood for
decent street basketball, check
behind the school when classes let
out. (Northwest)

MOUNT TABOR PARK
SE 69th Ave.
Shoot some hoops within the cone
of an extinct volcano atop this cool,
forested park. After the game,
enjoy a hike through the woods;
hike to the top and indulge in the
scenic views of downtown Portland to the west and Mount Hood to
the east. During summer months
check for what's playing at the
newly built outdoor amphitheater,
also in the charred volcano cone,
and bring a picnic. Access the park
at SE 69th Avenue from Belmont,
then turn west to the amphitheater
parking lot. (Eastside)

Bicycling

Portland has been named by *Bicycle* magazine as one of the best cities for bicycling, despite the bad rep the weather gets. Public transportation is bike-friendly, as are many roadways and bridges. And, nearby off-road opportunities for fun and scenic adventures are many, to be sure.

Bike racks can be found all over the city, including on all Tri-Met buses and MAX light-rail trains. But you'll need a permit, which costs $5; you can get it at the Tri-Met office downtown at Pioneer Courthouse Square, along with maps and everything you could want to know about city bicycling. Call 503/239-3044 or check out www.tri-met.org for more info on bikes on Tri-Met. Lockers are also available at some stations and can be rented overnight. Or, call Portland Bicycle Program for more information: 503/823-7082.

FOREST PARK
Far west end of NW Thurman
This is the largest forested city park in the United States, with nearly 5,000 acres. Numerous fire lanes and Leif Erickson Drive are open to mountain bikes. More than 50 species of mammals and at least 100 varieties of birds populate the more than 50 miles of winding hiking trails.

The park lies along the northeast slope of the Tuality Mountains, above the Willamette River and between Northwest Skyline Boulevard and Northwest Saint Helens Road (Highway 30 West). Access can be found on Northwest Thurman Street, where a large map is posted to help orient you. (Northwest)

POWELL BUTTE
SE 162nd Ave. and Powell Blvd.
From the top of this open 570-acre park you will find breathtaking views of the city and the Cascade Mountains. Nine miles of mountain biking trails await exploration, including one paved for wheelchairs. Watch for wildlife. (Eastside)

SPRINGWATER CORRIDOR
SE Johnson Creek Blvd and SE 45th Ave.
This bike path follows an old railroad route through countryside with nice views of Mount Hood. It's the flattest ride in town and without vehicle traffic, and therefore it's great for beginners, kids, or anyone wanting a pretty, leisurely ride. The bike ride first passes through Tidewater-Johnson Park, Beggars Tick Marsh, and Powell Butte Nature Park, the only decent single-track park in the city. Much of the trail is paved. Mountain bikes and hybrids are recommended, but road bikes are okay too, except for the trail east of Gresham, which is gravel. Pack a picnic or plan to stop in Gresham for lunch. For more information call 503/823-6183 or 503/823-5596.

Bowling Alleys

HOLLYWOOD BOWL
4030 NE Halsey
503/288-9237
Automated scorekeeping, rental shoes, and a snack bar are some of the amenities at Hollywood Bowl. Mon–Thu 9 a.m.–midnight, Fri–Sat

9 a.m.–2 a.m., Sun 9 a.m.–11 p.m. Fees are $2.75 per person, per game and $2 shoe rental. (Eastside)

SUNSET LANES
12770 SW Walker Rd.
503/646-1116
This place is a hit with kids thanks to its Cosmic Bowling nights, which include psychedelic disco lights (see chapter 8, Kids' Stuff). Mon–Thu 10 a.m.–11:30 p.m., Fri–Sat 9 a.m.–2 a.m., Sun 7:45 a.m.–11 p.m. Fees are $5 to get in, 25¢ for shoe rentals, 25¢ per game. Call ahead for the Cosmic Bowling schedule. (West Suburbs)

Canoeing/Rafting/Kayaking

It comes as no surprise that a city built at the intersection of two major Northwest rivers would be a popular site for water adventures. Whether you are a beginner and looking for flat-water leisure paddling with the family, an expert whitewater runner, or somewhere in the middle, you'll find your river near Portland. World-class rapids on raging rivers with waterfalls can be found typically in the Cascades' far reaches. Mellower opportunities are abundant close to home. But, even if you are a relative novice, consider a guided rafting trip suited for families. It's a great way to get intimate with the beautiful and more remote terrain of the Cascade and Coast Ranges.

ALDER CREEK KAYAK AND CANOE
250 NE Tomahawk Island Dr.
503/285-0464
Consider renting canoes and paddling in the nearby placid Columbia River Slough. Or, if you're more ambitious, ask about touring and whitewater trips. Rentals are available, as is instruction. (North Portland)

PORTLAND RIVER COMPANY
Riverplace Esplanade
503/229-0551

River kayaking

Lincoln City Visitor and Convention Bureau

www.portlandrivercompany.com
Whitewater adventure rafting trips abound in Oregon, where there is still wild water of all classes to enjoy. Portland River Company is one of a number of whitewater rafting guides. Adventures can range from primitive to extravagant and from several hours to several days in length. (Downtown)

Fitness Clubs

THE HOOP
9685 SW Harvest Court
Beaverton
503/644-2191
A one-week pass entitles you to use all of the facilities at The Hoop. You'll find basketball courts, a volleyball court, exercise machines, showers, lockers, and saunas. Mon–Fri 6 a.m.–10 p.m., Sat–Sun 10–8. $25 per week. (West Suburbs)

LLOYD ATHLETIC CLUB
815 NE Halsey
503/287-4594
In addition to its racquetball and squash courts, this athletic club has weights and exercise machines, a spa, and a sauna. Unfortunately, to visit Lloyd Athletic Club you must be a guest of a member. The fee is $8. Mon–Fri 5 a.m.–10 p.m., Sat–Sun 7 a.m.–7 p.m. (Eastside)

METRO YMCA
2831 SW Barbur
503/294-3366
This is probably the best deal in town. You can drop in for the day for $10 and get the benefits of a full-service athletic club: large indoor and outdoor tracks, large indoor swimming pool and spa,

sauna, machines, and weights. There are also basketball courts available. Mon–Fri 5:30 a.m.–10 p.m., Sat 7 a.m.–9 p.m., Sun 9–9. (Downtown)

MULTNOMAH ATHLETIC CLUB
1849 SW Salmon
503/223-6251
Probably Portland's most prestigious and elegant athletic club, the MAC, as it's commonly referred to, is a members-only private fitness club. Guests can come with a member for $12 a day. Facilities include three gyms, racquetball and handball courts, tennis, golf and batting cages, three weight rooms, a restaurant, whirlpool, saunas, and steam room. Open Mon–Thurs 5 a.m.–midnight, Fri 5 a.m.–1 a.m., Sat 6 a.m.–1 a.m., Sun 6 a.m.–10 p.m. (Downtown)

PRINCETON ATHLETIC CLUB
614 SW 11th Ave.
503/222-2639
Conveniently located in the heart of downtown, the Princeton Athletic Club is a full-service club with a swimming pool, Jacuzzi, steam rooms and saunas, an indoor track, and weights and machines. Princeton serves the Governor Hotel, private members, and non-members ($15 for a one-day pass). Mon–Fri 5 a.m.–10 p.m., Sat–Sun 7–7. (Downtown)

RESORT TO FITNESS
2714 NE Broadway
503/287-0655
This is a women-only club. It's not a big place, but it has plenty of machines and weights, a sauna, and a eucalyptus room, a small humid room with the searing scent of eucalyptus—refreshing! The

place is a little uptight—they shun nudity in the sauna and bathroom areas. (Eastside)

RIVERPLACE ATHLETIC CLUB
0150 SW Montgomery
503/221-1212
Riverplace is a large athletic club with an indoor swimming pool and spa; a track; racquetball, squash, and basketball courts; an extensive selection of machines and weights, and a sauna. By the Willamette River, it's a members-only club, but it honors guests from a number of downtown hotels for a $15 fee. Open Mon–Fri 4:30 a.m.–10 p.m., Sat 7 a.m.–8 p.m., and Sun 8–8. (Downtown)

Golf Courses

EASTMORELAND GOLF COURSE
2425 SE Bybee
503/775-2900
The Eastmoreland Golf Course, located next to Crystal Springs Rhododendron Gardens, is an 18-hole regulation course with 6,529 champion yards in a pretty setting. It's regarded as one of the top public courses in the country. Extra perks include a covered, lighted driving range and a pro shop. Greens fees: $21 for 18 holes and $11 for 9 holes Mon–Thu; $23 for 18 holes and $12 for 9 holes Fri–Sun. (Eastside)

GLENDOVEER GOLF COURSE
14015 NE Glisan
503/253-7507
The Glendoveer offers two par-73 18-hole courses, each 6,319 yards long. Also available are a heated and covered drive range, two pro shops, and a grill. Greens fees:

Mon–Fri $19, Sat–Sun $21; power carts are $9. (East Suburbs)

HERON LAKES
3500 N. Victory Blvd.
503/289-1818
tee-time reservations 503/292-8570
Two 18-hole championship courses contain lots of water and traps, not to mention long-limbed blue herons. The Great Blue Course is 18 holes, 6,916 yards, par 72. Greens fees: $35 for 18 holes and $18 for 9 holes; power carts are $24. The par-72 Greenback Course also has 18 holes over 6,595 yards. Greens fees: Mon–Fri $19, Sat–Sun $21; power cart is $24, trail fees $4. There is also a driving range and food grill. (North Portland)

PUMPKIN RIDGE GOLF CLUB
12930 Old Pumpkin Ridge Rd.
Cornelius
503/647-9977
www.pumpkinridge.com
Golf Digest called the par-71 Ghost Creek Golf Course at Pumpkin Ridge the best new course of 1992. The 18-hole, 6,839-yard course, designed by Bob Cupp, also includes a large clubhouse, grill, and pro shop, as well as a 15-acre practice facility. The golf club has hosted a number of championships, including the 1996 U.S. Amateur, which was won by Tiger Woods. To get there, take Highway 26 west from Portland to exit 55. The course is approximately 20 minutes from downtown. Greens fees are $115. (West Suburbs)

Hiking

Hiking doesn't get any better than in Portland and the surrounding area. You can easily spend vast amounts of time hiking in the city in Forest Park alone and never cover the same terrain. (For more details on Forest Park, the largest inner-city park in the United States, see chapter 9, Parks, Gardens, and Recreation Areas.) But if you seek additional hiking in the area, the Cascades and the Gorge area have great trails.

DOG MOUNTAIN

A popular trail (#147) with panoramic views and loads of wildflowers leads to the summit of 2,900-foot Dog Mountain. It can get windy and cool on marginal days, but it's a wonderful place to see a glorious display of brilliant yellow flowering balsamroot. Take Interstate 84 east to Bridge of the Gods in Cascade Locks. Cross the bridge to Highway 14 in Washington, then travel east toward Home Valley. (North Suburbs)

LARCH MOUNTAIN

Because of the realtively high elevation (approximately 3,000 feet), trails on Larch Mountain should be tackled only in summer and early fall. Groves of western hemlock and Douglas fir contain trees more than four hundred years old. Mount Rainier, Mount Saint Helens, Mount Adams, Mount Hood, Mount Jefferson, and Three Sisters are all visible on a clear day. Peak elevation is 4,055 feet. Take Interstate 84 east to Corbett (exit 22). Proceed 1.6 miles uphill on Corbett Hill Road, turn left onto Columbia Gorge Scenic Highway for about two miles, then bear right on Larch Mountain Road. Continue for 14 miles to the parking lot and trailhead. (East Suburbs)

WILDWOOD TRAIL

Wildwood Trail's 28 miles wind through Washington and Forest Parks and are easily accessible. You can reach the beginning of the Wildwood Trail near the Oregon Zoo. Take Tri-Met bus no. 63 from downtown or the Rose Quarter and get off near the Vietnam Veterans Memorial. A large sign notes the beginning of the trail up Knights Boulevard from the many parking lots near the zoo. To return to downtown, hike the Wildwood Trail three miles to where it crosses Burnside Road. Bus no. 20 stops nearby on its run between the Gateway and Beaverton transit centers. This section of the Wildwood Trail passes Hoyt Aboretum and the Japanese Garden, a busy part of town on a sunny summer day. Numerous trail intersections beckon, but the Wildwood Trail is well marked and easy to follow. (Northwest)

Ice-Skating Rinks

ICE CHALET
Lloyd Center
NE Ninth Ave. and NE Halsey
503/288-6073
www.icechalet.com
Figure skates can be rented, and skating lessons are available. Call for open skate hours as they vary. Skate rentals are $2.50. Rink-use fee is $6 adults, $5 children. (Eastside)

ICE CHALET
Clackamas Town Center
503/786-6000
www.icechalet.com
Fallen Olympic figure-skating hopeful Tonya Harding can occasionally be spotted gliding on the

ice here. The rink, in Clackamas Town Center mall, rents figure skates and hockey skates to those who need them. Ice-skating and hockey lessons are also available. Call for open skate hours. Skate rentals are $2.50, hockey skates are $3.50. Rink-use fee is $6 adults, $5 children. (East Suburbs)

In-Line/Roller-Skating Rinks

OAKS SKATING RINK
Oaks Amusement Park
SE Spokane at the Willamette River
503/236-5722
www.oakspark.com
This large wooden indoor rink can be packed with young people on weekend nights. Roller skates are available for rent. Buy a soda and a hot dog, and then skate to the music on this classic old-fashioned skating rink that draws them in from far and wide. The meticulously maintained 100- by 200-foot floor is in excellent condition. Each year in June, Oaks Park hosts the Northwest Regional Championship. Those skaters who place in the top three of their event qualify to skate the U.S. National Roller Skating Championships. (Eastside)

Rock Climbing

FIRST ASCENT CLIMBING SERVICES
1136 SW Deschutes Ave.
Redmond
800/325-5462
www.goclimbing.com
Climbing guides at First Ascent specialize in the world-famous Smith Rock, the mega-monolith in

central Oregon that challenges the very best climbers. But the company also offers a complete range of rock climbing and adventure programs, including private, group, teen, and women's programs. (West Suburbs)

PORTLAND ROCK GYM
2034 SE Sixth Ave.
503/232-8310
For the rock-climbing junkie or anyone who just wants to brush up on their skills before testing oneself on the real thing. The gym has various grades of faux rock for practicing in a safe setting. Not only for the serious, this is a fun place for kids, too, and group visits can be arranged. Open Mon–Fri 11–11, Sat 9–7, Sun 11–6. One-day pass costs $14. Harness and shoes cost $3–$5. (Eastside)

TIMBERLINE MOUNTAIN GUIDES
P.O. Box 1167
Bend
541/312-9242 or 800/464-7704
e-mail: climbing@transport.com
For the serious. If you're interested in climbing to the summit of Mount Hood or scaling faces in Smith Rock Park, call Timberline Mountain Guides. Guided climbs range from $190 to $570; climbing seminars (three to five days) cost anywhere from $470 to $800. This company also organizes and guides international expeditions.

Skateboard Parks/Ramps

BURNSIDE SKATE PARK
Burnside Bridge
It's not a park, and it's a little seedy, but it has some of the best skateboard ramps around. You'll find it

tucked beneath the east end of the Burnside Bridge. Built by kids who wanted their own park to skateboard in, and approved by the city (which previously refused such proposed parks at other sites), this park has the added benefit of being under the bridge, so that you can skate dry under cover on those many rainy days. National skateboarding magazines like *Thrasher* and even Nintendo video games have featured the Burnside skateboarding scene. (Eastside)

NEWBERG SKATEPARK
1201 Blaine St.
Newberg
Thrasher magazine rated Newberg the best in the world just after it opened in July 2000. It has 27,330 square feet of super smooth, and steep, concrete. There's a concession stand and the park provides free helmuts for you to borrow. You will be kicked out of this park if you don't wear one. (West Suburbs)

VANCOUVER WATER WORKS PARK
Fourth Plain and Fort Vancouver Way
Vancouver, WA
360/696-8171
Kids come from all over to ride these ramps and rails in the middle of a pretty park just 15 minutes from downtown Portland near Fort Vancouver. Take Interstate 5 north to the Fourth Plain exit, then drive east for about a mile. (North Suburbs)

Ski/Snowboard Resorts

Heading to "the mountain" offers both the good and the bad for

---

Skateboarding in Portland

Oregon has become the skateboarding capital of the country. Dubbed by Thrasher *magazine as "king of skateparks," the state is home to dozens of skateparks, including some of the best and most famous. Portland is working hard to become the epicenter of this kingdom with its new skatepark, slated to open in 2001. Located downtown at the base of the Steel Bridge (NW Everett and Naito), the park will complement the Burnside ramps (for advanced skateboarders) just across the river because it's specifically designed for street skating. Be forewarned that skateboarding is still illegal downtown and you will be ticketed if you get caught roaming around in undesignated areas. However, you'll see skateboarders nearly everywhere else—crossing bridges, along the waterfront, and throughout the neighborhoods. Just be careful downtown.*

skiers and snowboarders. On the up side, Mount Hood is one of North America's most spectacular natural wonders. Three major resorts hug its flanks and offer year-round fun for enthusiasts. However, weather and snow conditions on the mountain are often a challenge. Powder conditions are rare. Instead, skiers and boarders often must slog through deep "Oregon concrete," as the locals affectionately refer to the Northwest's wet snow. Good snow does fall, and the spring season— March, April, and May—offers up plenty of sunshine and some of the deepest snowpacks on the continent. Skiing is not just a winter sport in Oregon. Mount Hood's Timberline resort is open at least 11 months each year, and nearby Mount Hood Meadows usually operates well into May.

BENNETT RIDGE
CROSS-COUNTRY SKI TOUR

This is a favorite Mount Hood Nordic ski route. Ski down Forest Service Road 48. After you've crossed Iron Creek, turn onto Forest Service Road 530 and continue in either direction for some lovely tree groves and great views of Mount Hood above. Bennett Pass has the highest starting elevation for Mount Hood cross-country ski trailheads, at 4,647 feet. Stay out of the clearcut immediately below the trail during and after heavy snowfall or during very warm weather—the area is avalanche-prone. To get there, take Highway 26 east to Highway 35 north. Drive 4.5 miles on Highway 35 to White River East Snowpark on the east side of the road. (East Suburbs)

MOUNT HOOD MEADOWS
U.S. 35
Mount Hood
503/337-2222 or 503/227-7669
(snow report)

On the southeastern flank of magnificent Mount Hood, Mount Hood Meadows is the area's premier ski resort. Its snow is a little drier than its rivals and its high-speed lifts are unmatched. In addition, the resort offers the best expert skiing on the mountain (unless, of course, you want to hike into the backcountry). In particular, Heather Canyon offers up challenging terrain when it is open, which only happens when the ski patrol determines there is no chance for an avalanche. For mere mortals, Meadows offers four high-speed quad lifts to whisk you up the mountain. There are canyons and bowls even in the lower environs of the slopes and plenty of challenges for skiers and snowboarders of all levels. The recently expanded lodge now offers a large, outdoor deck for

Snowboarding on Mount Hood

Robin Klein

Cross-country skiing

and accessible skiing on Mount Hood. Situated in a mountain pass, SkiBowl also offers more night skiing than any resort in the nation. While the runs are relatively short and at a low elevation, there are some serious steeps and black-diamond terrain at the resort. It is a great place to bring children or learn how to ski or snowboard. SkiBowl also offers the luxury (for late risers) of a lift ticket that extends from 1 to 10 p.m. In the summer, SkiBowl's Action Park comes alive with great downhill mountain-biking terrain, bungee jumping, and a giant Alpine slide. Shift tickets are available. Check for prices and hours. The resort is usually closed Monday and Tuesday during the day but opens at 3:30 for evening fun. Because of its lower elevation, SkiBowl has the shortest season on Mount Hood but also the mildest weather. (East Suburbs)

those rare sunny days. But remember, this is Oregon skiing, so be prepared for ice, wind, fog, and all the other wonders of the mountain. Mount Hood Meadows does not offer any overnight accommodations but has arrangements with more than a dozen nearby hotels and bed-and-breakfasts, where you can buy package deals that reduce the cost of a lift ticket to only $20 per person. Regular adult lift tickets are $41; however, a number of partial-day options are available as well. Snowboard and ski rentals and lessons are available. Season usually runs about Thanksgiving through May. (East Suburbs)

MOUNT HOOD SKIBOWL
U.S. 26
Government Camp
503/272-3206 or 503/222-BOWL
(snow report)
SkiBowl offers the most affordable

TIMBERLINE LODGE AND RESORT
Timberline
503/231-7979 or 503/222-2211
(snow report)
www.timberlinelodge.com
What Timberline lacks in terrain it makes up for with incredible history and charm. Perched on the southern flanks of Mount Hood, Timberline is one of the oldest ski resorts in North America and a treasure chest of Oregon skiing history. It's also the only place in North America where you can ski all 12 months of the year.

Timberline has 32 runs, six lifts, and 1,000 skiable acres. Most of the terrain is beginner or intermediate with expert skiing in the summer on the Palmer snowfield high above the resort. Palmer attracts

Mount Hood—Endless Winter

*"If you can ski on Mount Hood in Oregon, you can ski anywhere,"
says Guillaume Gendre, a high school French teacher at Portland
Public Schools. Ski conditions in the Cascades can range from plat-
inum to brutal. Cascadian snow is often wetter than that in other
regions, sometimes making for heavy snow or icy runs. Overcast
skies are common during winter, and winds in open areas at higher
elevations can be harsh. In recent years, however, heavy precipita-
tion (a result of warm La Niña) has brought record-breaking snow-
pack to the area. In fact, the two deepest snowpacks ever recorded
were measured in 1999 in the Cascade Range, in Washington, and
in British Columbia. The result has been a skier's dream, with extra-
long seasons (almost year-round) and a lot of snow.*

top pro and Olympic athletes from all over the world for summer training. Add the many summer snowboard and ski camps, and Palmer snowfield can get quite busy in the summer. But there's nothing like spending a sunny July afternoon riding above the clouds, at 8,000 feet, for a near-mystic experience.

The main lodge was built in the 1930s at the request of President Franklin Roosevelt. Built by Italian laborers, it drips cozy warmth. It has also starred in some movies, including the bone-chilling *The Shining.* You can stay overnight at the lodge and enjoy the hot tub and sauna and one of the best restaurants in the state.

Lift tickets are a little cheaper here than at Mount Hood Meadows, and there are especially good deals in the spring and fall shoulder seasons. A regular adult

ski lift ticket goes for $34. (East Suburbs)

Swimming Pools

DISHMAN COMMUNITY CENTER AND POOL
77 N. Knott
503/823-3673
The fee to use this indoor pool is nominal ($1.50 for kids, $3 for adults) or free. Check for open and free swim times. A large pool with a shallow children's area, lanes, and a diving area, in addition to nice large clean showers and locker rooms and weight room, make this a popular local facility. Swim classes are offered in two-week sessions for all levels. You may frequently hear the searing rhythms of drums, as Dishman has also become the city's unofficial center

for African dance classes, which are held in the gym. For a treat, take a peek in the gym for a gander at the athletic dance if you hear those primal beats. (North Portland)

MONTAVILLA
8219 NE Glisan
503/823-3675
This large outdoor pool is open during the summer only. The fee is nominal ($1.50 for kids, $3 for adults) except during free swim. Situated in a park, this place is very popular, and on nice days you may have to wait in line to get in. No diving boards, but the large separated shallow area makes it easy for a parent to observe while lounging in the sun on one of the many chaises. Lessons run in two-week intervals for all levels of skill. Sign up in advance for best choices. (Eastside)

NORTH CLACKAMAS AQUATIC PARK
7300 SE Harmony
503/557-7873
This place is a water wonderland with slides, a wave machine, fountains, and diving boards. There is a full-size lap pool, a diving area, a grown-ups only hot tub, and a shallow play area. $9.50 adults, $6.50 seniors, $4.50 ages 3–8, $6.50 ages 9–17; family rates are also available. Call for open hours. (East Suburbs)

SOUTHWEST COMMUNITY CENTER
6820 SW 45th Ave.
503/823-2840
Features include an indoor six-lane lap pool, as well as a leisure pool with water slide and rope swing, a spa, locker rooms and family changing rooms, exercise equipment, child care, and a gym. Fees are $3 children, $4 adults. Swim lessons are offered for a variety of skill levels. Southwest Community Center is at Gabriel Park. (West Suburbs)

Tennis Courts

LAKE OSWEGO INDOOR TENNIS CENTER
2900 SW Dianne Dr.
Lake Oswego
503/635-5550
Open year-round 6 a.m.–10 p.m. daily. The facility is available for persons of all ages and abilities. The center offers tennis lessons for adults and youth. Reservations may be made up to one week in advance by calling while an attendant is on duty.

Fees are $13 per court hour; pay each time you reserve a court. During June, July, and August court time drops to $11 per hour. You can purchase a lump sum of court time in advance, then call to make a court reservation. (West Suburbs)

MOUNT TABOR PARK
SE Salmon, east of SE 60th Ave.
For tennis in a forested setting, try Mount Tabor Park's courts. Three courts are near the reservoir, and two more are on the west side of the park, free and open to the public. (Eastside)

PORTLAND TENNIS CENTER
324 NE 12th Ave.
503/823-3189
Open to the public, the Center has four indoor courts (two with ball

machines) and eight outdoor courts. Reservations are necessary for indoor courts and cost $6.25 per person before 4 p.m. and $7.25 per person after 4 p.m. The outdoor courts are free and do not require reservations. The Portland Tennis Center is run by the City of Portland. Mon–Fri 6:30 a.m.–10 p.m., Sat 7:45 a.m.–11:15 p.m., Sun 7:45 a.m.–9 p.m. (Eastside)

WASHINGTON PARK
400 SW Kingston Ave.
If you want to play tennis with a magnificient view overlooking the city, a number of courts sit next to the famous rose gardens in Washington Park. Unfortunately, though, it can be difficult to find a free court during prime times on sunny, rainless weekends, so be prepared for a wait. (Downtown)

Windsurfing the Columbia River Gorge

by Greg deBruler of Columbia River United

What makes windsurfing in the gorge so great? The Columbia River Gorge is one of the most beautiful places in the world, with cascading waterfalls, lush mountain forests, and snowcapped volcanoes like Mount Hood and Mount Adams. Just 30 minutes from Portland, it will take your breath away. The gorge is simply gorgeous.

Spring through fall, strong west winds—up to 40 miles per hour on any given day—funnel through the Cascade Mountains and past the towns of Stevenson, Cascade Locks, Hood River, Bingen, White Salmon, and Mosier. Powerful winds and warm temperatures—the gorge is drier and warmer than Portland—are what beckon windsurfers from all over the world to play in the Columbia's fresh water. Enjoy the sun while warm winds propel you back and forth across the river.

Some people think windsurfing is for kids, but in reality windsurfing can be enjoyed by people of all ages. Still, if you don't want to windsurf, the Columbia River Gorge has some great beaches for sunbathing, swimming, and taking in the sights. If you're looking for sun and fun, the gorge is the place to be!

Windsurfing

BIG WINDS
207 Front St.
Hood River
888/509-4210
www.bigwinds.com
Big Winds offers lessons to wind-surfers of all levels and claims to have the largest rental fleet on the West Coast. Pick up a free "Gorge Guide" when heading up the gorge. There are more than 50 approved windsurfing sites on the Columbia River. Look for many around the Hood River area.

The best-known spot is the Event Site at the Interstate 84 Hood River exit. Call 541/386-1336 for weather information.

A complete board with two sails will cost you about $50 a day to rent. Or, better yet for newcomers, for $59 you can take a three-hour lesson and all your equipment is included. More advanced lesson/equipment packages are offered and will cost you more. The best time to go is during the prime season, May through September, when the weather is warm, but some enjoy the sport year-round. (East Suburbs)

12

PERFORMING ARTS

Portland's thriving performing arts scene embraces not only a first-rate ballet, opera, theater company, and symphony but also a number of other prized performance troupes, such as the Northwest Afrikan American Ballet and IMAGO. But you'd be missing out on a burgeoning arts scene, including up-and-coming performers and directors, if you limited yourself to just the better-known options. Check out a student performance at Dance West, see the reinvented Jefferson Dancers, or take in a show at the well-liked Northwest Children's Theater.

THEATER

ARTISTS REPERTORY THEATRE
1516 SW Alder
503/241-1278
This professional company with a solid following stages performances throughout the season. The venue is a small and cozy theater downtown. For example, ART (as it's commonly known) recently presented a mixed-media work by an artist exploring her African American identity along with the ART theater performance of *A Raisin in the Sun.* (Downtown)

BROADWAY THEATER SERIES
1515 SW Morrison
503/241-1407
Each year, Portland Opera brings hit Broadway plays and musicals to Portland. "Portland Opera Presents Keybank Best of Broadway" was the series title for the 1999–2000 season of traveling shows. Among the shows performed that season were *The Wizard of Oz, Les Miserables, Sunset Boulevard, Jekyll & Hyde,* and *The Sound of Music.* Call for a current schedule. (Downtown)

Artists Repertory Theatre's 1998 production of Jean Cocteau's Indiscretions

IMAGO
17 SE Eighth Ave.
503/231-9581

Based in Portland, IMAGO Theatre has developed several internationally acclaimed productions. Its founders have created an "almost vaudevillian experimental style," blending theater, mime, comedy, dance, special effects and acrobatics. It's hard to say just what IMAGO is, but it is popular. Stage mime and agile bodies slithering and jumping in costumes while portraying lower life forms (sort of) come together for a truly entertaining experience. Call for upcoming shows, tickets, and prices. (Eastside)

PORTLAND CENTER STAGE
1111 SW Broadway
503/274-6588

Portland Center Stage claims to be Portland's only fully professional resident theater company. Six performances a year are held at the Newmark Theater between September and April. In any given season, you'll find a range of offerings from Shakespeare to contemporary to classic theater. Ticket prices are reasonable. Call for times and shows. (Downtown)

PORTLAND INSTITUTE FOR CONTEMPORARY ART
219 NW 12th Ave.
503/242-1419

Begun in 1995, the Portland Institute for Contemporary Art (PICA) brings avant-garde works and cutting-edge artists to Portland in the areas of dance, theater, music, and the visual arts. PICA strives to "advance the emerging ideas in new art by fostering the creative explorations of contemporary artists," according to its mission statement. Some PICA experiences are rich ones indeed; others might leave you wondering if the emperor has any clothes. Either way, PICA has been a refreshing and progressive addition to Portland's art scene. PICA's administrative staff and visual exhibition have settled into a new—and permanent—8,000-square-foot space in the Weiden and Kennedy building in the Pearl district. The building also houses a Resource Room, a "uniquely created" multimedia library of contemporary art materials. In addition to its regular season schedule, PICA offers three other individualized smaller series focused on dance, performance, and music. Each series takes place in venues throughout the city. (Northwest)

STARK RAVING THEATER
3430 SE Belmont
503/232-7072
For theater that's a little more offbeat than the big downtown performances and presented on a small stage, try Stark Raving Theater, a growing theater with a following. Tickets are cheap and prices are on a sliding scale. (Eastside)

Dada Ball

The Dada Ball, billed by its hosts as "an elegant evening of mayhem and merriment," is named after the avant-garde Dada art movement. Full of wild (and scant) costumes and silliness, this annual September fund-raiser for PICA works hard to surprise its guests. You never know what is planned. The first ball included a Lady Godiva, with long hair and nothing else, who greeted partygoers on her horse. Another year, a separate champagne bar was situated across from a photo booth/bed, where you could have pictures taken of you and your friends in bed together. Sometimes a very popular Brazilian percussion band shows up at the ball to lead guests in frenzied dance. Even the location is not revealed until the last minute, but the space is always huge, so there's plenty of room to accommodate the hundreds who come. Plan to attend. Bring friends, have fun, and don't worry about the food or odd entertainment—after all, the funds go for a good cause. Tickets are about $25 per person for the party. If you plan to attend the patron dinner and auction beforehand, tickets are $150. For more information contact PICA, 503/242-1419.

TYGRES HEART SHAKESPEARE THEATER
1111 SW Broadway
503/288-8400
Tygres Heart strives to make personal contact with its audience both literally and figuratively. The action often embraces, flanks, or includes the spectators. Performances are held in the Winningstad Theater. (Downtown)

MUSIC AND OPERA

CHAMBER MUSIC
522 SW Fifth Ave.
503/223-3202
Regular classical concerts are presented at Catlin Gabel School and Reed College. Call for a performance schedule. (Downtown)

OREGON SYMPHONY
921 SW Washington, Ste. 200
503/228-4294
The Oregon Symphony, founded in 1896, is led by conductor James DePriest. A variety of performance series are presented each season, including classical, pops, and family. The symphony performs at the Arlene Schnitzer Concert Hall. (Downtown)

PORTLAND BAROQUE ORCHESTRA
1425 SW 20th Ave., Ste. 103
503/222-6000
This much-loved local orchestra performs music from the seventeenth and eighteenth centuries at Reed College and Trinity Cathedral. (Downtown)

PORTLAND OPERA
1515 SW Morrison
503/241-1407
The popular Portland Opera has been presenting traditional opera for more than 35 years. Now venturing into modern productions, the opera performs at the Civic Auditorium. (Downtown)

PORTLAND YOUTH PHILHARMONIC
1119 SW Park Ave.
503/223-5939
The Portland Youth Philharmonic is the oldest (and one of the finest) youth orchestra in the country. More than 200 students comprise the Philharmonic and Conservatory orchestras and the Young String Ensemble. The 1999/2000 season was the Philharmonic's 76th year in existence. (Downtown)

DANCE

CONDUIT
918 SW Yamhill, Ste. 401
503/221-5857
"A contemporary dance site," the Conduit Dance Studio showcases cutting-edge work by its resident artists and choreographers. Look for creativity and experimentation here, with solid dance skills and technique. Mary Oslund, Linda K. Johnson, Keith Goodman, and Gregg Bielemeier are some of the established core artists at Conduit and among the best-known local contemporary dancers. (Downtown)

DO JUMP! EXTREMELY PHYSICAL THEATER
Echo Theater
1515 SE 37th Ave.
503/231-6605
Do Jump! blends gymnastics, dance, and theatrics into entertaining, acrobatic, and circuslike performances.

Performance Art in Portland

by Keith V. Goodman, Portland dancer and choreographer

In the last few years, a few new presenters have created a unique performance-arts scene in Portland. Portland Institute of Contemporary Arts (PICA), for example, has proven to be a very reliable source of the best in avant-garde and cutting-edge contemporary performances. Its shows range from dance and performance art to music. Another notable presenter with an even longer history is Howie Baggadonutz at Echo Theater. The newest presenter in town for dance is White Bird. Its focus is a little more traditional as it presents top-quality modern dance from around the nation. Local artists are occasionally featured in performances.

Another source of unusual entertainment is Conduit Dance Studio in downtown Portland. In addition to presenting its six core artists, the studio presents other local and national contemporary-dance artists and offers dance-technique classes.

Local colleges have joined the performing-arts scene, too. Reed College has a long history of producing and presenting performances. Portland State University has a student activity organization, the World Dance Office, which brings a variety of people to town to teach great workshops in folkloric dance and music forms including Afro-Caribbean and hip-hop.

Other performers and companies to keep an eye out for include: Imago, an excellent theater and movement company replete with puppets; Aero Betty, a contemporary dance and trapeze company; Body Vox; Northwest Afrikan American Ballet; and Daryl Grant, jazz composer and pianist. The Unitarian Church supports the arts and the city's artists and regularly integrates them and their art forms into services. Berbati's Pan is a nightclub with entertainment, excellent music, delicious food, and wonderful ambience. The list goes on and on. This is what we have in Portland—a great city with fantastic arts and supportive people.

Oregon Ballet Theater

The company has been gaining notoriety lately and recently received praise on its New York tour. (Eastside)

THE JEFFERSON DANCERS
5210 N. Kerby
503/916-5180

The Jefferson Dancers dance company stems from a Portland Public Schools program at Jefferson High School. It's been called a public-school version of New York's Julliard. The dancing, jazz, tap, African, and classical ballet performances have been top-notch, an amazing accomplishment for a public school. Unfortunately, however, Portland schools have suffered funding woes in recent years, and art programs, even ones as adored as this, have felt the strain. As a result, there has been a change in artistic directions. Still,

the Jefferson Dancers are not to be missed. A favorite of young people, the enthusiastic and talented group of dancers is a great role model and a constant inspiration. (North Portland)

NORTHWEST AFRIKAN AMERICAN BALLET
P.O. Box 11143
503/287-8852
e-mail: nwaab@teleport.com

If you have never seen a professional African dance performance, you are in for a treat. The athleticism and exploding energy of the dancers, combined with compelling drum rhythms, make for an incredibly exciting dance experience. You might find it hard to sit still in your seat. Bruce Smith, artistic director of the NWAAB, has led his company to national and international recognition. A master drummer himself, he draws on authentic dance techniques acquired from regular trips to Africa. Look for the troupe's Portland performance each February. (Downtown)

OREGON BALLET THEATER
1120 SW 10th Ave.
503/222-5538
www.obt.org
Oregon's premier ballet company, OBT has it all: scandal, politics, "sexy, revved-up" dancing, classical ballet, and great reviews. OBT has gained national recognition for its consistently solid dancing, excellent treatment of classical works, and controversial new choreography. The more dynamic of the newer works present challenging dancing done well and are usually a pleasure to see. There aren't any superstar dancers, but the company itself shines. Performances are held at several different venues in Portland. Most often they are at the Civic Auditorium, but some are at the Newmark Intermediate Theater or at Portland State University. OBT's season runs from October through May and includes an acclaimed version of *The Nutcracker* during the holidays. As *New York City Search* put it, "Rap meets the tutu, nice." (Downtown)

CONCERT VENUES

ARLENE SCHNITZER CONCERT HALL
SW Broadway and SW Main
503/248-4335
Known affectionately by locals as the "Schnitz," this beautifully renovated concert hall and historic landmark, now home of the Oregon Symphony, originally opened in 1928 as the Portland Publix Theater. The hall is ornate and elegant—

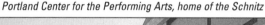

Portland Center for the Performing Arts, home of the Schnitz

Michael Dahlstrom

you're guaranteed to enjoy concerts here in style. A full bar and concessions are available during certain performances. For more details, see chapter 5, Sights and Attractions. (Downtown)

CIVIC AUDITORIUM
SW Third and SW Clay
503/274-6560 or 503/796-9293
This large venue hosts the opera, ballet, and a number of shows. Most seats have good views. A snack bar with overpriced candy and the like is swamped by long lines during intermission. An espresso stand and cocktail bar are open for evening performances. Parking can be difficult in the area, so come early and leave your car in one of the nearby garages. (Downtown)

PORTLAND MEADOWS
1001 N. Schmeer Rd.
503/285-9144
Portland Meadows occasionally hosts large outdoor concerts when the weather is warm. Otherwise, it functions as a horse racetrack. (North Portland)

ROSELAND THEATER
8 NW Sixth Ave.
503/224-2038
You name the band, they've been here. Or so it seems. A nightclub sometimes, a midsize concert venue others, the Roseland has two stages. The larger upstairs stage is in a dark hall and gets pretty hot on summer evenings. For a list of upcoming concerts, check out the free local newspaper, *Willamette Week*. (Downtown)

ROSE QUARTER
One Center Court
503/234-9291
This is Portland's largest concert venue, with a total capacity of more than 21,300. Just a few years old, the indoor Rose Garden Arena has hosted many big-name bands, including the Rolling Stones. It's also the home of the Portland Trail Blazers. (Eastside)

WASHINGTON PARK AMPHITHEATER
400 SW Kingston
Acoustics aside, and weather permitting, this is a lovely place to see a concert. Seating is outdoors only, so it's best to bring a blanket or folding chairs. For tickets, visit www.showman.com, or contact Ticketmaster. A rundown of the amphitheater series is found at www.oregonlive.com/ent/music/rosegarden/. Scheduled around Labor Day weekend at the end of the summer, the concerts are held amid the Washington Park Rose Test Gardens with Mount Hood as backdrop. The concerts benefit Portland Parks and Recreation. (Downtown)

Tri-Met

13

NIGHTLIFE

Portland's ever-growing night scene could almost be considered an explosion. Successful gentrification efforts in Old Town and the Pearl district, as well as Eastside growth coupled with a bit of an artistic renaissance and a young edge, make this once-provincial city a place with soul. An almost surprising undercurrent rich in music flows through Portland, and it is never so apparent as on a fine weekend summer eve when locals find the pubs, socializing, music, dancing, and clubs irresistible. You'll find whatever you're looking for from fetish nights to some of the finest jazz, memorable blues, cutting alternative, and the best beer on the planet. People carry on until late in some parts of downtown, bustling at 1 a.m. as though it were dinner hour. Someone once said, Portland isn't really pretty, but it has an underbelly, it has soul.

DANCE CLUBS

ANDREA'S CHA CHA CLUB
832 SE Grand
503/230-1166
Andrea's has Latin dancing most nights. It's also a good place to take dancing lessons. This is a very small place below the ground, underneath the Grand Café, and so it can get crowded. Sunday is '70s disco night. (Eastside)

BAR 71
71 SW Second Ave.
503/241-4242
It is not uncommon to find lines outside Bar 71 on weekend nights. It's a popular meat market for young suburban types. The convenient downtown location ensures a consistent flow of people throughout the night. Those who do not feel like checking out other places in the area might spend their time

lounging in Bar 71's comfortable chairs, playing pool, or hitting the dance floor in the back. Dance music ranges from techno to hip-hop. (Downtown)

COBALT LOUNGE'S XOTICA GO-GO, THURSDAY NIGHTS
32 NW Third Ave.
503/225-1003
Thursday nights after 11, the Cobalt turns into a popular disco with techno/hip-hop/retro sounds and live semi-exotic go-go dancers above the tables and dance floor. To round out the scene, old black-and-white sex movies are shown on TV screens, and cheap eats are served late.

Drawing a young, alternative crowd of both sexes, the place verges on seedy, but it is not a strip joint or hard-core bar. Owned by a young porn-guide entrepreneur, it's a great place to get down in Old Town. Xotica go-go can be irresistible and is nearly always entertaining. (Downtown)

EGYPTIAN ROOM
3701 SE Division
503/236-8689
Egyptian's Room is a girl's club. Swing lessons are offered some nights, and the pool tables are free on weekdays. Yes, this place caters to a lesbian crowd, but it's fun for guys and straight women too, because of its neighborhood friendly feeling. Call for information on swing nights. (Eastside)

EMBERS
11 NW Broadway
503/222-3082
Embers, in Old Town, is divided into two bar areas, with drag shows in the front bar. The other bar includes a great dance club no matter what your sexual persuasion. The dance floor can get crowded and wild on Saturday nights and can get sweaty in the summertime. Music is typically catchy '80s disco or Top 40. (Downtown)

OHM
31 NW First Ave.
503/223-9919
Techno, techno. The crowd at Old Town's Ohm is mostly young, but some older clientele left over from the bluesy Key Largo days still stop by. The redo has yielded appealing bar decor. A number of Northwest bands and deejays play here, but the music can be experimental and is not always dance-friendly, despite the large dance floor. Be aware also that the service is not always nice. The cover charge can be a little high for what you get inside. (Downtown)

MUSIC CLUBS

Jazz

ATWATER'S
111 SW Fifth Ave., 30th floor
503/275-3600

TRIVIA

For a near-comprehensive assessment of Portland's night scene, pick up a copy of the free *BarFly, the 'Zine on the Scene*, or check out its Web site at www.barflymag.com.

Atwater's is the bar (and restaurant) with the view. Corporate to upscale, this lounge is known for its romantic atmosphere and for having some of the best jazz in town. Drinks are pricey, but there is a happy hour from five to seven on weekdays. (Downtown)

BRASSERIE MONTMARTE
626 SW Park
503/224-5552
Loaded with ambience, the Brasserie, in the heart of downtown, is memorable for the Old Paris–nightclub atmosphere more than the music or food. Well worth a visit for that alone, it's nearly always busy. Step inside and see. The black-and-white tile, white-linen tables, and artwork recall another era in another place. For fun, and in keeping with the Montmarte theme, each table is supplied with plenty of Crayolas, and guests are encouraged to doodle at will on the white butcher paper lining the tables. There are also tableside magic shows. Stellar works of the past adorn the walls of the restaurant. (Downtown)

JAZZ DE OPUS
33 NW Second Ave.
503/222-6077
Small and cozy, this Old Town club has been showcasing Portland jazz favorites for years. Jazz de Opus also has a restaurant with an inexpensive menu. (Downtown)

JIMMY MAK'S
300 NW 10th Ave.
503/295-6542
What this bar lacks in ambience (it's rather nondescript, like an old banquet room in a cheap hotel) it makes up for in the music. Some of

Atwater's Restaurant

Catch Leroy Vinnegar and other jazz greats at Atwater's.

the best jazz bands in town play here, and the place is comfortably accommodating with a full bar and menu. (Northwest)

Blues

CANDLELIGHT CAFÉ AND BAR
2032 SW Fifth Ave.
503/222-3378
This smoky, crowded, and often uncomfortable dive gets down with some good music. The dance floor—if you can even reach it—is tiny. The Candlelight doubles as a pickup bar for an older crowd. Access is a little tricky as it's just near Interstate 405 downtown. Take the Fourth Avenue exit to College, then College to Fifth. (Downtown)

KELLY'S OLYMPIAN
426 SW Washington
503/228-3669
A smoke shop and shoeshine add to this old blues bar's ambience. (Downtown)

Music and Blues in Portland

by Albert Reda, musician and member of the
Cascade Blues Association Hall of Fame

Set in the Pacific Northwest, a part of the country known for its wealth of natural wonder, Portland is a city rich in diversity. A day spent driving around town and stopping in the many unique neighborhoods will make that clear. Nowhere, though, is Portland's diversity more on display than in the arts, especially music. On any night of the week, a visitor can satisfy any musical taste. Classical, opera, alternative, jazz, country, and the blues all can be enjoyed while out on the town.

The Arlene Schnitzer Concert Hall (or The Schnitz, as it's known to locals) and the Portland Center for the Performing Arts are both downtown, right across from the Hilton. The Crystal Ballroom is a restored treasure on Burnside. Listed in the National Register of Historic Places and boasting what may be the only "floating dance floor" left in the country, this is the place to go for a dose of alternative rock or swing dancing. Berbati's Pan, on Southwest Second just off Burnside, offers similar musical fare in more of a nightclub atmosphere. For jazz, if you're looking for a mellow vibe, check out the hotels. The Benson and Heathman both feature jazz nightly in their lounges. If you want to hear someone really cut loose, Jazz de Opus, Atwater's, Brasserie Montmarte, and Jimmy Mak's all feature world-class jazz.

And then there are the blues. Spearheaded by the Cascade Blues Association (CBA), the blues are a significant part of Portland's nightlife. The Waterfront Blues Festival takes place every Fourth of July weekend at Tom McCall Waterfront Park on the banks of the Willamette River and routinely features more than 40 national and local acts on four stages. In addition, at least a dozen clubs in town host live blues. Artists such as harp players Paul deLay and Curtis Salgado, pianist Janice Scroggins, singer Lloyd Jones, and guitarists Terry Robb and Jim Mesi can be found holding court at places like the Candlelight Café and Bar, the Trail's End Saloon, and the Tillicum Club.

Rock/Alternative/Reggae

ASH STREET SALOON
225 SW Ash
503/226-0430
If you want to support a local rock
'n' roll band, this Old Town bar and
club serves them up three or four
nights a week. It's usually loud and
local. A great selection of beer as
well as hard liquor is available. The
space is small, so you had better
like the band and be prepared to
shout at your friends to be heard.
There is a small space to dance
and an even smaller stage for the
young bands to strut their stuff.
This is rock 'n' roll the way it is supposed to be—close up and personal. (Downtown)

BERBATI'S PAN
231 SW Ankeny
503/248-4579
This popular music club attracts
some of the better bands in the
Northwest and beyond, including
alternative punk, rap, hip-hop, and
swing. The crowd morphs on any
given night depending on the
music. The bar is roomy and dark
and the dance floor is decent. The
lighter adjacent bar off the restaurant is a great place to visit
between sets, but it's also one of
the better bar destinations for
meeting, attracting a hipster crowd
and Pan overflow. There's a cover
charge for music in the Pan that
varies, but there's no cover charge
in Berbati's bar next door. The Pan
also offers some wonderful late-
night fare for cheap. (Downtown)

CRYSTAL BALLROOM
1332 W. Burnside
503/778-5625
This huge place could almost be
considered a concert hall.
Restored by the McMenamin
brothers of local beer fame, but still
not really fancy, the Crystal showcases local as well as national live
music. The bands vary widely and
some nights are for all ages.
Known for its "floating" dance
floor, the Crystal Ballroom offers
dancing lessons on Sunday swing
night. (Downtown)

THE GREEN ROOM
2280 NW Thurman
503/228-6178
The Green Room mixes the intimacy of an Irish pub with good
Northwest rock complemented by
a sprinkle of blues. The music here
can vary widely, but you can count
on something six nights a week.
The acoustics are not the best, and
if you don't care too much for the
band you may find yourself wincing
at the volume level. Thankfully,
there is a comfortable outdoor
deck now equipped with a full bar
and heaters. They pour a great pint
of Guinness at the Green Room
(yes, the owner is Irish) and serve
good pub grub, too. (Northwest)

MOUNT TABOR PUB
4811 SE Hawthorne Blvd.
503/238-1646
This Hawthorne Boulevard club
regularly serves up good, local
alternative rock with an occasional
big-name band thrown in for good
measure. There is usually music
here every night of the week, and
many nights feature three or four
bands. The club offers two venues:
a converted cinema with a small
stage, bar, and pool table, and an
acoustic theater for those seeking
quieter sounds. The cover charge

North by Northwest

by Monique Balas, writer for *The Oregonian*

If you are in Portland in September or October, you might think you're in a city full of Alfred Hitchcock fans. Think again. North by Northwest (or NXNW) refers not to the suspense-filled flick but to Portland's annual music event. The festival is a way of uniting everyone involved in the music industry, from bands to fans to music-business representatives.

North by Northwest consumes Portland's downtown night scene for three days. Bands showcase raw musical talent, predominantly from the Northwest but also from all over the United States and the world. More than 300 bands play at around 25 clubs over the course of three days. They each play a 40-minute set. Ground zero, the area densest in participating clubs, is around SW Third and Ash downtown. But clubs all over the city are involved. Best bet is to pick up a Willamette Week *newspaper anywhere in town for a schedule, club map, and band lineup. The event offers a full of array of music to choose from—from super-pop, punk,*

is usually low, and good microbrews as well old standards are featured on tap. (Eastside)

THE RED SEA
318 SW Third
503/241-5450
Praise Ja! This is the only regular venue for real roots-rock reggae and world beat. The Red Sea serves up true Rastafarian fare, not just white guys who only have dreadlocks because they are too lazy to wash their hair. The club usually features three to four live bands a week or deejays spinning reggae sounds for the dance floor. (Downtown)

SATYRICON
125 NW Fifth Ave.
503/243-2380
Live and loud punk-rock music can be had every night in this small, established venue in Old Town. Loads of murals decorate the walls. The club is conveniently located on the downtown bus mall. A cover is charged every night except Monday. (Downtown)

PUBS AND BARS

THE BAGDAD THEATER AND PUB
3702 SE Hawthorne Blvd.
503/232-6676

and alternative to country or lounge. Performances are all inside, and wristbands are checked.

NXNW began in 1995 as a spinoff of the South by Southwest festival, which takes place in Austin, Texas. The Portland event now attracts more than 300 bands, most of which hail from the West Coast and other parts of the United States (though some are from as far away as Denmark, Japan, and Australia).

Although the bands you'll see performing might not be playing on the radio next week, one of the most important and exciting parts of the event is networking. Bands meet publicists, attorneys, managers, and record-label representatives who can give them, if nothing else, useful career advice. Still, popular groups such as Black Lab, Cake, and Cherry Poppin' Daddies have been seen at NXNW.

Tickets (in the form of wristbands and badges) to the weekend's events cost about $30 and are available from local retailers such as Ozone Records, Music Millennium, and all Fred Meyer Fastixx outlets. A limited number of individual show tickets may be available at club doors, usually at the cover-charge price ($5 to $10), but wristband- and badge-holders have priority.

Good, cheap beer (20 taps), piping-hot pizza, and second-run movies for two bucks a head. There's nothing wrong with that formula. The McMenamins' flagship on hip Hawthorne Boulevard is the place to be seen for hopheads and cinephiles alike. The sidewalk picnic tables are always packed, but nothing beats settling back in the creaky old theater seats and enjoying a cold one in front of the silver screen. (Eastside)

BAR OF THE GODS
4801 SE Hawthorne Blvd.
503/232-2037
For mere mortals living on the cheap, this is a good spot for a brew. Guinness is always on tap and the rotating microbrews cost only two or three dollars a pint. The music is loud and usually from the 20-something genre. In the summer the back deck is a good escape from the high decibels and smoky air. Open daily, nine taps. (Eastside)

THE BARLEY MILL PUB
1629 SE Hawthorne Blvd.
503/231-1492
The first successful McMenamins pub, the Barley Mill captures the essence of the brothers' empire better than most. From the Grateful Dead concert photos and posters

dotting the walls to the laid-back service, the Barley Mill exemplifies Portland's pub scene. The miniature picnic tables on the sidewalk are a great place to hang on a warm Saturday afternoon, and, yes, the servings of fries are huge here, too. Open daily, 20 taps. (Eastside)

BELMONT'S INN
3357 SE Belmont St.
503/232-1998

Belmont's is a survivor. Nearly driven out of the growing neighborhood by noise complaints and violent patrons, Belmont's has transformed itself into a pool-hall pub. There is always good beer, a young crowd, and loud music even though the live acts are history. Try the pinball machines when you get tired of shooting pool. Open daily, 22 taps. (Eastside)

BEULAHLAND
118 NE 28th Ave.
503/235-2794

Beulahland exudes effortless cool. There's a pinball machine, a rotary phone, and a tiny hovel of a back deck. There may be only four beers on tap, but they are always better than average. There's cheap beer in bottles and good espresso too. Open daily. (Eastside)

CAPTAIN ANKENY'S WELL
50 SW Third Ave.
503/223-1375

Captain Ankeny's in Old Town is Portland's best place for a slice of pizza and a cold beer. Try the pineapple pizza for a real treat. There are more than a dozen taps and a fine variety of microbrews from Oregon and beyond. The crowd, which is usually young, comes here to get primed for late-night fun. Open daily. (Downtown)

CLAUDIA'S
3006 SE Hawthorne Blvd.
503/232-1744

Portland's best sports pub, Claudia's attracts a healthy crowd nearly every night of the week. The high-backed, swivel captain's chairs at the bar are a real experience; you can follow a half-dozen football games beamed down from the satellites. There are pool tables for those who don't mind missing a play or two. Good, simple pub food is also available. Open daily, 15 taps. (Eastside)

DUBLIN PUB
6821 SW Beaverton-Hillsday Hwy.
Beaverton/Raleigh
503/297-2889

There are 105 taps at the Dublin Pub, so if it doesn't have a beer you like, you don't like beer. In fact, you probably won't know half of them. They hail from every part of the globe and include a great selection of American microbrews, in particular those from California, Oregon, and Washington. It's a few miles out of town but worth the trip. (West Suburbs)

GOOSE HOLLOW INN
1927 SW Jefferson St.
503/228-7010

This neighborhood pub is owned by former Portland mayor Bud Clark (who offended uptight Portlanders with his "expose yourself to art" poster in which he flashes a downtown statue; sales of the poster retired his campaign debts). Bud knows beer even if his taste tends toward the lower end of the scale. Here you'll find everything from microbrew to Schlitz. Good food and a great mix of people make the Goose a winner. Bud also makes a killer vegetarian Reuben sandwich. Open daily, 13 taps. (Downtown)

GYPSY
625 NW 21st Ave.
503/796-1859
The Gypsy has two bar areas. The darker lower area is more of a meat market than a trendy lounge. An eclectic haunt for those in the know as well as local barflies, the lower bar lost its edge when the pool tables were yanked but gained in business and preppy appeal. Still, the pretty red upper bar with its tacky black velvet art and booths makes for a cool place to grab a martini without paying a cover. Basic food is served at the Gypsy-la. (Northwest)

HAWTHORNE ALE HOUSE
3632 SE Hawthorne Blvd.
503/233-6540
This is Bridgeport Brewing's only satellite location. The company may not brew any beer here, but it certainly knows how to pour a pint (Bridgeport ales only). This is a yuppie pub, especially popular among upwardly mobile couples in their thirties. What the pub lacks in gritty atmosphere, it makes up for with gravity-fed, cask-conditioned ales served at British temperatures. The great menu borders on the gourmet (as far as pubs go). Try the hummus plate or the crab dip with pita bread. Or go for the portobello mushroom sandwich. Open daily, six taps. (Eastside)

HORSE BRASS PUB
4534 SE Belmont St.
503/232-2202
The best English pub west of London (or is it east?), the Horse Brass is without peer. This is where the patriots of Portland's microbrew revolution plotted their historic undertaking. And this is where you can now enjoy the fruits of their labor. But the Horse Brass's beer selection doesn't stop at the city limits. There's great beer from around the world, English pub food, and a single-malt Scotch list that will tantalize your tongue while lightening your wallet. Be warned: This is where the FDA could demonstrate that secondhand smoke kills. Open daily, 42 taps. (Eastside)

HUBER'S
411 SW Third Ave.
503/228-5686
This older bar, of the San Francisco brass and dark wood ilk, is renowned for its flaming Spanish (rather than Irish) coffees and Trail Blazer sightings. Frequented by yuppies and very tall professional athletes, Huber's can get crowded on weekend nights. It is worth ordering a Spanish coffee just to watch the preparation. The waiter assembles the coffee tableside, complete with sugared rim, real cream, and flames. (Downtown)

KELLS
112 SW Second Ave.
503/227-4057
For that little taste of Ireland right in Portland's Old Town, Kells is as good as it gets. You'll find Guinness on tap (of course), rounded out with a fine selection of Northwest microbrews. The whiskey selection is staggering and impressively arrayed high above the bar. Ask your waiter to stick a dollar bill to

the ceiling (don't ask how it works—it's a secret) and you can go home knowing your money will end up at a deserving charity. Live Irish music or something similar to that starts each night around nine. The pub is open daily, with 14 taps. (Downtown)

LAURELTHIRST PUBLIC HOUSE
2958 NE Glisan St.
503/232-1504
This is one of Portland's best spots to drink great beer and catch a good local band. An enormous selection of on-tap microbrews lines the wall behind the bar. There's good, cheap food and a couple of busy pool tables in the back. The cover charge rarely exceeds two dollars, so come early if you want a seat. Open daily, 22 taps. (Eastside)

THE LOW BROW LOUNGE
1036 NW Hoyt
503/226-0200
The Low Brow is run by two refugees from the McMenamins' empire. The beer is good and cheap and the food is better than average. The low-slung booths and kitschy decor give the Low Brow a charm that lives up to its moniker. Outdoor seating is available on the sidewalk for warm summer nights of beer drinking. (Downtown)

MCMENAMINS TAVERN
1716 NW 23rd Ave.
503/227-0929
This place used to be a rare McMenamins' pool hall, but alas, the tables are gone, replaced by more booths for thirsty customers. Nestled on the quieter north end of bustling Northwest 23rd Avenue, this is a good place to chill on a

summer day (outdoor seating is available) or hunker down during one of Portland's winter gales. The usual pub grub and a full array of McMenamins ales are available. Open daily, 15 taps. (North Portland)

THE MEDICINE HAT
1834 NE Alberta
503/440-3514
Microbrews and bottled beers are available now, but the liquor license is forthcoming and two additional bars are being added. Although understated from the outside, this fairly new hot spot in the up-and-coming Alberta Street area is dripping with funky ambience. This nightclub/bar/restaurant at the site of the former Louisiana Kitchen (before its almost total transformation) has room to dance, ample seating for dining, and several sofas—perfect to accelerate the intimacy of that first meeting. Several pool tables and a couple of pinball machines (including one graced with Elvira) are in the basement. Live music varies from big-band to Goth from one night to the next. Similarly, the menu exhibits a wide scope, ranging from burgers to hush puppies, catfish and gumbo, assorted salads, grilled salmon, and a tarragon tuna melt. The extra-adventurous may want to choke down some gizzards with ranch dressing. (North Portland)

MONTAGE
301 SE Morrison
503/234-1324
This place is always busy until the wee hours on weekends. Montage's funky bistro/Cajun atmosphere and location beneath the east end of the Morrison Bridge add to the lively ambience. While

Neil Gilpin's Belmont Street Octet at Laurelthirst Public House

this is definitely a restaurant, it is also a good place to grab a drink, beer, or glass of red wine. Long tables, set European-style so that you sit right next to your neighbor, make Montage a fun place to meet. Montage answers the question, How many different ways can you serve macaroni and cheese? (Eastside)

MUU MUU'S
612 NW 21st
503/223-8169
This chic and diverse little bar serves tasty food, too. It's a great place to go on a blind date—not too cozy or romantic, but not too noisy, either. Booths allow for intimate conversation. (Northwest)

OBA!
1210 NW Hoyt
503/228-6161
This swanky, fashionable bar might be just the place to bring a date before a show or after a First Thursday gallery tour. Bathed in fiery lighting, the bar area glows. But it can get packed and finding a seat can be difficult. If you come on a weekday or early in the evening, however, you should be fine. Have a martini made with fresh mixers. (Northwest)

PADDY'S BAR AND GRILL
65 SW Yamhill St.
503/224-5626
Paddy's gives Kells a run for its money, but it doesn't quite feel as Irish here. Still, you will find a good selection of microbrews and enough hard liquor to stagger any Irishman. Paddy's serves better food than most bars and provides sidewalk seating during Portland's short summer. Open daily, 10 taps. (Downtown)

PRODUCE ROW
204 SE Oak St.
503/232-8355
This was the McMenamin empire's first outpost; now it is just a great place to drink beer. The selection

Laurelthirst Public House

here is big on quality and quantity. The local, national, and international brew could satisfy any thirsty soul. In the summer, the back deck is the spot to eat a burger and fries and quaff a cold one. Open daily, 27 taps. (Eastside)

ROSE AND RAINDROP
532 SE Grand Ave.
503/238-6996
This relatively new addition to the Portland pub scene is co-owned by Horse Brass publican Don Younger. The excellent beer selection shows off Younger's unparalleled taste. Unfortunately, the food menu fails in its attempt to move beyond the normal pub fare. Stick to the beer and you'll be more than satisfied. Open daily, 15 taps. (Eastside)

ROSE AND THISTLE PUB
2314 NE Broadway
503/287-8582
This English alehouse is a pretty good knockoff of its British cousins. Thankfully, the food is not limited to the English isles. Try the crab cakes or scallops and don't miss the cheap late-night pub menu. The beer comes from both sides of the Atlantic and, of course, the Pacific Northwest. Open daily, 13 taps. (Eastside)

SAUCEBOX
214 SW Broadway
503/241-3393
Dark, sleek, trendy, and upscale, this restaurant brings out a deejay and becomes a bar after 10. Think cocktails made with strange but delicious fresh ingredients: lime, mango, coconut, and ginger. Saucebox is *très* cool and, because of its central location, is a great launching point for an evening of clubbing in downtown Portland. (Downtown)

SHANGHAI TUNNEL
211 SW Ankeny
503/220-4001
This dark and cavernous underground bar in Old Town attracts a hip crowd but can feel a little claustrophobic. There's a pool table and discreet nooks for clandestine meetings. (Downtown)

SPACEROOM
4800 SE Hawthorne
503/235-8303
Meet the Jetsons. The Spaceroom's dated rocket decor works oh so well today. This is your 1960s-style smoke-filled cocktail joint with big booths, black lights, and a rockin' juke box. There's no sign that this eclectic establishment, which doubles as a hipster hangout and an old neighborhood bar, won't fall the trendy way of so many others. (Eastside)

SWEETWATER JAM HOUSE
3350 SE Morrison
503/233-0333
This warmly lit, inviting place attracts a young, alternative, laid-back bar crowd. Tables are painted picnic. The theme is sort of island: Jamaican, Creole, and '70s kitsch. A restaurant is attached, but you can order food in the bar. For a satisfying light meal with a kick, try the side dish of curried avocado on jasmine rice. Sweetwater's has a great selection of rums and rum concoctions, and the Jamaican Red Stripe beer is great. Open every evening at that magical time: 4:20. (Eastside)

TIGER BAR
317 NW Broadway

Ten Best Places to Drink Beer in Portland

1. Kells
2. Dublin Pub
3. Horse Brass Pub
4. Produce Row
5. Full Sail/Pilsner Room at Riverplace
6. Beulahland
7. Captain Ankeny's Well
8. Bridgeport Brewing Company
9. Laurelthirst Public House
10. Hawthorne Ale House

503/222-7297
This super-hip, dark lounge with its tiger-stripe bar and terrific spring rolls draws a young, alternative crowd. Deejays spin techno or hip-hop all night long. TV screens frequently run soundless snowboard and surfing footage and old movies. (Downtown)

UPTOWN BILLIARDS CLUB
120 NW 23rd Ave.
503/226-6909
You'll find loads of pool tables (reserve in advance) in this spacious, upscale, and comfortable bar. Aside from being a great place to play pool, Uptown Billiards is a fine place to sip a drink or cognac in the elegant library area. Located above a Christmas store, it's not obvious from the busy Northwest 23rd Avenue below. Free parking is available in nearby retail parking lots after store hours. (Northwest)

WHITE EAGLE SALOON
836 N. Russell St.
503/282-6810
One of the latest McMenamins acquisitions, the White Eagle drips Portland pub history. For nearly a century, Portlanders have cooled their heels and wet their whistles before the elaborate wooden bar of the Eagle. The upper portion of the building is said to be haunted by a ghost, but you're more likely to hear the wailing guitars of a blues band when you settle in here for the night. (North Portland)

COMEDY CLUBS

COMEDYSPORTZ
1963 NW Kearney
503/236-8888
ComedySportz offers interactive competitive comedy, complete with two teams, a referee, and a scoreboard. This is "clean improv comedy, suitable for all ages, persuasions, and species." Portland won the 1999 Comedy League of America National Tournament. Comedy-Sportz Portland is a member of the Comedy League of America, with teams in more than 25 cities.

DINNER THEATERS

SYLVIA'S
5115 NE Sandy
503/288-6828

www.sylvias.net
Sylvia's dinner theater presents musicals, mysteries, comedies, and dramas. Italian dinners are served with the show. Groups of up to 100 people can make a reservation ($31.95 per person). (Eastside)

MOVIE HOUSES OF NOTE

BAGDAD THEATER
3702 SE Hawthorne
503/777-FILM
www.mcmenamins.com/Edge/ thsched.html
You can buy a slice of pizza and a

Bagdad Theater

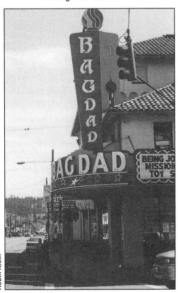

Robin Klein

beer to enjoy while watching a movie in this theater owned by the McMenamin brothers of local beer fame. It has the funky old McMenamin ambience with roomy seating and laid-back atmosphere. Look for double features and super-cheap movie prices—like a buck. (Eastside)

CINEMA 21
616 NW 21st Ave.
503/223-4515
Featuring independent and alternative films, old classics and documentaries, Cinema 21 is a comfortable older theater in the heart of Northwest 21st sandwiched between popular clubs and restaurants. (Northwest)

KENNEDY SCHOOL THEATER
5736 NE 33rd Ave.
503/777-FILM
www.mcmenamins.com/Edge/ thsched.html
Like the Bagdad Theater and the Mission Theater, Kennedy School is owned by the McMenamin brothers. See the Bagdad Theater listing, above, for more details. (North Portland)

KOIN CINEMAS
SW Third Ave. at Clay St.
503/225-5555, ext. 4608
Downtown's KOIN Center Cinemas, on the second floor of a glass office building, holds six small cozy theaters accommodating 70 to 150

moviegoers each. KOIN shows some of the best newly released independent and foreign films. So-called crying rooms are available in two of the theaters—sound-proof rooms that allow parents with infants a place to watch the movie without interrupting the audience—what a great thing! (Downtown)

LLOYD CINEMAS
503/225-5555 ext. 4600

This is major-motion-picture central, with 10 screens showing the most popular releases and conveniently located on the MAX light-rail line and next to Lloyd Center Mall. And if you can't find a movie to see, just walk across the street into the mall and check out what's playing on the eight movie screens inside at the Lloyd Mall Theater. (Eastside)

MISSION THEATER
1624 NW Glisan
503/777-FILM
www.mcmenamins.com/Edge/
thsched.html

This movie house is similar to others owned by the McMenamin brothers. See the Kennedy School Theater listing, above, for more details. (Northwest)

MOVIE HOUSE
1220 SW Taylor
503/225-5555, ext. 4609

Showing so-called art movies, this older, laid-back, 260-seat theater is roomy and comfortable. Foreign films and some occasional fine or offbeat American flicks can be seen here. However, movies shown are generally popular, not obscure. Runs are usually long. (Downtown)

SUNDANCE CINEMAS
Pioneer Place
Fourth and Yamhill

Robert Redford's Sundance Cinemas, a seven-screen theater with stadium seating, tops the major new additions to Pioneer Place, Portland's upscale shopping mall. The joint venture between Redford and General Cinemas Theaters Inc. of Massachusetts shows documentaries, indies, and international films. The 150,000-square-foot complex occupies the third, fourth, and fifth floors complete with bistro, a movie-related bookstore, private screening rooms, and an outlet that sells merchandise from Redford's Sundance catalog. Portland was selected to be the site of the first theater of the chain to open west of the Mississippi. (Downtown)

Tri-Met

14

DAY TRIPS

Day Trip: Mount Hood

Distance from Portland: 45 miles (Timberline and Trillium Lake); 70 miles (Lost Lake)

Portland lies in a valley with the Cascade Mountains looming to the east and stretching north and south. The nearest and highest of all the peaks is 11,240-foot Mount Hood. **Timberline Lodge,** set on its flank at an elevation of 6,000 feet, is the highest point to which it's possible to drive on the mountain. It takes a little over an hour to reach the lodge from Portland.

In nice weather, take a hike on one of the many trails emanating from the lodge area. Afterward, ride the Magic Mile chairlift (to 7,016 feet) for a spectacular view of the Cascades and beyond. Then step inside the main lodge to enjoy a snack, beer, or hot drink as you rest on an oversize chair and gaze through colossal windows at skiers and snowboarders far up the Palmer Glacier (8,540 feet). Or, if you're so inclined, go ahead and try the terrain yourself. Skiing, snowboarding, and mountain climbing are all popular and accessible from Timberline (see chapter 11, Sports and Recreation). For a real treat, consider staying in the historic lodge or dining in the **Cascade Dining Room.** With its award-winning chef, it's one of Oregon's best restaurants.

When you've had your fill, proceed down Timberline Road then turn east on Highway 26 and drive a couple of miles to the south end of the beautiful and serene **Trillium Lake.** There you'll find spectacular views of Mount Hood, perfectly centered and framed over the lake's north end. An easy 1.5-mile trail (easy even for children) leads around the lake through wildflower meadows, wetlands, and forests.

Alternatively, for a day trip or an overnight camping experience to remember, visit the equally picture-perfect **Lost Lake** on the other side of Mount Hood. There you'll find one of the most impressive remnants of ancient forest in the area, an old grove of giant Douglas fir and western red cedar. To see the biggest trees, take the easy three-mile Lost Lake Nature Trail clockwise around the lake (to the left when facing the lake from the campground) through forests and marshes. In addition to the trees, there are more excellent views of Mount Hood. You'll find a campground, a general store, and a boat-rental service on the lake.

Getting there from Portland: To get to Timberline Lodge, take U.S. Highway 26 east from Portland to Government Camp. Just past Government Camp, take a left onto Timberline Road and follow it to the

Mount Hood with orchards in winter

lodge. To get to Lost Lake, take Interstate 84 east from Portland to exit 62 near Hood River. There catch Highway 30 east (it soon becomes Cascade Street, then Oak Street). Turn right at 13th Street and follow signs to Odell. After five miles turn right on Dee Highway. Go six miles and bear right at a sign for Dee, then turn left onto Lost Lake Road. After another five miles you'll arrive at Forest Service Road 13. Turn left and follow it 5.5 miles to Forest Service Road 1341, which leads directly to Lost Lake.

Day Trip: Hood River and the Columbia River Gorge

Distance from Portland: 60 miles

Make your way up the **Columbia River Gorge** to the town of **Hood River** by taking the scenic **Historic Highway** east of Troutdale. The old highway, rising high above the Columbia River and hugging the gorge cliffs, offers spectacular views. Along the way, be sure to stop by the **Vista House** at **Crown Point** for a little gorge history and to take in just one more mind-boggling vista. Then continue eastward to the falls area, one of the densest concentrations of waterfalls in North America and a great place to enjoy a picnic or an easy hike. The trails to **Horsetail** and **Bridal Veil Falls** are two of the best.

East of the falls area, the old highway reconnects with Interstate 84 and continues to Hood River, where the pace is easy and the windsurfing fine. Hood River has a bit of the Old West in it, yet feels oddly more like Solana Beach in Southern California than an outpost in Oregon, with a surfer

PORTLAND REGION

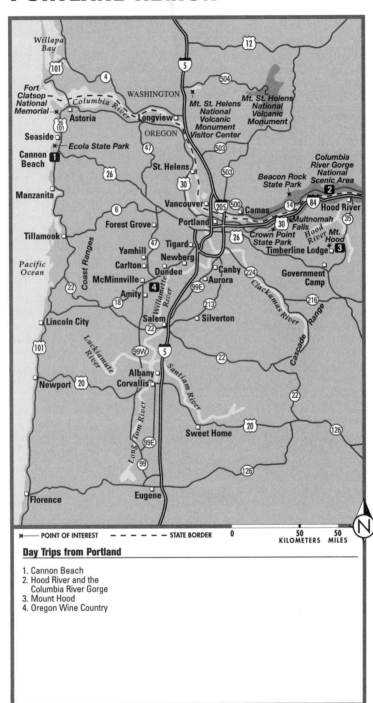

Day Trips from Portland

1. Cannon Beach
2. Hood River and the
   Columbia River Gorge
3. Mount Hood
4. Oregon Wine Country

culture permeating just about everything, not to mention hot summer weather typical of SoCal. Remember, though, you *are* in "rainy" Oregon—just 40 minutes from snowboard country and drizzly Portland. And therein lies Hood River's appeal.

Hood River has been called the nation's windsurfing capital. Though the windsurfing is some of the best in the continental United States, it does not quite compare with Hawaii's world-class conditions. Nevertheless, during warm months, boarders come from near and far to ride the Columbia's waves and swallow the strong gorge winds. May through September the town bustles with festivities: music concerts, brewfests, and the **Gorge Games** competition, which attracts participants from far and wide to such events as mountain biking, rafting, and windsurfing.

Multnomah Falls

Portland Oregon Visitors Association

If windsurfing is not your thing, don't worry. Hood River can be fun for just about anybody with its shops, restaurants, and brewpubs. Check out **Brian's Pourhouse** on Oak Street for great casual dining, or the cozy **Sixth Street Bistro** for lunch or a drink. **Full Sail Brewing** is based in town, so check it out if you're in the mood for a microbrew. Before you leave town, be sure to grab an ice-cream cone at **Mike's Ice Cream** on Oak between Fifth and Sixth Streets.

From Hood River, head north across the toll bridge to Bingen, Washington, and take State Route 52 west to the **Bridge of the Gods**. Cross this toll bridge back into Oregon at Cascade Locks. This will give you a perspective of the gorge from the Washington side of the river, where the views are at least as beautiful as those from Oregon. Take Interstate 84 west (toward Portland) a few miles to **Bonneville Dam**, where you can tour the powerhouse and see the fish ladders that allow

The Columbia River Gorge is worth the trip, even if it's raining in Portland. Typically, the weather takes a dramatic change for the better the closer you get to Cascade Locks. It's not unusual for Hood River to be hot and sunny while back in Portland it's dark and pouring rain. Check the weather forecast.

The Oregon Coast

salmon to climb the river to their spawning grounds. The best time to view the fish is in late spring and early summer (see chapter 8, Kids' Stuff).

After checking out the fish, continue on Interstate 84 west to **Multnomah Falls,** Oregon's most popular tourist attraction and one of the tallest waterfalls in the world (see chapter 5, Sights and Attractions). Take a moment to stop and feel the spray. When you're through, continue on Interstate 84 west back to Portland.

Getting there from Portland: Take Interstate 84 east to Troutdale and Lewis and Clark State Park (on the Sandy River). Follow signs to the Columbia River Historic Highway.

Day Trip: Cannon Beach

Distance from Portland: 75 miles
The Oregon coast is simply not to be missed when visiting Portland. The beaches are near legendary—not the sort where you'll find bikini-clad sun lovers, wall-to-wall families, or honky-tonk boardwalks, but the kind that inspire great novels, or at least grand thoughts. The ocean, sky, and beach all seem bigger in Oregon.

Despite its beauty, the Oregon coast is a remote and wild place, pummeled by wind and lined with winding cliffs and huge rock formations that jut out of the sea just offshore. **Cannon Beach,** the closest beach to Portland, is no exception, with its signature Haystack Rock, which provides a resting stop for birds and sea lions. Fly a kite, ride a horse, play in the water, or dream all day on the beach. The water is cold, but on hot days during summer and early fall it feels welcome. The town of Cannon

Beach is loaded with boutiques, galleries, bookshops, eateries, and hotels.

Ten minutes farther south on U.S. Highway 101 you'll find the quiet town of **Manzanita** and another quieter, larger beach. Ride a horse along the shore or pedal a reclining beach bicycle (just five dollars per hour) through the wet sand. Not much of a business district, Manzanita is, nevertheless, home to a few retailers. Among others, you'll find Manzanita News, which has a decent selection of magazines; an ice-cream store; a toy store; a kite store; a small grocery store; and a restaurant.

Getting there from Portland: Take Highway 26 west to Highway 101, then follow 101 south a few miles to Cannon Beach.

Day Trip: Oregon Wine Country

Distance from Portland: 35 miles

The combination of lush, fertile countryside and a long, warm growing season makes the Willamette Valley an ideal place for growing both wine grapes and berries. Prime northern Willamette Valley wines are Pinot Noir (Oregon's premier red wine), Chardonnay, Pinot Gris, Riesling, and Cabernet Sauvignon, but there are many others. Oregon's cool climate yields crisp wines with a long finish. Now a well-recognized supplier of excellent wine, Oregon is also recognized for its superb berries used in some winemaking processes.

Highway 99 will take you into the heart of the northern Willamette Valley wine country. It would be well worth picking up an excellent map and brochure from the Portland Oregon Visitors Association detailing the

---

Oregon Wine Facts

Number of Wineries: 120

Acreage: 9,000

Cases: 836,029

Major Varieties Produced: Pinot Noir, Chardonnay, Pinot Gris, Riesling, Cabernet Sauvignon, Merlot, Gewürztraminer, Zinfandel, Muller-Thurgau, Sauvignon Blanc, Chenin Blanc, Marechal Foch, Semillon, Pinot Blanc, Cabernet Franc, Loganberry/Raspberry Fortified Wine, Nebbiolo, Grenache, Syrah

Leading Varietals: Pinot Noir, Chardonnay, Riesling, Pinot Gris, Cabernet Sauvignon

---

Northern Willamette Valley Wineries

ARGYLE
691 Hwy. 99W, Dundee, 503/538-8520

The Dundee Wine Company, founded by an Australian vintner and formerly a hazelnut processing plant, produces wine under the popular Argyle label. Enjoy samples in the restored Victorian farmhouse. Open year-round. Tours are by appointment.

CHATEAU BENOIT WINERY
6580 NE Mineral Springs Rd., Carlton, 503/864-2991

A picturesque setting with panoramic views of Yamhill County and a French chateau on the premises make this one worth the visit. Tasting year-round, and picnicking is okay. Emphasis is on dry whites like Sauvignon Blanc and Chardonnay, as well as Pinot Noirs.

REX HILL VINEYARDS
30835 N. Hwy. 99W, Newberg, 503/538-0666

The pretty setting at Rex Hill calls to mind Italian countryside. Sit outside at the picnic tables and enjoy wine samples while overlooking the vineyards. The winery specializes in Pinot Noirs, but other varieties are available as well. Open most of the year.

SOKOL BLOSSER WINERY
5000 Sokol Blosser Lane, Dundee, 800/582-6668 or 503/864-2282

Sweeping Willamette Valley views enhance the ambience of this, one of the oldest and largest in the state. This winery can accommodate large groups and frequently hosts outdoor concerts during warm weather. You can take a self-guided tour and enjoy samples in the tasting room, which is open year-round.

YAMHILL VALLEY VINEYARDS
16250 Oldsville Rd., off Hwy. 18, McMinnville, 503/843-3100

A 300-acre estate in the foothills of the Coast Mountains, this family winery produces Pinot Noir, Pinot Gris, and Riesling, and others. Picnic area available. Open mid-March to Thanksgiving. No fee.

Barrel making in Willamette Valley

Doreen L. Wynja

wineries in the area. Many are open daily for tasting and purchases during the summer and early fall months.

One suggested trip: Take Highway 99 to Dundee, turn right onto Ninth Street (Worden Hill Road), and follow the signs to **Erath Winery**. Sample the wines while sitting outside on one of the tables overlooking the vineyards on the hillsides in the beautiful Yamhill Valley. If you blink, you might think you're in the Italian countryside. When leaving, just before you reach the end of the winery drive turn right into Crabtree Park, a wonderful place for a picnic. Afterward, drive west on Highway 99 to **Argyle and Dundee Wine Cellars** in Dundee, and then continue west again to the **Sokol Blosser Winery and Vineyards,** one of the oldest and biggest wineries in Oregon. Even farther west on Highway 99, you'll find the **Chateau Benoit Winery** on Mineral Springs Road, with its panoramic hilltop view of Yamhill County.

Another winery-rich destination is the beautiful area surrounding **Gaston,** offering sweeping views of rolling green hillsides, old farm houses, and goat and llama farms. From Newberg, take Highway 240 west to Yamhill and Highway 47 north to Gaston. As you approach Gaston you'll pass **Elk Cove Vineyards,** which is worthy of a visit. *Wine Advocate* claimed, "For the pure beauty of its setting, no winery in Oregon can match the breathtaking views from Elk Cove's splendid wine tasting room."

Getting there from Portland: Take Interstate 5 south to Highway 99, then drive west to Newberg, Dundee, and McMinnville.

APPENDIX: CITY·SMART BASICS

EMERGENCY PHONE NUMBERS

Police/Ambulance/Fire
911

Poison Control
503/494-8968

Coast Guard
503/240-9300

FBI
503/224-4181

Multnomah County Mental Health
503/215-7082

Crisis Hotline/Mental Health Multnomah County
503/228-5692

HOSPITALS AND EMERGENCY MEDICAL CENTERS

Dentist Referral
503/223-4738

Doctor Referral
503/222-0156

Legacy Emanuel Hospital and Children's Hospital
2801 N. Gantenbein Ave.
503/413-4687

Oregon Health Sciences University
3181 SW Sam Jackson Park Rd.
503/494-7551

Providence Hospital
4805 NE Glisan
503/215-6000

RECORDED INFORMATION

Air Quality
503/229-5630 or 503/229-5696

Road Conditions
503/222-6721

Time and Weather
503/225-5555

POST OFFICE

Main Office
715 NW Hoyt
800/275-8777

East Portland Station
1020 SE Seventh Ave.
800/275-8777

VISITOR INFORMATION

City of Portland Information
503/823-4000

Portland Chamber of Commerce
503/228-9411

Portland, Oregon, Visitors Association
503/222-2223

Portland Visitor and Convention Bureau
503/275-9750

Visitor Assistance
503/251-8350

Visitors Information Hotline
503/257-7798

CITY TOURS

Ecotours
503/245-1428

Raz
503/684-3322

VanGo Tours
503/292-2085

CAR RENTAL

Avis
800/831-2847

Budget
800/527-0700

Dollar
800/800-4000

Hertz
800/654-2280

National
800/227-7368

Thrifty
800/367-2277

DISABLED ACCESS INFORMATION

Disability Services Helpline
503/248-3646

MULTICULTURAL RESOURCES

African American Chamber of Commerce
503/244-5794

African American Convention and Tourism
503/244-5794

African American Health Coalition
503/413-1850

Black Educational Center
503/284-9552

Black United Fund of Oregon
503/282-7973

Jewish Family and Child Service
503/226-7079

Jewish Outreach and Welcome
503/246-5070

Multnomah County Asian Family Center
503/235-9396

BABYSITTING/CHILD CARE

Babysitting Service
503/786-3837

NEWSPAPERS

The Business Journal
503/274-8733

Cascadia Times
503/223-9036
www.cascadia.times.org

The Columbian
503/224-0654
www.columbian.com

The Oregonian
503/221-8240

The Scanner
503/285-5555

Willamette Week
503/243-2122

MAGAZINES

Exotic Magazine
503/241-4317

Fresh Cup
503/236-2587

NW Palate Magazine
503/224-6039

Oregon Future
503/731-9938

Oregon Wine Magazine
503/232-7607

Sports Car Market Magazine
503/252-5812

BOOKSTORES

Academic Book Center
5600 NW Hassalo St.
503/287-6657

Annie Bloom's Books
7834 SW Capital Hwy.
503/246-0053

Author's Ink
13611 NW Cornell Rd.
503/626-4743

B. Dalton
Washington Square
503/620-3007

1021 Lloyd Center
503/288-6343

Barnes & Noble
3333 NW 35th
503/335-0201

1720 Janzen Beach
503/283-2800

Borders Books & Music
708 SW Third, Mohawk Bldg,
First Floor
503/220-5911

Broadway Books
1714 NE Broadway
503/284-1726

Cameron's Books and Magazines
336 SW Third Ave.
503/228-2391

A Children's Place
1631 NE Broadway
503/284-8294

Future Dreams
1424 NE 103rd Ave.
503/255-5245

Great Northwest Book Store
1234 SW Stark St.
503/223-8098

Hanson's Books
814 NW 23rd Ave.
503/223-7610

In Other Words
3129 Hawthorne Blvd.
503/236-3211

Laughing Horse Books
3652 SE Division St.
503/236-2893

Looking Glass Bookstore
318 SW Taylor St.
503/227-4760

Morrison Books
530 NW 12th Ave.
503/295-6882

Murder by the Book
3210 SE Hawthorne Blvd.
503/232-9995

Nature Store at Portland Audubon Society
5151 NW Cornell Rd.
503/292-6855

New Renaissance Book Shop
1338 NW 23rd Ave.
503/224-4929

Oregon History Center Museum Store
1200 SW Park Ave.
503/222-1741

Paperbacks Etc.
8622 N Lombard
503/978-3999

Portland State University Bookstore
1880 SW Sixth Ave.
503/226-2631

Powell's Books For Cooks and Gardeners
3747 Hawthorne Blvd.
503/235-3802

Powell's Bookstore
1005 W. Burnside
503/228-0540

Powell's Travel Bookstore
701 SW Sixth Ave.
503/228-1108

Reed College Bookstore
3203 SE Woodstock Blvd.
503/777-7287

Riverplace Book Merchants
0315 SW Montgomery St.
503/248-5674

Tower Books
1307 NE 102nd Ave.
503/253-3116

23rd Avenue Books
1015 NW 23rd Ave.
503/224-5097

Waldenbooks
2116 Clackamas Town Ctr.
12000SE 82nd Ave.
503/659-3138

Water Tower Books
5331 SW Macadam Ave.
503/228-0290

Wrigley-Cross Books
1809 NE 39th Ave.
503/281-9449

RADIO STATIONS

KNRK FM 94.7: new rock/alternative
KBBT FM 107.5: '80s mix
KBOO FM 90.7: community issues
KISN FM 97.1: rock/pop oldies
KKJZ FM 106.7: jazz
KNEWS AM 620: news
KOPB FM 91.5: public radio
KOTK AM 1080: talk
KUPL AM 970: country
KUPL FM 98.7: country
KXL AM 750: talk

TELEVISION STATIONS

KATU 2: ABC
KGW 8: NBC
KOIN 6: CBS
KOPB 10: PBS
KPTV 12: UPN

INDEX

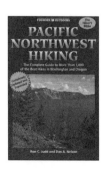

FOR TRAVELERS WITH
SPECIAL INTERESTS

GUIDES

The 100 Best Small Art Towns in America • Asia in New York City
The Big Book of Adventure Travel • Cities to Go
Cross-Country Ski Vacations • Gene Kilgore's Ranch Vacations
Great American Motorcycle Tours • Healing Centers and Retreats
Indian America • Into the Heart of Jerusalem
The People's Guide to Mexico • The Practical Nomad
Saddle Up! • Staying Healthy in Asia, Africa, and Latin America
Steppin' Out • Travel Unlimited • Understanding Europeans
Watch It Made in the U.S.A. • The Way of the Traveler
Work Worldwide • The World Awaits
The Top Retirement Havens • Yoga Vacations

SERIES

Adventures in Nature
The Dog Lover's Companion
Kidding Around
Live Well

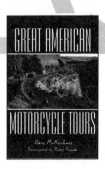

MOON HANDBOOKS

provide comprehensive coverage of a region's arts, history, land, people, and social issues in addition to detailed practical listings for accommodations, food, outdoor recreation, and entertainment. Moon Handbooks allow complete immersion in a region's culture—ideal for travelers who want to combine sightseeing with insight for an extraordinary travel experience.

USA

Alaska-Yukon • Arizona • Big Island of Hawaii • Boston
Coastal California • Colorado • Connecticut • Georgia
Grand Canyon • Hawaii • Honolulu-Waikiki • Idaho
Kauai • Los Angeles • Maine • Massachusetts • Maui
Michigan • Montana • Nevada • New Hampshire
New Mexico • New York City • New York State
North Carolina • Northern California • Ohio • Oregon
Pennsylvania • San Francisco • Santa Fe-Taos • Silicon Valley
South Carolina • Southern California • Tahoe • Tennessee
Texas • Utah • Virginia • Washington • Wisconsin
Wyoming • Yellowstone-Grand Teton

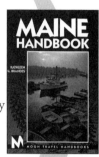

INTERNATIONAL

Alberta and the Northwest Territories • Archaeological Mexico
Atlantic Canada • Australia • Baja • Bangkok • Bali • Belize
British Columbia • Cabo • Canadian Rockies • Cancún
Caribbean Vacations • Colonial Mexico • Costa Rica • Cuba
Dominican Republic • Ecuador • Fiji • Havana • Honduras
Hong Kong • Indonesia • Jamaica • Mexico City • Mexico
Micronesia • The Moon • Nepal • New Zealand
Northern Mexico • Oaxaca • Pacific Mexico • Pakistan
Philippines • Puerto Vallarta • Singapore • South Korea
South Pacific • Southeast Asia • Tahiti
Thailand • Tonga-Samoa • Vancouver
Vietnam, Cambodia and Laos
Virgin Islands • Yucatán Peninsula

www.moon.com

Rick Steves shows you where to travel and how to travel—all while getting the most value for your dollar. His Back Door travel philosophy is about making friends, having fun, and avoiding tourist rip-offs.

Rick's been traveling to Europe for more than 25 years and is the author of 22 guidebooks, which have sold more than a million copies. He also hosts the award-winning public television series *Travels in Europe with Rick Steves*.

RICK STEVES' COUNTRY & CITY GUIDES
Best of Europe
France, Belgium & the Netherlands
Germany, Austria & Switzerland
Great Britain & Ireland
Italy • London • Paris • Rome • Scandinavia • Spain & Portugal

RICK STEVES' PHRASE BOOKS
French • German • Italian • French, Italian & German
Spanish & Portuguese

MORE EUROPE FROM RICK STEVES
Europe 101
Europe Through the Back Door
Mona Winks
Postcards from Europe

WWW.RICKSTEVES.COM

ROAD TRIP USA

Getting there is half the fun, and Road Trip USA guides are your ticket to driving adventure. Taking you off the interstates and onto less-traveled, two-lane highways, each guide is filled with fascinating trivia, historical information, photographs, facts about regional writers, and details on where to sleep and eat—all contributing to your exploration of the American road.

*"Books so full of the pleasures of the American road,
you can smell the upholstery."*
~ BBC radio

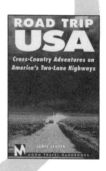

THE ORIGINAL CLASSIC GUIDE
Road Trip USA

ROAD TRIP USA REGIONAL GUIDE
Road Trip USA: California and the Southwest

ROAD TRIP USA GETAWAYS
Road Trip USA Getaways: Chicago
Road Trip USA Getaways: New Orleans
Road Trip USA Getaways: San Francisco
Road Trip USA Getaways: Seattle

www.roadtripusa.com

TRAVEL ✦ SMART®

guidebooks are accessible, route-based driving guides. Special interest tours provide the most practical routes for family fun, outdoor activities, or regional history for a trip of anywhere from two to 22 days. Travel Smarts take the guesswork out of planning a trip by recommending only the most interesting places to eat, stay, and visit.

"One of the few travel series that rates sightseeing attractions. That's a handy feature. It helps to have some guidance so that every minute counts."
~ San Diego Union-Tribune

TRAVEL SMART REGIONS

Alaska
American
Southwest
Arizona
Carolinas
Colorado
Deep South
Eastern
Canada
Florida Gulf
Coast
Florida
Georgia
Hawaii
Illinois/Indiana
Iowa/Nebraska
Kentucky/Tennessee
Maryland/Delaware
Michigan
Minnesota/Wisconsin
Montana/Wyoming/Idaho
Nevada

New England
New Mexico
New York State
Northern California
Ohio
Oregon
Pacific Northwest
Pennsylvania/New Jersey
South Florida and the Keys
Southern California
Texas
Utah
Virginias
Western Canada

Foghorn Outdoors

guides are for campers, hikers, boaters, anglers, bikers, and golfers of all levels of daring and skill. Each guide contains site descriptions and ratings, driving directions, facilities and fees information, and easy-to-read maps that leave only the task of deciding where to go.

"Foghorn Outdoors has established an ecological conservation standard unmatched by any other publisher."
~ Sierra Club

CAMPING Arizona and New Mexico Camping
Baja Camping • California Camping
Camper's Companion • Colorado Camping
Easy Camping in Northern California
Easy Camping in Southern California
Florida Camping • New England Camping
Pacific Northwest Camping
Utah and Nevada Camping

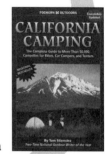

HIKING 101 Great Hikes of the San Francisco Bay Area
California Hiking • Day-Hiking California's National Parks
Easy Hiking in Northern California
Easy Hiking in Southern California
New England Hiking
Pacific Northwest Hiking • Utah Hiking

FISHING Alaska Fishing • California Fishing
Washington Fishing

BOATING California Recreational Lakes and Rivers
Washington Boating and Water Sports

OTHER OUTDOOR RECREATION California Beaches
California Golf • California Waterfalls
California Wildlife • Easy Biking in Northern California
Florida Beaches
The Outdoor Getaway Guide For Southern California
Tom Stienstra's Outdoor Getaway Guide: Northern California

WWW.FOGHORN.COM

CiTY·SMaRT™

The best way to enjoy a city is to get advice from someone who lives there—and that's exactly what City Smart guidebooks offer. City Smarts are written by local authors with hometown perspectives who have personally selected the best places to eat, shop, sightsee, and simply hang out. The honest, lively, and opinionated advice is perfect for business travelers looking to relax with the locals or for longtime residents looking for something new to do Saturday night.

A portion of sales from each title
benefits a non-profit literacy organization in that city.

CITY SMART CITIES

Albuquerque	Anchorage
Austin	Baltimore
Berkeley/Oakland	Boston
Calgary	Charlotte
Chicago	Cincinnati
Cleveland	Dallas/Ft. Worth
Denver	Indianapolis
Kansas City	Memphis
Milwaukee	Minneapolis/St. Paul
Nashville	Pittsburgh
Portland	Richmond
San Francisco	Sacramento
St. Louis	Salt Lake City
San Antonio	San Diego
Tampa/St. Petersburg	Toronto
Tucson	Vancouver

www.travelmatters.com

User-friendly, informative, and fun:

Because travel *matters.*

Visit our newly launched web site and explore the variety of titles and travel information available online, featuring an interactive *Road Trip USA* exhibit.

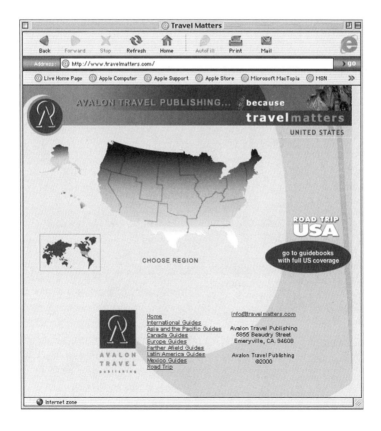

www.ricksteves.com

The Rick Steves web site is bursting with information to boost your travel I.Q. and liven up your European adventure. Including:
- The latest from Rick on what's hot in Europe
- Excerpts from Rick's books
- Rick's comprehensive Guide to European Railpasses

www.foghorn.com

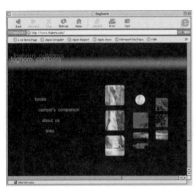

Foghorn Outdoors guides are the premier source for United States outdoor recreation information. Visit the Foghorn Outdoors web site for more information on these activity-based travel guides, including the complete text of the handy *Foghorn Outdoors: Camper's Companion.*

www.moon.com

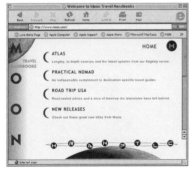

Moon Handbooks' goal is to give travelers all the background and practical information they'll need for an extraordinary travel experience. Visit the Moon Handbooks web site for interesting information and practical advice, including Q&A with the author of *The Practical Nomad*, Edward Hasbrouck.

ABOUT THE AUTHORS

Robin Klein is co-publisher of Portland-based *Cascadia Times,* a regional newspaper covering the Northwest. She has also worked for a number of years in the Portland area's booming high-tech industry as an optics/laser engineer. A dance enthusiast, she enjoys Portland's diverse offerings, including African dance and ballet. Robin is also involved in regional environmental and political causes, particularly nuclear site cleanup. She came to Portland in 1991.

Paul Koberstein is editor and co-publisher of *Cascadia Times,* which he helped found in 1995. A journalism graduate of the University of Oregon, Paul has been a reporter for the *Oregon Journal* and *The Oregonian,* and has written for numerous other publications and magazines, including *Outside* and *Time.* Paul was born and raised in Portland.

Oregon Literacy was founded over 30 years ago as a nonprofit organization dedicated to promoting free tutoring for adult learners. Their primary focus is to provide advice and technical support to local and statewide literacy efforts. They also offer information and referral services to organizations, volunteer, and students through Literacy Line, a toll-free hotline. New services include book scholarships for students and free Web hosting for volunteer tutoring programs. Oregon Literacy is based in Portland and maintains collaborative relationships with affiliated literacy groups throughout the state.

For more information, please contact:
Oregon Literacy, Inc.
9806 SW Boones Ferry Rd.
Portland, OR 97219
Phone: 503/244-3898
Fax: 503/244-9147
Literacy Line: 800/322-8715
Email: info@oregonliteracy.org
Web: www.oregonliteracy.org